The River Running By

Published by Wedderburn Art Ltd
on behalf of Joan Fleming-Yates

ISBN 1 905037 05 8

All rights reserved. No part of this publication may be reproduced, stored in a retrieval system or transmitted in any form by any means, electronic, mechanical, photocopying, recording or otherwise without prior permission of the publisher.

© Copyright: Joan Fleming-Yates

Printed in the U.K. for
IMPRESSIONS OF MONMOUTH LTD
Tel: 01594 839407
print@impresscoleford.demon.co.uk

The River Running By

By

Joan Fleming-Yates

*Dedicated to my dear husband Brian without whose help
and encouragement this book would never have been written.*

MONNOW

I know the secret! How thy shivering rill
Leaps high on Cusop bluff, among the stones;
Till swelled by Escley brook, from Vagar hill,
Then, where by Craswall Chapel sleep the bones
Of grey-frocked friars, is heard a larger sound:
'Tis Olchon, dimpling o'er his stony bed,
Olchon, from many a rood of moorland ground,
From heathery dingles, bare, unvisited,
Him too thou dost enfold, and onward thou art bound.

A C Benson (1862-1925)

CONTENTS

The River Monnow 1
Early History 4

THE PARISHES
Llanveynoe 16
Craswall 11
Longtown 20
Clodock 26
Oldcastle 29
Walterstone 31
Llancillo 32
Rowlestone 34
Ewyas Harold 36
Pontrilas 40
Llangua 44
Grosmont 49
Kentchurch 53
Garway 57
Garway Hill 63
Skenfrith 69
Llanrothal 76
St Maughans 78
Rockfield 81
Monmouth 87

THE KNIGHTS TEMPLARS AND
HOSPITALLERS IN THE PARISH OF GARWAY 99

THE CATHOLIC MARTYRS
Recusancy 123
The Riot 135
The Cwm 139
The Plot 143
The Martyrs 148
Matthew Pritchard 156
Coed Anghred 161
Dan-y-Graig 170
Return to Pembridge Castle 172

RIVER ROAD AND RAIL
Travel in the 18th Century 179
River Navigation 181
Toll Roads 190
Railways 211

BIBLIOGRAPHY AND REFERENCE 225
GLOSSARY 230
INDEX 231

FOREWORD

I suppose that I am one of the lucky ones, for I was born and still live in the beautiful Valley of the Monnow where generations of my family rest beside the tranquil churches of Grosmont and Skenfrith. But here is a book by a resident of just thirty years – not quite a foreigner, for she resides on the English bank of the river – but a newcomer all the same!

Newcomer or not, Joan Fleming-Yates clearly loves the Monnow Valley and must surely have spent a considerable part of her thirty years' residency in researching its history. The volume is crammed with information but it is not just a series of gleanings from dusty records but a lively trip down the river, presented in such a charming and readable way that it is hard to put down. There is also much that is new for local historians and other enthusiasts who will probably find themselves taking notes.

The River Monnow – Yr Afon Mynwy – rises in the misty mountains of Wales and meanders through an enchanting border country as rich in myth and legend as it is in history and the magic of nature.

Today, Herefordshire is 'Welsh-ified' and Gwent is 'English-ified', so the two live at peace. But this was not always so, for here is a borderland that had (and needed) more castles, mottes and forts than most countries in the world. Our valley has its share of them and Mrs Fleming-Yates recalls the history and atmosphere of those ages as well as of the more recent past and of the people who lived on the banks of the river.

This is no place for a review, but I am sure that after flicking through the pages you may well find that the book will accompany you home.

I can imagine how much my grandfather would have enjoyed this book, so I am buying a couple of extra copies for my grandchildren – when they arrive!

Stephen Clarke M.B.E
Monmouth Archaeological Society

PREFACE AND ACKNOWLEDGEMENTS

The Monnow valley has been my home since I moved to Herefordshire some thirty years ago. It is a very beautiful quiet backwater off the main tourist route, with narrow roads, few villages and except for Monmouth, no towns. Its history has been essentially rural. There are no stately homes owned by titled aristocracy, no industrial heritage and the only great battle was fought at Grosmont. My interest in local history started when I went to Hereford Record Office and tentatively looked up Garway in the reference cards. I was hooked! I gradually realised that although there had been histories written about a few individual parishes in the Monnow valley and on subjects such as castles, nothing had been written about the valley as a whole.

Local history takes the researcher down many unexpected paths and I have found that life in the valley has not always been so uneventful. When the Norman invasion and the Marcher Lordships superseded the Celtic and Saxon rulers, the great period of castle building began of which there is still evidence throughout the valley today. The largest possessions of the Knights Templar in the country were at Garway. Between the Reformation and the Restoration there were riots, persecution and martyrdom of the Catholics and the struggle to keep their religion alive continued into the 20th century. As the Industrial Revolution gathered momentum, an attempt was made to make the valley into a trade route with plans to make the Monnow a navigable river, to extend the road system and finally to build a railway from Monmouth to Pontrilas.

Each parish is unique and special to the people who live there. A complete history of the nineteen parishes that border the river Monnow is beyond the scope of this book but hopefully this account will make visiting these parishes more interesting and perhaps tell some stories that have not previously been known.

I have been greatly helped in this endeavour by many people but mostly by my husband, Brian Thomas whose interest in and knowledge of local history has been invaluable. He has spent many hours checking my work and making constructive suggestions for its improvement. I have made extensive use of his book and postcard collections and he has taken many of the photographs. It is due to his encouragement and enthusiasm that I have at long last finished this book.

I would like to thank Sue Hubbard, Elizabeth Semper O'Keefe and the staff of the Hereford Record Office, Mr D Rimmer and staff of the Gwent Record Office and Andrew Helme and Sue Miles at the Monmouth Museum. I am very much indebted to Mrs Mary Hopson of Tregate Castle for allowing me to use her research on Coed Anghred and to Mr Bill Price of Skenfrith for lending me photographs and documents. I am very grateful to the following people who have answered my letters, phone calls and questions; Bruce Coppleston-Crow, Steve Clarke, Keith Kissack, Heather Hurley, the late Elizabeth Taylor, David Lloyd Jeans, Margaret Kelly and Mary Walsh of the Cwm, David Hancocks, Rev Brian Dooley, Les Gardiner of Orcop, Miss Cooke of Pembridge Castle and Father Luke and the Librarian at Belmont Abbey. Mike Whitehead and John Hughes rescued me several times when I couldn't understand my computer. David Brain and his colleagues at Impressions of Monmouth could not have been more helpful and patient in guiding me through the technicalities of producing a book.

A word of gratitude also to the authors and local historians of yesteryear who recorded their findings for posterity and whose work I have used extensively.

LOCATION MAP FOR THE MONNOW VALLEY

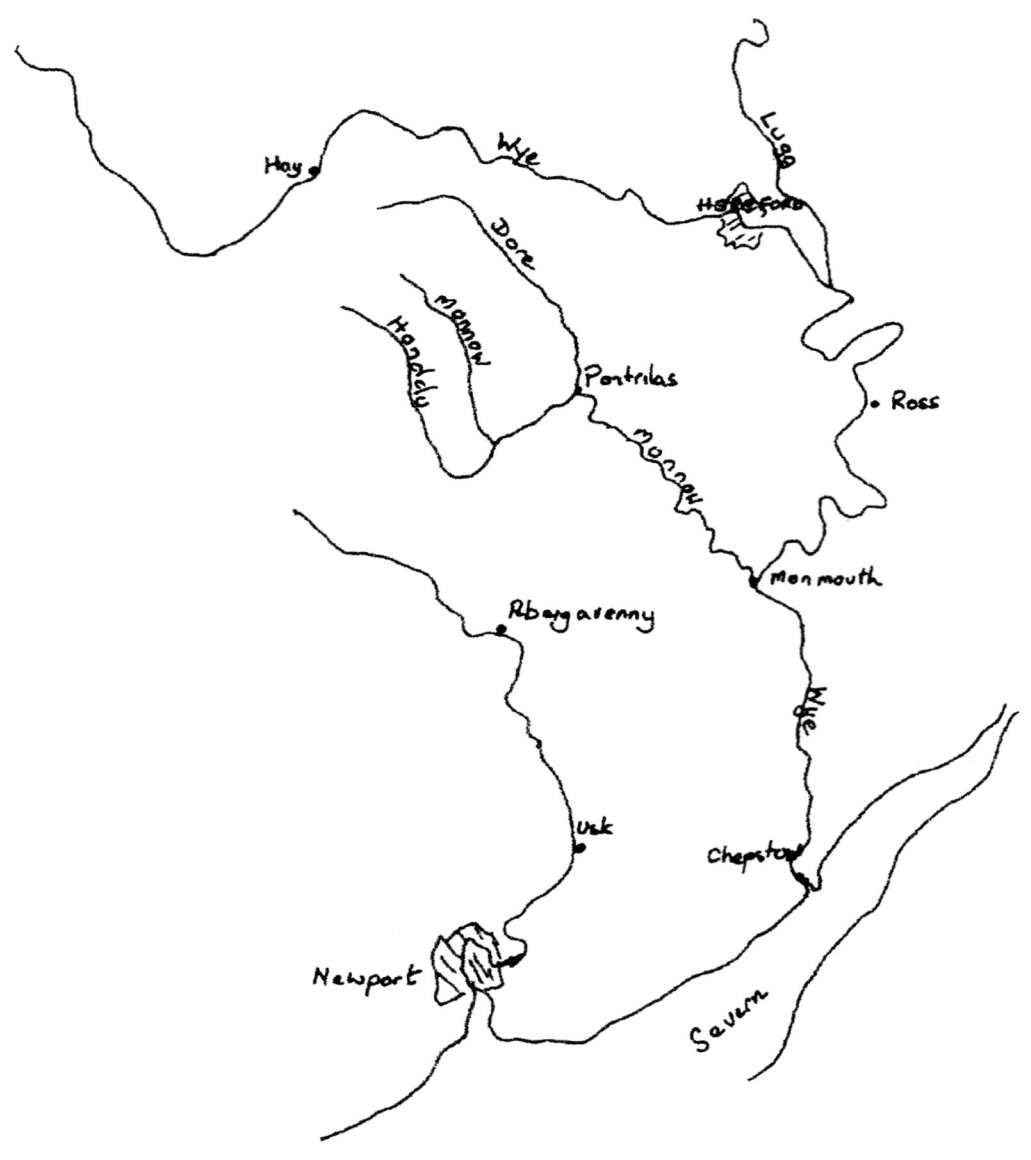

THE RIVER MONNOW

High in the Black Mountains the river Monnow begins its thirty-mile journey to meet the river Wye at Monmouth. On the escarpment in the shadow of the Black Hill many tiny streams and bubbling springs rush down the mountainside over miniature waterfalls and gradually flow together to form a single stream, the infant river Monnow. Flowing south from Craswall, continually swelled by more streams, the river reaches Longtown where it is joined by the Escley brook, the first of its real tributaries. Just a few hundred yards downstream the Monnow is joined by a second tributary, the Olchon brook which rises at the end of the beautiful and remote Olchon Valley where the ridge of the Cat's Back (Crib y Garth) and the high hills of the Black Mountains gradually close in and the land rises to the high plateau of Hatterrall Hill.

Continuing its' journey southwards through Clodock, the river, which has so far been entirely in Herefordshire, crosses and re-crosses the county border of Brecknock at the very edge of the Brecon Beacons National Park.

The river Honddu rises in Brecknockshire on the south side of Ffynnon Beacon (Hay Bluff) at a height of 2100 feet above sea level. It flows down the vale of Ewyas through Capel-y-ffin and past Llanthony Priory to Cwmyoy. Below Cwmyoy the river turns in a semi-circle to join the Monnow at Alltyrynys, the ancestral home of the Cecil family of Elizabethan fame. Immediately to the south of this loop in the river Honddu is a large moraine lying across the valley which marks the limit of an ice tongue which moved southwards down one of the valleys of the Black mountains during the last ice age, before which the river Honddu flowed on down this valley towards Abergavenny.

The river Monnow now alters course from its southerly direction to north easterly, flowing slowly along a wide mature plain until just south of Pontrilas it is joined by the river Dore which, flowing along the Golden Valley appears to have been the original headstream of the river Monnow.

The stretch from Pontrilas to Monmouth is exceptionally beautiful. The river has excavated a deep cleft through the ridge of sandstone that runs from the Graig to Dinedor Hill. The sides of this valley rise to 1100 feet in the west on the wooded slopes of the Graig and on the eastern side is Garway Hill with its steep bracken covered slopes of common land rising to 1202 feet. Both summits are within a mile of the valley floor that lies at only 200 feet above sea level.

The river has several meanders, especially at Grosmont, Skenfrith and Rockfield. Looking down from the summit of Garway Hill the eye can follow the river winding its tree-fringed course like a green ribbon through the valley. At Skenfrith the river makes a large sweep around Coed Anghred Hill. Steeply wooded slopes rise up from the river in an unspoilt and rather inaccessible part of the valley, as the only road is very narrow and steep and tends to discourage all but the most intrepid travellers. As the river turns into its last meander just above Rockfield it ceases to be the county and country boundary and for the rest of its journey to Monmouth is entirely in Monmouthshire and Wales.

The old county town of Monmouth takes its name from the fact that it is here that the Monnow, one of its major tributaries, flows into the river Wye. The most famous bridge on this river is the ancient 13th century medieval gatehouse bridge crossing the Monnow into Monmouth

Towards the Black Montains

The Monnow had long been a renowned angling river. Because of its clean, well-oxygenated water it was considered one of the premier rivers in the country for the indigenous brown trout and the greyling. The greyling, a fish with the appearance of a small salmon, lives in swift rivers and mountain lakes and requires even cleaner water than the trout.

Over the last century there has been a steady decline in the presence of wild fish and other wildlife. In consequence, restocking takes place on a regular basis by the fishing syndicates who lease stretches of the river. Many factors have contributed to the decline of fish stocks. Farming methods such as the use of herbicides, pesticides and nitrates have caused contamination of the water and the Government subsidies on sheep, have resulted in a much higher density of livestock being kept. If these animals have access to the riverbanks then the vegetation which once grew there is lost, leading to the river banks widening and the river beds becoming shallower. Another problem is the dense growth of alder trees along the bank-side, especially in the upper reaches of the river, where they cause deep shade preventing the growth of the long grasses and the sort of vegetation which would have hung over the water where the fish could find shelter. These alder trees were once part of the rural economy being used for the production of charcoal and domestic fuel.

The run off of silt from the cultivated river meadows makes the water, especially after heavy rain, brown and muddy and this silt settles on the river bed. Trout lay their eggs in the river gravel and to survive need a good supply of clean, uncontaminated well oxygenated water.

Concern about the decline in the fish stocks in the river Monnow brought together people interested in reversing the damage. In 2003 the River Monnow Project was launched with funding from DEFRA together with other interested organisations and the £1.5 million project for the restoration of the river and the enhancement of the fish habitats was commenced. Work consists of tree coppicing and double bank fencing on the rivers Dore, Monnow, Escley and Olchon and the work will be finished by June 2006.

There is all the usual bird-life one would expect to find on such a river with kingfishers, dippers and herons. Spring brings a very good hatch of mayfly, known as the lady of the river, and the Monnow is also home to the very rare soldier fly (oxycere terminata) which can be seen in June and July on sunny shingle banks of the river bed.

A small number of otters are also present on the river but as they are shy creatures leading a largely nocturnal existence they are not often seen. Unfortunately, wild mink, classified as vermin have become established in the lower reaches of the river causing serious problems for birds and small fish.

The river is slow running and deep in parts while some stretches are shallow and rapid. After heavy rain in the mountains the river can rise rapidly and the racing orange coloured water leaves it's debris on the tree lined banks. In the winter of 2000 the Monnow featured in the national news as being on high flood alert and there was serious flooding at Monmouth and Skenfrith causing much damage to the newly refurbished Bell Inn.

Apart from Monmouth there are no towns in the valley and the most of the villages are now much smaller than they were. Although there has been some new building there are no major developments. The countryside still retains its essentially rural character with agriculture as the main industry. The farmhouses are scattered throughout the valley and most farms are of between 100 and 500 acres. The hilly topography of the area probably discouraged the enlargement of fields by the grubbing out of hedgerows, thus saving the wildlife from a devastating loss of habitat. The heavily wooded hills provide an ideal breeding environment for the pheasants being reared by the various shooting syndicates.

A quiet stretch of the river Monnow at Garway

EARLY HISTORY

The river Monnow forms part of the national boundary between England and Wales and the county boundary between Herefordshire and Monmouthshire. Even today, the two areas feel different with separate identities, each looking in opposite directions for the administrative and cultural aspects of life.

By the time of the Domesday survey in 1086 there had already been some Norman intrusion into the Welsh Marches including the Monnow valley where settlements were soon established. The Saxons occupied land between the Wye and the Dore but in the three ancient kingdoms known as Ewias, Archenfield or Ergyng and Gwent Uwch-Coed, the Welsh people of Celtic origin still lived undisturbed.

Edward the Confesssor who ruled between 1042-1066 was brought up in the Norman Court in France and was instrumental in bringing many Frenchmen to this country. He was married to Eadgyth, the daughter of Earl Godwin who also had five sons, Sweyn, Harold, Tostig, Leofwine and Gyrth all of whom achieved the rank and office of Earl. Earl Harold eventually succeeded his brother-in-law Edward the Confessor as King. Earl Godwin, who was virtual ruler of the kingdom until his death in 1053 succeeded in removing Herefordshire and its dependencies of Archenfield and Ewias from the Kingdom of Mercia and in 1043 created a new Earldom of Hereford which he gave to his son Sweyn. However, Sweyn was soon in disgrace and after seducing the Abbess of Leominster fled to Denmark. King Edward gave the Earldom of Hereford to his nephew Ralph, the son of his sister Goda. Ralph was very anti English and pro Norman and brought with him from Normandy many Frenchmen two of whom, Osbern Pentecost and Richard Fitz Scrob received grants of land on the Herefordshsire border at Ewyas Harold and Richard's Castle. On taking possession of their new lands both these men commenced building motte and bailey castles following the pattern of those they were accustomed to in their native Normandy. These timber framed castles were the first of their type in the country being built 20 years before the Norman Conquest.

The imposition of a new way of life for the local population would not have been popular. The native Welshmen were accustomed to a more egalitarian existence with their leaders living amongst them. They were not prepared for these ruthless alien invaders ensconced in these fortified positions, imposing a harsh and oppressive regime. In 1052 the Welsh invaded Herefordshire and defeated the Saxon and French settlers. Osbern Pentecost and his followers fled to Scotland and the castle at Ewyas Harold known as Pentecost Castle was dismantled. Ralph however returned to his Earldom of Hereford.

Just three years later in 1055, Gruffydd, Prince of North Wales, attacked and sacked Hereford and his army marched through Ewias and Archenfield laying the country to waste. Edward sent Earl Harold Godwin to Hereford and after refortifying the city caused the Welsh marauders to retreat back into Wales. Earl Ralph died in 1057 leaving a five-year-old son, also called Harold and it was he who gave the name to 'Ewyas Harold'.

After the defeat of King Harold at the battle of Hastings in 1066, bringing his short reign to an end, William the Conqueror became King of England. The border land was still very troubled with raids by the Welsh and William Fitz Osbern was appointed to hold this troublesome frontier. He was a palatine Earl, a cousin of the King and acting with Royal authority on the Welsh border administering the royal manors of Hereforshire and granting tithes, churches and small pieces of land to his monastic foundations at Lyre and Cormeilles in Normandy. Although William Fitz Osbern's rule was brief, he died in 1071, he was instrumental in building castles at Chepstow, Monmouth, Clifford and Wigmore and he reinforced the castle at Ewyas Harold.

The system of occupation by the Marcher Lords was conducted in a different way from the rest of England where each manor was given by direct grant from the King. As each Marcher lord defeated a Welsh ruler he took over his kingdom as his own property creating his own laws and making himself a petty king with royal rights. The Marcher Lords set up a system, new to the area, of feudal methods of land tenure, large scale agriculture, towns with trade and a church organised on diocesan lines. Territorial bishoprics were introduced and Llandaff claimed all the ancient Kingdom of Gwent including all of Archenfield causing a conflict with the Bishop of Hereford.

Land was granted to tenants-in-chief who had this property in return for knights service. Each tenant-in-chief had to find a knight or knights with their retainers, fully armed for forty days whenever they were needed. The tenants-in-chief sublet parts of their land to other tenants who would share the burden of supplying knights. This was eventually compounded to a money payment as it was found that mercenary soldiers were more reliable.

In Ewyas Harold, land had been granted to Alured de Marlborough and at Ewias Lacy, later known as Longtown, to Walter de Lacy. When the owners took possession of these feudal holdings they invariably built a castle of the motte and bailey type, very necessary in these districts that were still populated by the hostile Welsh. The tenants-in-chief went on to build strong stone castles in place of the wooden tower on the motte, especially in places of strategic importance. The smaller tenants also built motte and bailey castles for protection and status but generally never progressed beyond wooden defence works. There are a number of these small mottes along the river, for example, Walterstone, Llancillo, Rowlestone, Kentchurch, and Llanrothal.

The administrative division of a shire was a Hundred, a system probably established in the 10th century. The Hundred Court, presided over by the Reeve, met monthly to consider criminal cases, levy and collect taxes and to deal with ecclesiastical matters. These meetings were usually held in the open-air at a boundary stone, a large tree or at crossroads. At the time of the Domesday survey in 1086, there were two areas of Herefordshire that were only partially incorporated into the Hundred scheme. They were Archenfield and Ewias. Until the Norman Conquest almost all the area of the Monnow Valley was part of the autonomous Welsh territory.

There were only two interruptions in the long history of the Welsh society in Gwent. The Roman invasion had made a considerable impact but the Anglo Saxons had much less effect upon the kingdom although there was some Saxon infiltration into Ergyng. There was a completely different structure to the society that had developed out of the Celtic tribal system. Gwent was divided into three cantrefs, Gwynllwg, Gwent Uwchcoed and Gwent Iscoed, and each cantref was divided into commotes. Gwent Uwchcoed, meaning above the woods had four commotes, Abergavenny, Monmouth and the Three Castles, Ergyng and Ewyas. This was the political and administrative organisation and each commote had its lord who held court at the commote centre and administered the old Welsh laws. There were fifteen officials at each court consisting of:

Captain of the bodyguard	Page of the chamber	Doorkeeper
Chaplain	Bard of the court	Cook
Steward	Candlebearer	Handmaiden
Chief falconer	Chief huntsman	
Judge of the court	Physician	
Chief groom	Butler	

Each commote had a number of Trefydd or townships, which were really small hamlets or centres of population and most Monmouthshire villages have descended from these. Society was organised on a tribal basis and kept together by blood relationships, even up to the 9th degree of kinship. A tribe inhabited a particular tract of country and held it in common with other members of the tribe who had the use of, but not the ownership of this land. The structure of this society consisted of Princely families, free Welshmen and bondsmen who were the remnants of the Celtic tribal structure. Common ownership took precedence over individual holding. Agriculture was pastoral with some cultivation and Ergyng and Ewais were very much part of this society.

The Norman invasion had a considerable impact, especially on the Wye and Monnow valleys. Most of the old Welsh commotes had been absorbed into the Marcher lordships by the 13th century and these lordships divided up into Englishries and Welshries. The Englishry was centred on the castle where the lord resided with his retainers. This castle may have been surrounded by a town with burgesses and include a church. Around the town would be the town fields and open pastures. Walls and dykes were used as boundaries for the town field and the limits were clearly set out. Some of these medieval castle towns have disappeared but Monmouth and Abergavenny are two local examples that have survived with many of their original features intact. Fortified villages were also created around a motte and bailey castle ruled over by a minor lord.

The remaining lands formed the Welshry, usually the uplands and a Welsh population, both free and bond, inhabited these areas. Tribal society was slowly changing but old customs long remained, with the blood bond the basis of the society and a deeply rooted Celtic concept of land. There were no villages in the English sense, and there were no castles or towns. It was a pastoral economy with very few common fields and only small farmsteads; all the best land would have been included in the Englishry. The tribe was made up of family groups and on the death of the head of the family all the sons would divide the land equally between them as would happen again with their sons thus creating very small holdings. This system of inheritance was known as gavelkind and was not legally abolished until 1925.

The land known as Ewias and subsequently, Ewyas Lacy had been given to Walter de Lacy following the Norman Conquest. Walter died rather tragically in 1085 by falling from the walls of St Peter's Church in Hereford which he was having built. He was succeeded by his son Roger de Lacy, a powerful baron who owned a great deal of land in the Welsh Marches.

The territory of Ewias was a large area that stretched from the Black Mountains to Ewyas Harold and from the river Monnow to Cusop. Ewias was still Welsh and included what are now the parishes of Longtown, Clodock, Llanveynoe, Newton, St Margarets, Michaelchurch Escley and Craswall.

There is only one small item with reference to Ewias in the Domesday Survey, which states that

Roger also has one land called Longtown within the boundary of Ewias. This land does not belong to the Castlery nor to the Hundred. From this land Roger has 15 sesters of honey, 15 pigs when men are there and (administers) justice over them.

(The Castlery was an area organised for the protection of its castle and a sester is a vessel for holding liquid believed to have contained 32oz).

The Normans had not yet wholly occupied Ewias and would have infiltrated westwards from the stronghold of Ewyas Harold castle, gradually increasing their influence and eventually building the imposing castle at Longtown. When reading the Domesday Survey it is possible to see a subtle distinction between the land which had long had English settlement and the districts which were still Welsh. The land in the English areas was measured in hides and virgates, a hide being the amount of land that could be ploughed in a year with an eight-ox team and would be, depending on soil conditions, between 60 and 120 acres. The Welsh areas used the alternative word carucates. These were not the same as the carucates of the former Danish lands which were equivalent to the hide. In the Welsh borders and Herefordshire carucates were especially associated with castles and newly occupied land that had not yet been hidated.

One of the areas occupied subsequent to the Conquest was Walterstone, a parish that was possibly named after Walter de Lacy and where a motte was constructed to guard the southern end of this new territory. Other lands sub-let to tenants in chief but still under the jurisdiction of Roger, were Llancillo and Rowlestone. These two churches, along with Walterstone church were given to Llantony Abbey by Roger de Lacy.

At the time of the Domesday survey in 1086 Archenfield (Ergyng) was politically in Herefordshire but still economically and ecclesiastically in Gwent. The Welshmen in Archenfield were spiritually in the care of the Bishop of Llandaff and it was not until 1130 that the Bishop of Hereford secured the area for his diocese. This was the last official tie with Wales, but this did not extinguish the Welshness of the people. There seems to have been very little English settlement, for as late as 1400 a complaint was made to the Bishop of Hereford that in Garway the curate spoke only English while his parishioners spoke only Welsh. Throughout the area Welsh names have persisted in the names of farms, fields, hills and dales showing a resistance to change throughout the medieval times and well into modern times.

The Domesday survey for Archenfield spells out quite clearly that this area was very different with its own laws and customs that would be preserved.

In Archenfield the King has three churches. The priests of these churches bear the King's dispatches into Wales and each of them sings two masses each and every week for the King. If any one of them dies, the King has 20 shillings from him by custom.

If any Welshman steals a man, a woman, a horse, an ox or a cow, when he is convicted of it, he first restores what he stole and gives 20 shillings in forfieture; but for stealing a sheep or a bundle of sheaves he pays a fine of 2 shillings.

If anyone kills one of the King's men or commits housebreaking, he gives the King 20 shillings as payment for the man and 100 shillings in forfeiture. If anyone has killed a thane's man, he gives 10 shillings to the dead man's lord.

But if a Welshman has killed a Welshman, the relatives of the slain man gather and despoil the killer and his relatives and burn their houses until the body of the dead man is buried the next day about midday. The King has the third part of the plunder but they have all the rest free.

Otherwise, a man who has burnt a house and is accused of, proves his innocence through 40 men; but if he has been unable to, he will pay a fine of 20 shillings to the King.

If anyone has concealed a sester of honey from the customary due and this is proved, he pays five sesters for one sester if he hold as much land as ought to produce them.

If the Sheriff summons them to a meeting of the Shire, six or seven of the nobler ones of them go with him. A man who is called and does not go, gives 2 shillings or 1 ox to the King; a man who stays away from the Hundred (meeting) pays as much.

Anyone who does not go when ordered by the Sheriff to go with him into Wales, is fined the same. But if the Sheriff does not go, none of them goes.

When the army advances on the enemy, these men by custom form the vanguard and on their return the rearguard.

These were the custom of the Welshmen in Archenfield before 1066.

The Domesday Book is a statistical survey of England taken in 1086. Its purpose was to record a census of the population and the productive resources of the country. However, the major part of Archenfield was not surveyed and Garway is the only area mentioned in the southern half of this ancient kingdom.

Throughout England, the commissioners took on oath, details from the Sheriffs, the barons, the priests, the reeves and six villagers from each village. The King wanted to know what he had and who held it. French speaking Normans aided by Anglo Saxons in a wholly Welsh-speaking district must have caused considerable problems when surveying Archenfield.

Monmouth remained important enough to become the county town and of the other three Norman castles, Grosmont and Skenfrith are now small villages with ruined castles, reminders of long forgotten power while White Castle, which was a military garrison castle, and never appears to have acquired a village and stands isolated on a hill, its massive white walls which gave it its name now washed clean and grey.

Following the Act of Union in 1536, Wales was linked to the English Realm bringing it under a single government system. The Marcher Lordships were combined to form shires and these were divided into Hundreds. From the Feast of All Saints 1536, the new county of Monmouth was born. Monmouthshire was divided into six Hundreds of which Skenfrith was one. The Skenfrith Hundred included all the parishes of Grosmont, Llangua, Llantillo Crossenny and the lower division was comprised of Welsh Bicknor, Dixton, Hadnock, Wonastow, Rockfield and St Maughans. The Monmouth County Council came into being on 1st April 1881 and the Skenfrith Hundred ceased to exist. The Parish Council Act of 1894 saw the establishment of Rural District Councils and Parish Councils. In the Local Government Act of 1974 Monmouthshire was renamed Gwent.

Part One

The Parishes

The Monnow at Skenfrith

DIAGRAMATIC REPRESENTATION OF THE MONNOW VALLEY PARISHES

CRASWALL

LLANVEYNOE

LONGTOWN

CLODOCK   EWYAS HAROLD

OLDCASTLE   WALTERSTONE   LLANCILLO   ROWLESTONE
                                                    PONTRILAS

                              LLANGUA

                         GROSMONT

                                              KENTCHURCH

                         SKENFRITH

                                              GARWAY

                       ST MAUGHANS

                                              LLANROTHAL

                       ROCKFIELD

                                M O N M O U T H

CRASWALL

Craswell or Craswall is a small village or township in the parish of Clodock situated near the source of the river Monnow, and the Black Mountains, which here rise to 2306 feet, form the boundary between Herefordshire and Brecknockshire. Historically Craswall formed part of the parish of Clodock for ecclesiastical purposes only. For civil purposes it had its own officers and looked after its own poor. Although it lacks parish status it also lacks the elements of a village, the small population being scattered over a large area.

High in the Black Mountains, in a small valley called Cwm-y-Canddo (the fox dingle) in which flows a tiny brooklet, a tributary of the newly formed Monnow, lie the ruins of Craswall Priory which belonged to the Order of Grandmont. The initial impression greeting the visitor is that of an ancient site possibly pre-dating the magnificent ruins of Llantony Priory. The reality is quite different with the reasons for its demise being similar but not the same. The fate of Craswall Priory was sealed by the so-called One Hundred Years War (1337-1453) between England and France, when Religious Orders with an allegiance to France were disbanded and the assets seized by the Crown.

St Stephen of Muret founded the Order of the Grandmont. He lived as holy hermit in a hut until his death in 1124. His followers believed they heard a divine voice saying "to Grandmont" and they moved to the desolate mountain in 1125 taking the body of their founder with them. The first priory appears to have taken the form of a church with an adjoining hermitage but by the mid-12th century the cells were replaced by more conventional monastic buildings grouped around a cloister.

Prior Gerard Itier writing about 1135 describes Grandmont in Normandy thus.

Grandmont is stern and very cold unfertile and rocky misty and exposed to winds. The water is colder and worse than in other places, for it produces sickness instead of health. The mountain abounds in great stones for building in streams and sand but there is scarcely any timber for building. The land around the monastery scarcely ever suffices to provide necessaries for the soil is so unfertile, sterile and barren. The place which was chosen by God is a solitude for penitence and religion, and those who dwell there lead a hard life.

It would seem that Craswall was chosen as a site to build the priory because it had many of the same attributes as the original house.

As such desolate sites were chosen by the Grandmontines only a small number of brethren could be accommodated in each priory and the number of cells increased rapidly as a result. By the late 12th century there were over 140 and the Order had become established. The Order was divided into clerks and lay brothers. The clerks were exempt from all of the day-to-day work and might spend all their time on prayer and contemplation. The lay brothers took charge of the money, did all the manual work and were wholly responsible for the business of the house.

The first English house was founded in 1204 at Grosmont, in Eskdaleside Yorkshire. The second English house was at Craswall, founded in 1225 on land given by Walter de Lacy a few miles north of his castle at Ewias Lacy (Longtown). There was originally an endowment to maintain 10 priests and 3 clerks and there would be an equal number of lay brothers. Shortly after the foundation of Craswall there was a third house founded at Alderbury near Shrewsbury.

The Priory was subordinate to the Abbey of Grandmont in Normandy and for more than two hundred years it flourished. Many of the great lords of Herefordshire enriched it with gifts of land. All of the revenue from these alien priories excepting a very small amount for their own use was sent back to the foreign Abbey in France. The Priories were very unpopular with the English Bishops as the brothers cared little for the priest of the parish or for the Bishop. In the reign of Edward IV the alien priories were confiscated to the Crown.

Edward IV in 1462 granted the revenues of Craswall to God's House College, Cambridge (now Christ's College), but it does not appear that this grant was ever confirmed. The priory was then abandoned and became a ruin and most of the stone would have been taken, over the years, for building in the locality.

The Woolhope Naturalists Field Club visited Craswall Priory on Tuesday June 28th 1904 for their second Field Meeting of the year. Woolhope outings were very different affairs in 1904 from the comfortable coach trips we experience today. The members (all men, of course!) left Hereford on the 9.22 train to Hay on Wye which was on the Brecon line. There had been a choice of route to get to Craswall. One option was to travel by train from Pontrilas station to Peterchurch on the Golden Valley line, followed by an arduous walk of six miles across country. Another possible route was from Pandy station on the Hereford Abergavenny line along a good metalled road through Clodock and Longtown as far as the Bull's Head Inn at Craswall. This was a distance of ten miles then two more miles of rough road to the Priory. (Apparently, people travelling to Hay market by this route preferred to leave their wheeled conveyance at or near the Inn, travelling the remainder of the journey by horseback as the next six miles of road to Hay was indifferent, tortuous, hilly and suggestive of a switchback).

The route eventually chosen by the Woolhope Club was by train from Hereford to Hay. From here some 60 members set off to walk the 4 miles to the Priory up the Cusop dingle of the Dulas brook and past Birches Farm to the highest altitude of the road at 1450 feet and then down a track to the ruins of Craswall Priory. Mr Lilwall of Lllydyadyway, Cusop who had recently been excavating at the site and unearthed some interesting finds from the long buried ruins, met the party at the station. (Mr Lilwall continued to excavate on the site for several years and his finding are reported in the Woolhope transctions.)

The first impression upon reaching the ruins of Craswall is the remarkable seclusion of the situation. Hidden by trees, especially massive Yews, with weird gnarled roots and boles, the ruins are not seen until you find yourself almost walking over them. Overgrown by ivy, grass, thistles, nettles, mosses, lichens, and other vegetation, they have apparently been undisturbed, uncared for, and unnoticed since their roofs fell in, and their walls fell down in all directions inwards and outwards. Around the side of the apisidal east end of the excavated building the congregation assembled to hear the paper prepared by Mr Lilwall. (Woolhope Transactions 1904)

The party then walked on to Craswall Church. By this time it was 2.30pm and most of the party started the walk back to Hay. However, some intrepid members could not resist the temptation to walk to the top of the Black Mountains even though it was an ascent of one thousand feet and a further one and a half miles. At 4.30, with stragglers coming in at intervals the party sat down to luncheon at the Crown Hotel

Hay. They caught the train at 6.35 pm for the journey back to Hereford. The day's walk had been at least 12 miles an achievement which these erudite gentlemen performed with the stoicism of this bygone age when travel to remote areas was not easy.

Nearly sixty years later in 1962, fifteen students from the Liverpool School of Architecture, led by my good friend, Mr Cecil Wright who was lecturer in Medieval Architecture, spent the first two weeks of July re-examining Craswall Priory. They made careful record of those parts of the ruin uncovered by Mr Lilwall in his excavations of 1904 and made further excavations to reveal the true form of the North and South Chapels and collected profiles and details of the stonework to be found on or near the site. The Priory was densely overgrown with ash saplings and was littered with fallen timber. Since the 1903 excavation large quantities of rubble had fallen from the exposed walls and buried the church floor to a depth of several feet.

Photographs taken in 1906 showing a corbal and a springer for three ribs from inside the Chapterhouse.

St Mary's church, Craswall was founded sometime in the 14th century, probably by the monks of the Priory. It is an old stone building with a chancel, a nave and a weather-boarded belfry, the west end of the nave now being walled off to form a vestry. On the exterior of the south and east of the church can be found low stone seating. On the north side of the church is the outline of a disused cockpit where is it alleged that cockfights were held up to the beginning of the 19th century after the service on a Sunday. In October 2001 it was reported in the Hereford Times that thieves stole one third of the Welsh black slates covering the one side of the roof.

About five large stone flags used for seating around the perimeter of the church were also removed. This was the second attempt to steal from the church; the first time the looters were disturbed and left, leaving the tiles stacked on the ground.

Craswall Church

The Bull's Head Inn at Craswall is very near the church on a sharp right hand bend just before the road crosses the infant Monnow. This is a unique country public house which, until 1997 had hardly changed in a century. The Hereford Times, writing in 1997, described it as a "way of life" pub. It had been in the ownership of the same family for at least 125 years. This family combined the running of a pub that was popular with walkers, pony trekkers and tourists, with farming a 95-acre farm with grazing rights on the Black Hill for 850 sheep.

In 1997 following the decision of the landlord, Mr Wilfred George Lewis to retire, the Inn and farm were put up for auction in two lots on June 27th 1997 by the auctioneers Sidney Phillips. Sadly, Mr Lewis died during May of that year.

The Inn was reported as having been sold to Miss Denise Lewis of Rottingdean, Sussex for £118,000. The following year having successfully blended updating without loss of atmosphere, CAMRA voted it 'county pub of the year'. The judges were as much taken with 'its' timeless atmosphere' as the quality of its ales. The Bull's reputation for good food is now well established.

There was also a public house called The Three Horseshoes in Craswall. This was open before 1876 and was still in operation in the 1940's. It was situated just opposite the turning leading to Michaelchurch Escley and very near the Forest Mill and was occupied in 1867 by William Shaw who was a farmer and blacksmith. The naming of a pub or beer house, the Three Horse Shoes, was often an indication that this was a place where horses could be shod. The Forest Mill probably ceased working as a water mill in the early 19th century. There were three mills altogether on the river Monnow in Craswall. In addition to the Forest Mill there was the Old Mill which was referred to as 'old' in 1840. This mill was near Old Mill Farm. Nearer to Longtown is the Cwm Mill the remains of which are near Upper Cwm Farm. This building was partly destroyed by fire in 1976. In addition to being a corn mill it was a fulling mill sometime in the early 19th century. Fulling was the process of thickening the cloth that had been produced by the cottagers who had spun and woven it in their homes. The cloth was beaten in a mixture of water and fuller's earth in order to shrink it and increase its denseness and durability. The process was also known as tucking, hence the commonly found 'Tuck Mill'. In Monmouthshire these mills were often called 'Pandy Mills'. Mills frequently changed their function over the years, being at different times used for grinding corn, fulling, and papermaking.

The Bull's Head Craswall

LLANVEYNOE AND THE OLCHON VALLEY

The Olchon brook joins the river Monnow at Longtown. During its short journey it flows down a narrow gorge in the beautiful Olchon valley. A very quiet, narrow lane leaves the road north of Longtown and after a short distance Llanveynoe church is reached. St Peter's church, Llanveynoe is a small Welsh-style chapel with a single bell-gable. (Plate 1) The name Llanveynoe comes from the original dedication of the church to St Beino (or Beuno). King Ynyr of Gwent granted lands in Ewias to Beuno where the saint built a church of which Llanveynoe church is the successor. St Beuno went on to found eleven churches, mostly in North Wales. He died at Clynog on the Lleyn peninsular but it is quite likely that his remains were returned to Llanveynoe. There are three crosses of considerable antiquity to be found in the church and churchyard. One is an ancient churchyard cross of early medieval date with a grooved shaft and truncated arms. It is thought that these short-armed types of cross were designed to support a wooden cross superstructure. On the south wall inside the church are two much earlier stone slabs with inscription in runic script. The notice on the wall says that they are tenth century Hiberno-Saxon work. The church was extended in 1912 and its seating capacity increased from 45 to 86.

Ancient Cross in Llanveynoe Churchyard.

Continuing along the Olchon valley with the sharp ridge of the Black Hill or Cat's Back on the right and the long hillside of the Hatterrall ridge on the left, it is noticeable how few farms and houses there are in this remote valley. (Plate 3)

In 1887 there was a very strange book published entitled the *History of the Old Baptist Church at Olchon together with the Life and Martyrdom of Sir John Oldcastle and the life of Mr Vavasor Powell* by John Howells who was Baptist Minister for this area. In this book Mr Howells, in a very longwinded discourse and with typically Victorian verbosity, claims that the Olchon Valley was the birthplace of Nonconformity. He says that *'there is evidence that there were Baptists in Olchon at a very early period, and a probability that there were Baptists there even while some of the apostles were living'*.

It is claimed that the 'original' Primitive Baptist chapel stood on the hillside above Olchon Court. By 1900 the only evidence was the ruin of an old barn and it is only local legend that names this place as the site of the old chapel. When John Howells became Baptist minister in about 1872, there was no chapel in the Olchon valley. He writes about the ruins of what he describes as the oldest chapel belonging to the Primitive Baptists standing on the banks of the swift-flowing stream from which the narrow and romantic valley of the Olchon takes its name. Howells claimed that this ancient site was known as the Gellis.

They had for many years very sadly needed a place of worship. Though so far back as the year 1630 the church dates, yet they had no chapel nor any kind of meeting-house to worship God in for the last one hundred and fifty years. Such were the straightened means of the little church and congregation – consisting mainly of shepherds and other very poor people – that they could not attempt the task of building a chapel. So after ten years' experience of worshipping in farm houses, cottages, darrens and waysides, as the people had done for the long period of one hundred and fifty years – I was constrained to undertake the onerous task of erecting, to the glory of God, a soul-saving sanctuary, believing that Christian friends, likeminded with myself, would rally around me, and that He who "came to seek and to save that which was lost" would most assuredly add His all-enriching benediction. Now I am happy to say that after labouring all these years for a remuneration less than £10 per annum, a neat and comfortable chapel has been completed – beautifully and conspicuously situated – and here the prayer of faith is offered, the songs of Zion are sung, and the glad tidings of salvation are proclaimed.

Unfortunately, I have been unable to find out how long the Baptists worshipped at their new chapel but I have been told that by 1920 this chapel had been turned into a cottage and was lived in by a family called Hydes. In recent times this cottage has been extended again but the walls and roofline of the original chapel can be seen and the inscription stone is still in the end wall, 'Salem Chapel 1888'.

The Rev F G Llewellin, who was Vicar of Clodock and Longtown in 1919, in his book the *History of Saint Clodock, British King and Martyr*, wrote very dismissively of the theories of John Howell accusing him of confusing the Lollards with the Baptists.

Sir John Oldcastle was born in Herefordshire in 1378 and was the son of Sir Richard Oldcastle. His ancestors were Lords of the Manor of Almeley, three miles north of Eardisley. He fought for the English during the Scottish campaign of 1400 and during the Welsh wars he became a close friend of Henry, Prince of Wales. In 1409 he married the Kentish heiress, Joan Lady Cobham, and thus obtained a seat in the House of Lords as Lord Cobham, also retaining his original name and knightly style. Sir John belonged to a religious sect known as the Lollards. They were followers of John Wycliffe whose radical religious views included the denial of transubstantiation and stressed the importance of preaching and reading the Scriptures. The Lollard tradition facilitated the spread of Protestantism and helped influence public opinion in favour of Henry VIII's anticlerical legislation during the English Reformation.

Salem Baptist Chapel, Olchon Valley

In 1414 Sir John Oldcastle was indicted for maintaining Lollard preachers. Largely because of past friendship between Oldcastle and Henry when he was Prince of Wales, the new Henry V appealed to Oldcastle to submit and renounce his beliefs. This he refused to do and was brought to trial and convicted as a heretic. He was imprisoned in the Tower of London but managed to escape and took refuge with a Lollard bookseller called William Fisher at Smithfield. Managing to evade capture, he fled into the border country of Wales, which at that time was a stronghold of the Lollards. The next four years were spent in this area probably travelling between his ancestral home at Almeley and the Olchon Valley were he was given refuge by Walter Brute who lived at Olchon Court or, as it was then known, Court Walter. Tradition has it that Sir John escaped through a window at Olchon Court and evaded his pursuers. However, he was recaptured and returned to London in November 1417 and was hanged over a fire that consumed the gallows.

In 1932 a very significant find was made on the hillside just west and south of Olchon Court. Mr James Smith, then aged 79 had been the owner and occupier of

Olchon Court for over 50 years. It was on one of his fields on May 24th 1932 that the plough struck a large stone just a few inches below the surface. This large slab was removed with a crowbar and proved to be the covering of a small cist, an Early Bronze Age burial chamber. Mr Smith promptly reported his find and carefully kept the remains untouched until the experts could examine them. On the floor of this cist was the skeleton of a man in the usual crouched posture with a beaker fallen on its side, but intact, in the space behind the thigh-bones. At the bottom of the beaker was found a beautifully made tanged and winged arrowhead. Another cist of similar dimensions was found three feet to the east. The capstone was missing from this cist and although partly filled with fine silt the contents were undisturbed but nearly perished and the beaker, which contained a flint, was in a very poor condition.

The Beaker people are thought to have been groups of immigrants arriving from the Rhine basin in the Late Neolithic period bringing beaker drinking vessels, copper knives and daggers and maybe woven cloth. Their burial custom was generally a round barrow for single inhumations. A beaker was placed with the body often with arrowheads and ornaments. This group of objects could have been intended to indicate high status.

These burials date from the Early Bronze Age and have been dated between 1700 BC and 1600 BC. Professor Sir Arthur Keith studied the bones that were found in the cist and he reported that the man was of rather short stature, but that his mentality was considerably above the average for his race. He was thought to have been between 25 and 30 years of age. There is evidence that Neolithic man was already living in this area when the Beaker people arrived and that they probably amalgamated.

Mr Alfred Watkins photographed the finds in the field and the chamber and artefacts were presented to Hereford Museum where they were put on display. On enquiring at the museum I was told that although the artefacts would still be in their care they were not now on display to the public.

LONGTOWN

The village of Longtown occupies a ridge-top position at the foot of the Hatterrall Hills, known as the Black Mountains, at about 500 feet above sea level. The rivers Monnow, Olchon and Escley flow through the township and unite a little below the oldest part of the village. To the east of the village is a hill called Mynydd Fferdden (meaning, sloping mountain), or Merlin's mountain, the traditional burial place of Merlin of Arthurian legend. Longtown is described fairly as having 'all length and little breadth' as it straggles up the hill towards the castle which was built on a spur commanding the valleys of the Monnow and Olchon.

In the 11th century this whole area, known as Ewias Lacy, stretched to beyond Ewyas Harold and belonged to the de Lacy family. Walter de Lacy, the founder of this local dynasty, came to England with William the Conqueror and was granted lands in the Welsh Marches where he became Lord of Ewias Lacy. Apparently, it was the King's policy to install his most troublesome knights as Marcher Lords along the Welsh border where they would be less of a threat to his authority. These fighting lords were not so easy to restrain and as a result each lordship of the Marches had a court of its own with jurisdiction completely independent of the King. At various times the Kings tried to abolish the rights of the Lords of the Marches without success until the reign of Henry VIII.

Longtown castle occupies a strong defensive site and was built between the years 1185 and 1195. The large circular keep, which is perhaps the oldest in the country, is built on a massive earthwork that is thought to have been pre-conquest or even Roman in origin. At the southern end of the village at Pont Hendre and known as the Mound, is a motte that may have been the original castle. One account of the castle being under attack was recorded in a history of Wales written in 1584 and quoted by the Rev Llewellin in his book about St Clodock.

In the year 1146, Cadelh, Meredith and Rhys, sons of Gruddydh ap Rhys ap Theodor, brought an army before the castle of Gwys or Gwais, (Ewais) in Herefordshire, but finding themselves too weak to master it, they desired Howell, son of Prince Owen Gwynedd of North Wales, a person famously remarkable for martial endowments, to come to their assistance. Howell, who was very desirous to signalise himself and to evidence his valour in the world, readily consented to their request; and having drawn his forces together, marched directly towards Gwys, where being arrived, he was joyfully received and honourably esteemed by such lords as desired his help. Having viewed the strength and fortification of the castle, he found it was impracticable to take the place unless the walls could be destroyed, and therefore he gave orders that certain battering engines should be provided; whilst the rest should gaul and molest the besieged by throwing great stones into the castle. The enemies perceiving what irresistible preparations the besiegers contrived, thought it to no purpose to withstand their fury, and therefore to do that voluntarily which must be done by compulsion they presently yielded up the castle.

Castle building in Herefordshire went through several stages. The first stage, within a few years of the Conquest, saw new castles being built at Wigmore and Clifford while pre-conquest castles were rebuilt at Hereford and Ewyas Harold. During the second phase the de Lacy's established a castle and borough at Weobley and a new borough beside their castle at Grosmont. There is some evidence that there were also settlements established at White castle and Kilpeck castle.

Longtown Castle pre 1914

The settlement near Longtown castle soon developed into a small township with burgage plots and a small triangular market place abutting the church of St Peters that was once the chapel of the castle. Running at right angles to the main street were the burgage plots. The occupiers of these plots, known as burgesses paid an annual rent to the Lords and their successors. A burgage plot was an allotment of land near a market on which the burgess could build a tenement. Originally the burgesses had the monopoly of trade in these small towns except on market and fair days. On these days they were excused the payment of the tolls that were paid by the other traders to the Lord of the Manor.

The town passed out of the ownership of the de Lacys about 1230 and continued to prosper, so much so that in 1310 the population was about 500. The population is believed to have declined following the outbreak of the plague known as the Black Death which ravaged the country in the middle of the 14th Century. By 1540 the town was known as Longa Villa in Ewias Lacy and eventually just as Longtown.

The parish or township of Longtown is in the ecclesiastical parish of Clodock along with Craswall and Llanveynoe and the majority of the burials were sent to the mother church of Clodock causing the graveyard to have such a crowded appearance.

The 12th Century church of St Peters was restored in 1869 during the period of prolific Victorian church 'improvements'. A very long and detailed description of the opening ceremony was given in the *Hereford Journal on 25th September 1869*. The Journal reported on the fearful state of the building prior to restoration

In fact, if a church was ever thoroughly prostrate and in the dust it was this one. It consists of a nave and chancel only, and, previous to its restoration, a portion of the west end of the nave was portioned off to serve the purpose of a school house. There

was no flooring at all save the virgin earth, and no seats or benches; the only accommodation in this way being some low rough forms, which were transferred from school to service, and from service to school, as occasion might require. In addition to all this, the walls and roof were in a deplorable state, the weather having found its way through to such an extent as to render the building more uncomfortable even to the worshipper than many a well-kept barn could possibly be.

The earth on the north side of the church was five feet higher than the floor level while on the south side the ground fell away so steeply that a flight of a dozen steps were needed to reach the porch.

The church externally is consequently bare and exposed, and the approach is exceedingly uninviting through the fact that it is faced on the south side by a regular old rookery of tumble-down houses, which must be of a date coeval, or nearly so, with the castle; probably they formed the huts of some of the serfs belonging to it.

The alterations were carried out under the direction of Mr T Nicholson FIBA, the diocesan architect. There was the construction of a new roof, a new bell-gable and the bells were recast and toned. A new stone porch was erected on the south side of the church. The seat, which ran from the porch to the stone buttress, was restored to its original state. New windows were inserted; the one on the west side is where there used to be the fireplace of the school.

A new a very commodious school-room has been built at a short distance from the church, on a site the gift of the Earl of Abergavenny, the Lord of the Manor.

The work was carried out by a local builder, Mr Pritchard at a cost, school and church combined, of £1060 'only £160 of which remains to be wiped out'.

Before leaving this part of our subject we must be allowed to make a few remarks on what must be considered as somewhat of an oversight. We do so not in a spirit of fault-finding, and we are aware that the architect has good grounds for his manner of treating the church porch, in erecting which he has adhered to the conventional form of treatment maintaining it on the south side, where was the original entrance. This is in consonance with architectural propriety; but if there ever was a case where an exception might reasonably have been made it is in the case now under notice. We have remarked that on the north side the soil rises, and that on the south side it slopes away towards the village in such an abrupt manner as to render a flight of steps necessary; and also that on this side there are some wretched houses in close proximity. But this is not all; for in addition to the inconvenience and trouble of mounting the steps to the female and aged portion of the congregation, the 'gate of heaven' as the church entrance is sometimes not inaptly called, abuts on a low pot-house, with an unsavoury pigs-cot at its very door, and with the parish well in the midst of a small, filthy, triangular space of ground, used on fair-days as a rendezvous for all profaneness. An instance of the unworthy character of this vicinage was but too painfully apparent on the day of which we write, when some drunken idiot, not yet recovered from the fumes of his carousal of the previous market day, was making himself the sport of a lot of boors at the pothouse door; their ribald laughter distinctly heard by that part of the crowded congregation which was assembled within the church porch. Of course the policeman, with his proverbial invisibility, was nowhere to be seen.

After the service to which the Lord Bishop and his wife and many of the 'great and good' from around the county attended, there was a luncheon given in the schoolroom. By the early 1980's the church had become redundant and in 1983 it was being converted into a private house. The village school built in 1869 was in the precincts of the castle and opposite the castle green which had served for over a hundred years as a sports field and school playground; the ancient green outside the church being only a very small area with the village well in the centre. Livestock fairs on the castle green were held on 29th April and 22nd June and a Statute Fair was held on 21st September for the hiring of servants. By the 1970's, the village needed a new school and a modern building was erected further up the road. The old school was converted into private cottages. The castle green became very overgrown but was restored in 1994 by the Longtown Village Pride group who also restored the dip-well on the north side of the green. This group also created a medieval herb garden, known as Broome's Garden. It is on the left as you approach the entrance to the castle and is open to the public. This garden was formerly the cottage garden of William Broome during the 1920's and it won the Parish Pride Competition in 1996.

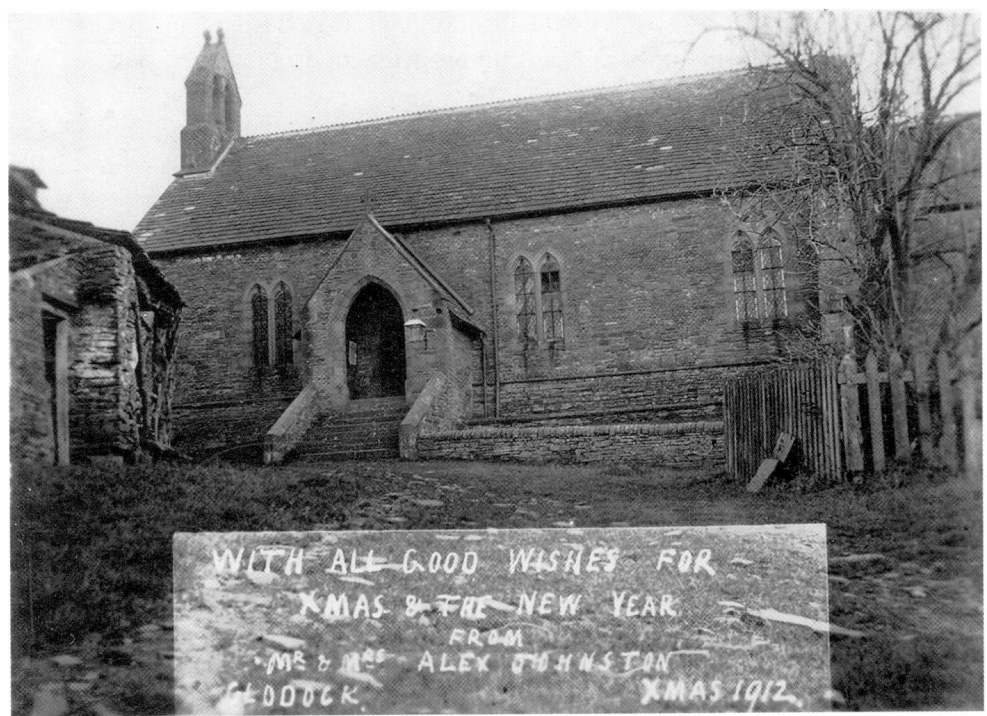

Longtown church pre-1912 showing the steps and the 'hovels'.

In 1876 there were five inns listed in the Directory for Herefordshire. They were the Crown Inn, New Inn, Black Lion Inn, Rising Sun, and Greyhound Inn. The

Crown Inn is now the only one remaining open. A list of the commercial activities in Longtown shows how self-sufficient these villages were in the late 19th century.

Grocer, draper, tailor and sub-postmaster. Post Office.
Saddler and harness maker
Blacksmith
Schoolmaster
Carrier
Tea dealer, family grocer at the New Shop
Road surveyor and registrar of births, marriages and deaths.
Insurance Agent
Carpenter and wheelwright
Miller
Coal, lime and manure merchant
Police sergeant
Boot and shoemaker
Mason and letter cutter
Stonemason
Blacksmith
Shoemaker
Watch and clock dealer, ironmonger, boot and shoe warehouse.
Shopkeeper
Horse breaker
Laundress and lodgings
Medical assistant
Carpenter, wheelwright and sawing machine proprietor
Grocer and provision dealer.

There were twenty-five farms listed. One of the Inns, the New Inn, which was once used as the Courthouse, is now the Longtown Education Centre which was opened in 1964 by the Northampton Education Authority as an outdoor education centre. Its first warden was John Van Laun In 1965 the centre became a Mountain Rescue Post (Post no 57), and John Van Laun decided that as Longtown was now an official Mountain Rescue Post he should form a local Mountain Rescue Team. These teams are made up of volunteers and John invited a number of people who regularly used the hill to become team members. During the 1960's and 70's the number of callouts gradually increased and by the 80's the team membership had risen to about 40 people, both male and female and had become a fully mobile response team with two vehicles used as equipment carriers. These vehicles enabled the teams to make a quicker response than when all the equipment was kept at the Longtown centre. By the year 2000 it was clear that a permanent base was needed and the new base at Abergavenny was opened in 2001. There are now over fifty volunteers and membership is steadily increasing.

During the last few years a number of new houses have been built at Longtown and others have been beautifully restored. After the last two shops closed it was feared that this was the end of an era. Fortunately, in May 2004 the new stores and post office was finally completed and Hopes of Longtown opened to the public. This is a beautiful new building full of local goodies. It is supported by the England Rural Development Programme and has already won an award from Flavours of

Herefordshire. It is advertised as 'the convenience of a supermarket sustaining a local economy'. We wish them the utmost success in this very worthy venture.

Longtown Church with a view of the village well in the foreground. On the reverse of the postcard it says, 'Chapel of ease to the more ancient Parish church of St Clodock. The mother-church is in danger of ruin. The Vicar needs £600 to save it. Will you help?'

CLODOCK

The present day ecclesiastical parish of Clodock is very large and it incorporates the smaller parishes of Craswall, Longtown and Llanveynoe. It is the largest and broadest parish in Herefordshire covering more that 27 square miles. This is an area of such diverse countryside, covering as it does mountains, vales, streams and rivers and it must rank as one of the most beautiful of parishes.

Clodock is now in the diocese of Hereford but this was not always so. In earlier times Clodock has belonged to three different dioceses. For its first five hundred years the parish was in the diocese of Llandaff, then when the boundaries were changed it transferred to the diocese of St David where it remained for the next seven hundred years. In 1858 the parish finally became part of the diocese of Hereford. As will be seen from the above, this church has a very long history and was founded on this site about 1500 years ago.

St Clodock has been known by various names of Clitauc, Clydawg, Clydog. The usual spelling in the Book of Llandaff was Clydawg. He was the son of Clydwyn who had invaded all the South Wales area and was the grandson of Brychan, the famous King of Brecon. Clydawg was King of Ewyas in the 5th century and was respected for his wisdom and justice ruling over a peaceful kingdom. Ewyas was the name given to the "hundred" or district which included Clodock, Craswall, Cusop, Llancillo, Llanveynoe, Longtown, Michaelchurch Escley, Newton, Rowlestone, St Margarets and Walterstone. This group of parishes were part of Wales until the reign of Henry VIII when they were transferred to England.

The story recounted in the 12th century Book of Llandaff (Liber Landavensis) tells how a young lady of noble birth wished to marry King Clydawg and no other. A friend of the King was consumed with jealousy and killed him whilst out hunting. (Other sources say Pagan Saxons killed him). The story continues that his body was placed on a cart to which two oxen were yoked, and driven towards the river where there was a ford. This river was known as the Mynwy, now the river Monnow. On approaching the river the yoke broke and the oxen refused to go any further so Clydawg was buried there beside the river. This spot soon became a place of veneration and pilgrimage and eventually a small church was built called the Merthyr Clydawg, the church of the Martyrdom of Clydawg. The parish church of St Clodock is still on this same site.

The present day red sandstone Norman church of St Clydawg or Clydog dates from around 1100 AD. There is one relic from an earlier era and this is a memorial stone that was dug up during the restoration of 1916-1919. Its date is thought to be somewhere between 750 and 850 AD. It was cut on sandstone by local craftsmen of the 'monastic' school. Translated it reads something like.

This tomb has the remains of that faithful woman the dear wife of Guinnda who herself was resident in this place.

The interior of Clodock church has many interesting and quite rare features. The Communion Rails and Housel Bench date from about 1650. They are called 'Laudian' because they reflect the attempt by Archbishop Laud to prevent the Communion Table being brought down from the chancel to the people in the nave

Interior Clodock Church, Herefordshire.

where sometimes it would be left and used for other purposes. To stop this practice, the Archbishop commanded that rails be placed around the Communion Table and that it should be left at the east end of the church and that the congregation should gather around it there. The rails at Clodock are unusual as they are three sided instead of the usual form of being straight across the chancel. The Rev Llewellin, writing in 1919 describes these rails as being of solid oak which had been painted white a dozen times and which he hoped could be restored. The Housel Bench is where the waiting communicants would sit. The word 'housel' is from the anglo-saxon 'husel', a sacrifice, and means the taking or administering of the Eucharist.

In the nave are fine furnishings from the 17th and 18th centuries. There are box pews arranged in three series with fine carvings and a variety of mouldings. There is a very fine three-decker pulpit with a sounding board and carved swags in the Grinling-Gibbons style which apparently also needed the stripping away of many layers of paint in the 1919 restoration.

At the west end of the church is a musician's gallery which is of the same date as the pulpit (1650-1680). This gallery is divided into two sections, one for the musicians or orchestra with a table in the centre to hold the music and surrounded by seating for the said musicians. The other section is for the minstrels or village choir with seats facing the chancel. It is very steep so that the singer behind could sing over the head of the one in front.

The churchyard is notable for its array of memorial stones that are still in very good condition and have not been moved from their original positions. The churchyard is enclosed by an ancient dry-stone wall in which there is a Lych-gate or Lich gate. The name is derived from the Old English 'Lich' meaning corpse. The term 'corpse-gate' was in common usage until recently when applied to any opening or stile by which a cortege might gain access to the churchyard. It was a requirement in the 1549 Prayer Book that the priest should meet the corpse at 'the church style' and commence the Order for the Burial of the Dead. In the days when most bodies were carried on a bier from home to church the covered lych-gate gave a opportunity to rest the bier under cover and the mourners could rest on the seats while waiting for the clergyman. Due to the rocky nature of the churchyard at Craswall, burials tend to take place lower down the valley at Clodock church.

Just a short distance from the church and across the Monnow Bridge on the left hand side is Saint Clydawg's well. This is a dip-well fed by a spring from a rock close to the river Monnow. It is reputed never to run dry. In times of flood the Monnow invades the well. Prior to the early 1930's when the Rural District Council supplied a piped supply, all drinking water in the village had to be fetched from this well.

Bridge over the River Monnow at Clodock

OLDCASTLE

Oldcastle, with its Welsh name Hen-gastell, is a small parish on the east slope of the Hatterrall ridge just south of Clodock. It takes its name from the ancient earthwork on which Oldcastle Court and the church are built. This may have been a Roman station on the road from Abergavenny to Kenchester and it is alleged that Roman coins have been found there. The Manor was part of the large possessions of Llantony Priory and at the Reformation, the Manor of Oldcastle, together with the manors of Walterstone, Llancillo St Margaret's, Longtown, Michaelchurch Escley, Rowlestone and Kenderchurch were all granted with their estates to Sir Nicholas Arnold who was rewarded for supporting Thomas Cromwell, the Elizabethan statesman. His son, and then his grandson, John Arnold lived at Llanvihangel Court.

Sir Joseph Bradley, writing in 1913, said that the neighbourhood of Oldcastle was peopled with descendants of Sitsyllt, the younger son of Sir Gilbert Wyston of Tre-Wyn. This Sitsyllt had two sons, ffilo or Philo and Grono, whose descendants were known in Welsh as the ffiloed and Gronowaid. These two clans were constantly in conflict with each other and killings were not unknown. A branch of the Gronowaid was long resident at Oldcastle Court.

The original old house of Oldcastle Court was rebuilt long ago. The present Court is a farmhouse offering Bed and Breakfast. Right next to the Court is the parish church that was rebuilt in 1864 on the site of the ancient church which was completely demolished. Until 1830 the services were in Welsh and English on alternate Sundays. The churches of Oldcastle, Llantony and Cwmyoy that were formerly in the diocese of St David's were transferred to the diocese of Llandaff in 1844. The church at Oldcastle is now a private dwelling.

Tre-Wyn in the Parish of Oldcastle

The Manor house of Tre-Wyn is in the hamlet or township of Bwlch Tre-Wyn. Bwlch which means a 'gap in the mountain'. Originally the area was in the County of Herefordshire but an Act of Parliament in 1844 transferred it to Monmouthshire. The house is said to have derived its name, the Wyn, from Sir John Gwyn or Wyn, the original owner who also owned Allt-yr-ynys. Apparently, a branch of this family whose name became Wynston went to live in Gloucestershire and Sarah, the daughter of Henry Wynston married into the Churchill family. Thus the name Wynston or Winston became the Christian name of our famous war-time Prime Minister, Sir Winston Churchill. In the 18th century Tre-wyn and Allt-yr-Ynys were both owned by the Delahay family and they were responsible for planting the avenue of Scotch Firs that at one time extended across both estates.

The original mansion was erected by the Harleys in the reign of Henry VII and the present house was built in 1694, the date being recorded in the stonework. The house is an unusual design for this part of the country with its lofty windows, high-pitched roof and the broad flight of steps with intervening terraces which lead up to the front door. The gardens were laid out in a formal style and a stream was diverted to form a canal. In a meadow near the house is a brick-built pigeon house with nests for 831 birds. H. Thornhill Timmins in his book *Nooks and Corners of Herefordshire* published in 1892 describes the interior of Tre-Wyn as having a beautiful panelled hall with a mantelpiece supported by huge pillars brought from the ruined chapel of Allt-yr-Ynys. In the grounds of Tre-Wyn, traces of a Roman road were found which was thought to be part of the highway from Abergavenny to Kenchester. Part of that same road was exposed during the building of the Golden Valley Railway near Abbey Dore from where it continued through Madley and to the river Wye at New Weir.

Allt-yr-Ynys

WALTERSTONE

Allt-yr-Ynys is in the parish of Walterstone in a beautiful setting almost surrounded by water as the stream called the Nant Cravell and the river Honddu both flow into the river Monnow on the south side of the house. The name Allt-yr-Ynys means a meadow partially surrounded by a river, or 'Hill of the Island'. It is from this place that the river Monnow becomes the boundary between England and Wales for most of its journey to Monmouth.

Allt-yr-Ynys is an ancient place with a long history. The estate became the property of the Cecils through the marriage of Robert Sitsylt (Cecil), to an heiress, said to be the daughter of Sir John Gwyn of Tre-Wyn. One of the descendants of the Cecils migrated to Lincolnshire in the early 16th century and became the grandfather of Sir William Cecil, the Lord Burghley who was Lord Treasurer to Queen Elizabeth I. Another branch of the family could be found at Dyffryn in Grosmont. In the 14th century the Grandison's lived in the house. John Grandison, Bishop of Exeter was a native of this place. He died in 1369. A survey of the house in 1647 described it as 'the ancient capital house'. By 1876 the Herefordshire Directory describes the property as having some of the remains of its ancient grandeur and had 'until recent years the arms of Burghley in stained glass in the window'. It is claimed that Queen Elizabeth was a guest at Allt-yr-Ynys. This ancient abode is now a four star Country House Hotel that retains much of the fine workmanship of the original house which was built in about 1550. There is a beautiful ceiling and fine old panelling in the lounge and massive oak beams throughout the house.

St Mary's church in Walterstone is quite a plain building with a Victorian bellcote. Very near the church are the remains of a motte and bailey castle with the motte rising 30 feet from the bottom of the ditch. The Carpenters Arms is a very welcoming and unspoilt public house with a log fire and real ales where we have on several occasions partaken of an excellent Sunday lunch. Another ancient feature in Walterstone is the Iron Age hill-fort covering about 10 acres and enclosed by three concentric ramparts.

In 2002 the rural tranquillity of the parish of Walterstone was disturbed by a very controversial planning application that was submitted to Herefordshire Council seeking permission to build a 'fairy tale castle'. The Hereford Times described the plans for Monnow Court, as it was to be called, 'as a mock-medieval moated manor house on a grand scale reminiscent of grand Tudor palaces. The moated court will be the first of its kind in Herefordshire for 600 years and will stand in 25 acres of landscaped gardens complete with a moat and maze and bordered by a deer park.'

These plans received a mixed reception by the general public and caused a lot of interest and speculation. However, the majority of the parishioners of Walterstone were quite united in their opposition and in early 2002 the Herefordshire Planning Committee refused the application; a blessing or a lost opportunity – we shall never know!

LLANCILLO

Llancillo is a very small parish of about 1000 acres with the only dwellings being just a few farms. The main buildings are Llancillo Hall and Llancillo Court with the parish church adjacent. The only road in the parish is the minor road from Rowlestone to Walterstone that just passes through the north of the parish. The main line railway carves a route very near the southern boundary of the parish, which is the river Monnow.

St Peter's Church, Llancillo

St Peter's Church Llancillo must be one of the best-kept secrets in Herefordshire. It is totally secluded with no road to it and hidden in a tranquil vale in a parish that few people have even heard of. The Book of Llandaff refers to Lann Sulbiu. In 1733 the spelling is Llansilo, which may indicate that the original dedication of the church was to St Tysilio, the same dedication as at Sellack church. St Tysilio was a Welsh prince who lived in the 7th century and was Abbot of Meifod in Powys.

In the 1876 Directory of Herefordshire, the church was described as being in a bad state of repair and unfit for divine service. By 1890 the Bishop advised closure. Conditions became even worse when the church was not used. A wall fell in, the roof tiles were blown off and sheep wandered in through the open door. It was assumed that the building would be left to decay but the Vicar of Rowlestone who also preached at Llancillo, the Rev Robert Whinning, set up a restoration fund and was able to raise enough money to have a considerable amount of work done. By 1905 the Directory was describing the church as *'an ancient building of stone, old and curious, in the Early English style. For some time ruinous and disused but now restored. The west wall was rebuilt and surmounted by a modern bell-cote.'* Sadly, when I visited the church in the summer of 2004, it was again showing signs of damp as a missing tile on the roof was letting in the rain which was seeping into the nave. There are very few services held in the church now, and it must be very difficult to keep such an old building in good repair. The visitor's book shows that there are a few visitors who manage to find their way here.

To the east of the church, about 90 yards away, is a castle site on which sits a circular motte of about 43 yards in diameter. A dry ditch and an outer rampart surround it. In 1930 when the Royal Commission for Ancient Monuments surveyed the site there were still traces of the rubble walling of a former keep and these are still visible. There are other ditches and banks around the site which may have enclosed the bailey or even a village.

Llancillo Court is an ancient house that was remodelled in the 18th century with further additions in more recent times. Llancillo Hall is about a mile to the west of Llancillo Court and dates from the 15th or early 16th century but it has been altered and modernised.

In the early 20th century Col. Edward Scudamore Lucas-Scudamore was the Lord of the Manor. He lived at Cap House, Llangua (formerly the Cap Inn). The Scottish Union and National Insurance Company of London were the principal landowners.

The parish was not always a quiet backwater. From the late 17th century there would have been a great deal of noise and activity generated by a forge on the banks of the river Monnow. The exact dates for the beginning and ending of Llancillo forge are unknown but in 1670 John Scudamore leased 'Lansyllo Forge' to William Hall for 21 years. (Foley papers HRO). The forge continued working probably into the 19th century.

The first consideration when choosing the site of a forge would have been the availability of water to turn the water wheels that operated the furnace bellows and the tilt hammers. A weir was built to hold back the water of the river Monnow so that a controlled flow was always available.

Llancillo forge was a works where molten iron, which had been smelted in a blast furnace and then converted into pigs, was converted into bars of wrought iron. The pig-iron was rich in carbon and other impurities and consequently rather brittle. After being heated and 'soaked' for a prolonged period in a furnace known as a finery, most of the carbon would oxidise from this cast iron leaving a more pure and malleable iron which was then reheated in the chaffery and forged to close the grain structure and thus greatly increase the tensile strength. This process was superseded by the introduction of the reverbatory furnace in the 1780's and the process known as 'puddling'. Even so the iron forges did not totally disappear and survived at Sticklepath in Devon up until the 1960's. The pig-iron was heated and then forged by means of water powered tilt hammers into bars of wrought iron which had considerable tensile strength. The pig-iron was brought to Llancillo from Llanelly near Abergavenny as well as from the furnace at St Weonards and from as far away as the Forest of Dean. These journeys must have been very difficult considering the poor state of the roads at that time. The wrought iron was taken to Monmouth to be sold on from there. Much of the iron from the local ironworks was transported by barge down the river Wye, destined for Bristol.

By 1672 the lease of Llancillo forge had been assigned to Paul Foley whose family were operating the forge until at least the 1730's as part of their industrial empire. For the years 1725-31 the total output of iron from Llancillo forge was almost 300 tons. The remains of the forge were still visible in the early 1970's when Stan Coates visited the site.

ROWLESTONE

Rowlestone is a small parish with part of its boundary on the river Monnow. I have found two explanations as to the derivation of its name. According to Preb. Lambert in the Woolhope Transaction of 1906, Rowlestone probably marks the spot where two Viking warriors, Walter and Rowl, or Rowley were buried and a stone erected over each one. A similar name, Rolleston appears in the heart of Nottinghamshire, by the river Trent, up which the Vikings certainly settled. Bannister, in his Place Names of Herefordshire gives a more plausible explanation. He suggests that Rowlestone and neighbouring, Gilbertson (Longtown) were the settlements of Ralph and Gilbert, two of the five knights who are mentioned in the Domesday Book as knights holding land in the Castelry of Ewias.

The church of St Peters is extremely interesting. From the outside it is a plain Norman building situated in the centre of the parish on high ground where three roads meet. On entering the church porch a glance upwards will be rewarded by a most remarkable tympanum over the door representing Christ in Glory. In His left hand Christ holds the Book and His right hand is held high in an attitude of a blessing. Four angels surround Him in adoration; two looking up from below and two look down from above. On each side of the doorway is a circular jamb decorated with birds and a green man with foliage proceeding from his mouth. These wonderful carvings and those within the church have been attributed to the Herefordshire School of Sculpture which flourished in the 12th century and whose work can be seen at its best at Kilpeck church.

Inside Rowlestone church the chancel arch has been beautifully carved. Here as elsewhere in the church birds feature in the carving. On the left of the chancel arch next to a carving of a dove are two figures about eight inches high with intricately carved dresses in deep folds, thought to be an angel and a bishop. On the other side of the arch is a similarly carved stone of the same size, once again depicting an angel and possibly St Peter. The difference is that this stone is upside down. Was this an accident or was it intended to represent St Peter being crucified upside down?

A most unusual feature in the chancel is the pair of iron candle brackets four and a half feet long, which are on the north and south walls. Each bracket holds five candles and they are decorated, one with cocks and one with swans each bird separated with a fleur de lis. These wrought iron brackets are thought to be of 15th century origin. They have been refurbished in recent years and are in splendid condition.

The church was restored in 1865 by the Vicar, the Rev James Martin Kennedy under the supervision of G C Haddon, Architect of Hereford and Malvern. A new vicarage was erected in 1869 at a cost of £1200. The Rev Kennedy was assisted in all his restoration work and the building of the new vicarage by his cousin Baron Martin of the Exchequer and other influential friends who contributed £2000 towards the project. The new vicarage was a very attractive Victorian country house. Unfortunately, in 1968 it was partly destroyed by fire and subsequently a new brick vicarage was built on the site. James Martin Kennedy was born in 1815 in Londonderry, Ireland and he completed his education at King's College, London. He was instituted into the living of Rowlestone and Llancillo in 1864 and retired to Hereford in 1892 after 28 years of service to the community. He died in 1905. His son, Dr James Kennedy and his grandchildren commissioned a stained glass window in his memory which was dedicated in 1964. The small circular window at the top depicts the Kennedy crest, a dolphin and the motto, 'Advise La Fin', which means 'Consider the End'

In the Herefordshire Directory for 1890 it states that 'the yew trees in the churchyard are extremely fine, some of them perhaps the finest in England'. If this was the case then they are long gone. There are now four yew trees of a moderate size to be found in the churchyard, but they are certainly not as eye-catching as those of Capel-y-ffin.

Rowlestone Church

EWYAS HAROLD

The Village, Ewyas Harold

Ewyas or Ewias as it was until the 13th century, was the name by which the area that stretched from the Black Mountains to the Golden Valley was known. (See chapter 1)

When Edward the Confessor came to the throne in 1042 he brought with him from Normandy, where he had lived for 25 years, many of his closest friends and supporters. Of these, a great favourite was his nephew Ralph, son of his sister Goda. When in 1046, Godwin's son Sweyn, Earl of Hereford was banished, Ralph was appointed Earl of Hereford in his place. Ralph granted lands to many of his native Normans who flooded to this country when Edward was crowned King. One of them, Osbern named Pentecost, was given lands in Ewias. Here he built a motte and bailey castle on the earthworks of an English burgh (an old English term for fortified land). This was the first castle to be built at Ewyas Harold.

The Norman friends of the King were very unpopular with the local population who considered them a threat to their freedom. Earl Godwin, who with others, decided to make a stand against the foreign favourites, persuaded King Edward to banish many of his Norman followers including Osbern Pentecost. His castle was dismantled and his lands given to Alured of Marlborough who still held them at the time of the Domesday survey.

In 1055 Gruffydd, Prince of North Wales attacked Herefordshire laying waste much of Ewias and Archenfield before attacking Hereford. The superior foot forces of the Welsh soon routed Earl Ralph's mounted army who turned and ran earning Ralph the nickname of 'Ralph the Timid'. The Welsh entered the city of Hereford which they sacked and burnt. The cathedral was destroyed and six canons were slain on the cathedral steps. Two years later in 1057 Ralph died leaving a young son who was to give his name to Ewyas Harold.

When King Edward, known as Edward the Confessor (1042-1065), died without an heir there were several claims to the English throne. Edward had, according to Norman sources, promised the throne to William of Normandy. King Harold of Norway considered himself the rightful heir and in England, Earl Harold, a member of the powerful Godwin family had a strong claim. With three contenders for the throne there could be just one winner. Harold Godwin, newly crowned King of England, convincingly defeated Harold Sigurdsson, King of Norway at the battle of Stamford Bridge where King Harold the Norwegian was killed. Three days after the victory William of Normandy landed at Hastings and it was Harold Godwin's turn to be defeated and killed in battle.

It was at the end of the 11th century when Harold, son of Ralph, succeeded Alured of Marlborough in the lordship of Ewyas. This was just one of his many manors and he owned lands in several English counties. It seems that Harold made Ewyas his main residence and ended his days there aged three score years and ten. Of his successors his son Robert was known for his stand against the Welsh all along the border. He founded the Abbey of Dore at the beginning of King Stephens's reign and built the parish church of Ewyas Harold. Sybilla de Ewyas, the eventual heir of the family married Robert de Tregoz of Eaton Tregoz, a manor in the parish of Foy. By 1200 there was no male issue and the Tregoz heirs eventually married into the la Warr family whose lands after a short interval became part of the Lordship of Abergavenny.

Gradually the castle fell into decay and does not seem to have been occupied after about 1400. By the time of Henry VIII it was already a ruin although many of the walls were still standing. Over the years it became a quarry where local people could get their building stone so the re-cycled castle of Ewias undoubtedly survives to this day, albeit in a more benign form.

In the summer of 1100 at the Abbey of Gloucester, there was a dedication service to commemorate the completion of the new church of St. Peter after 11 years of building. Many important people were present and after the service the Bishop of Hereford, together with others, including Harold of Ewias, made a grant of lands to the Abbey. Harold endowed the monks of Gloucester Abbey with the tithes of his desmesne and with other lands and possessions of St Michaels Church in Ewias. In return the monks undertook to serve the church of St Michaels and to provide a chaplain for the church and for the chapel of St Nicholas in the castle of Ewias.

After Harold's death in about 1120, the monks negotiated with his son Robert, the new lord of Ewyas, for a site on which to build monastic buildings. He granted them 'all that land where stood my father's barns and mine.' Robert also granted the monks free use of his mill. The Priory is thought to have been built somewhere between the castle bailey and the church.

Just eighty years later at the end of the century the Priory needed rebuilding but Harold's grandson refused to confirm the grants unless at least a Prior and one monk were sent to serve the churches. The monks continued to serve the church until 1358 when the Priory, 'poor in spirit and revenue' was suppressed and all reverted to Gloucester Abbey except a small portion sufficient to support a Vicar for St Michaels church. A contributory factor to the failure of the Priory may have been the abuse of hospitality by the neighbouring Welsh with few donations to help with the obligation to provide accommodation. There was also a problem with many of the outlying

Priories of Gloucester Abbey. Monks were sent out to these Priories from the parent Abbey either as a punishment for their misdemeanours or for their health and the rule was that no monk should stay for more than a year. The Prior was to provide all these brethren with all their necessities including clothing and shoes such as they were accustomed to receiving at the Abbey. It seems that these instructions were not always carried out often due to the great poverty of the Priory. This may well have been the case at Ewyas Harold. By the early part of the 13th century there was only the Prior and one monk at Ewyas Harold and the Abbot of Gloucester, at his own expense had to supply the monks with clothes and even their food.

During the English Civil Wars (1642-51) Ewyas Harold, in common with Hereford, supported the Royalists cause. Because of its strategic position at the end of the Golden Valley the village became an important place through which supplies were diverted into Radnorshire, thus bypassing the more dangerous route near Hereford and Ludlow and evading the Parliamentary army which was besieging Hereford.

Of the years between the abandonment of the castle and Priory up until the 17th century little detail is known about the village. Great changes must have been experienced during Tudor times with the closure of Dore Abbey and the departure of the Cistercians. The Lord's Wood, as Ewyas Harold common was originally known, would have gradually been cleared of trees. Cottages and smallholding would have been built round the edges of the common and the use of the common gradually becoming customary rights.

The population of the village did not vary very much throughout the centuries. In the year 1300 the parish contained 37 free tenants and 75 villeins amounting to approximately 400 people. This changed little over the centuries as in 1876 the population was 548 and in 1926 it was 445. However, by the end of the 20th century the population was nearer 900 due to the village being designated a development area by the Herefordshire Planning Authority, with many new houses and some small factories being built.

In the late Victorian era the church, as so many were at the time, was in a state of decay. In 1868 the Vicar, the Rev W R Lawrence was responsible for implementing a programme of restoration which cost £1220. This restoration included taking down much of the tower and rebuilding, replacing stone for stone in its original position. The ceilings were removed revealing a framed roof of oak.

For other denominations a Baptist Chapel was built in 1862 seating 200 and a Primitive Methodist chapel in 1864 seating 110. There is also a small modern Catholic church that is served from Belmont Abbey dedicated to St. John Kemble.

Perhaps the most illustrious and erudite Vicar appointed to Ewyas Harold was Canon Arthur Thomas Bannister, a classical scholar. In 1898 at the age of 36 he and his wife Alice came to live at the Vicarage. Although they only lived at Ewyas Harold for 11 years they were very active in all aspects of village life. Before taking up his duties at Ewyas Harold, Bannister had been teaching young students in his spare time. At Ewyas Harold he ran a private cramming establishment for students preparing to take the entrance examinations for Oxford University. One of his students was Brian Hatton who became famous as an artist and who was tragically killed near the Suez Canal during the First World War.

Bannister's busy life included being very involved with the village school and church choir. His most lasting legacy must be his book 'The History of Ewyas Harold' which was published in 1902. He later went on to publish 'The Place-Names of Herefordshire' in 1916. On resigning his living in Ewyas Harold in 1909, Bannister and his wife moved to the Cathedral Close in Hereford and he became a Residentiary Canon in Hereford Cathedral.

Arthur Bannister was an important man in the academic life of Hereford. He was President of the Woolhope Club in 1918 and very involved with the Cantilupe Society. He was Vice-President of Hereford Orchestral Society and in 1924 become President of the Herefordshire Branch of the Workers Educational Association. He wrote numerous theological books and articles and translated from Medieval Latin many documents in the Cathedral archives. Bannister died at his home at St Katherine's, Ledbury in 1936 and was buried at St Mary's, Donnington.

TEMPLE BAR INN, EWYAS HAROLD

PONTRILAS

Pontrilas is a hamlet in the parish of Kentchurch, and following the construction of the Hereford to Abergavenny Railway line in 1854 its name became well known. From relative obscurity the hamlet developed in the late 19th and early 20th centuries into a busy and industrious place. Today, with its almost deserted main street, while the traffic hurtles by on the new road, it presents a different picture to that of just a generation ago. Its busy railway station of yesteryear is no more as modern trains flash past with apparent indifference to the potential passengers from this populous area.

The name Pontrilas, according to Bannister in his book 'The History of Ewyas Harold', developed from the 14th century name Heliston then to Ailstone and eventually to Elstones Bridge in 1577 and Elston Bridge in 1670. Bannister suggests that the change to the name Pontrilas may have come about through the Welsh name for Heliston which was Tref-heilas. The bridge would have been called Pont-tref-heilas and then corrupted to Pontrilas. The other explanation is that it is called after a bridge of three streams. This Bannister considers misleading.

The earliest record of industry in Pontrilas was at Pontrilas forge which was situated at the confluence of the rivers Dore and Monnow.. The first record of a forge or iron mill was in 1623 when it was leased by Walter and James Baskerville to Benedict Hall for 12 years. James's son Humphrey Baskerville continued the lease in 1664 for another 21 years and in 1672 William Hall, son of Benedict, assigned the forge to Paul Foley. During the year 1677 the forge produced 89 tons of bar iron. The last mention of a forge at Pontrilas was in the year 1695. It is interesting that the forge was working at the same time as the Llancillo forge and was less than 2 miles distant. All traces of this forge have now disappeared.

The railway brought industry and prosperity to the then small hamlet of Pontrilas. The first railway – really a tramway – through Pontrilas was between Hereford and Abergavenny and owed its existence to the need to deliver Welsh coal to the City of Hereford and beyond. Prior to this Hereford relied upon its barge traffic on the river Wye for coal from the Forest of Dean. As these barges could only operate for about four months of the year when water levels were suitable, an alternative source would have been vital for the expansion of Hereford. Two large doors now hang in the wall at Pontrilas Court on the spot where the tramway is said to have been. Coal was first hauled by horse drawn trams on the cast iron plateway of the Hereford Railway through Pontrilas in September 1829. On almost the same route, in 1854, was built the Newport, Abergavenny and Hereford Railway that became part of the West Midland Railway in 1860. This in turn, became part of the Great Western Railway in 1863. Pontrilas was the chief intermediate station between Hereford and Abergavenny.

The opening of the Golden Valley Railway in September 1881 from Pontrilas to Dorstone and eventually to Hay-on-Wye in 1889, brought even more traffic and business through Pontrilas. The convenience of moving raw materials and manufactured goods by railway made Pontrilas an attractive place to set up business. In 1876 William Kear, a timber and bark merchant from Hereford traded from a stores and offices at Pontrilas. He advertised as a manufacturer of Rind Hoops, Dry Cask Hoops and all kinds of Helves and Hammer Shafts for colliery purposes and

Views of Pontrilas Court from the drive and from the garden c. 1900

workshops. He was also agent for the Star Brewery in Maylord Street which was owned by George Horne who advertised as a brewer of East India pale and mild ales and porter.

The Pontrilas Chemical Works was sited alongside the railway near the station with it's own private siding in use from 1874 to 1929. It was owned by Captain Richard Rees of Abergavenny. The works produced a range of materials; charcoal, acetate of lime, naphtha, pitch and tar made by a process described as 'destructive distillation of wood'. The chemical works was sold at an auction held at the King's Head Hotel, Newport at 3 pm on 17th October 1872 the reason being 'in consequence of the death of the resident partner'. The description was of a valuable works in full working order.

Twelve ovens or Retorts with all the plant and machinery necessary for the manufacture of naphtha, acetate of lime, charcoal etc in the Parish of Kentchurch, together with 6 cottages, offices, warehouses and stabling. The works stand in 9 acres of ground in the midst of thickly wooded district and are abundantly supplied with water. They are held under lease for 21 years from 2nd February 1858 at the rent of £30 pa, with the right of renewal for a further period of 21 years at the rent of £40 pa.

Large brickworks stood near the junction of the Rowlestone – Pontrilas road from the mid 19th century. G J Wilson advertised his works in the 1876 Hereford Directory. He had works at Hampton Park, Hereford and Pontrilas. The works manufactured pressed bricks, crested tiles, flooring squares, draining pipes, wall copings etc. A row of red brick houses known as Brickyard Row is all that remains today.

Near the station George Thomas was a coal, coke, lime and manure merchant. Miss M Bampfield was a grocer and provision dealer with a drapery and shoe warehouse. In addition to the Pontrilas Inn, which was near the railway, there was a beer retailer at the Royal Oak situated on the hill leading towards Orcop. The Pontrilas Inn was also at one time called the Scudamore Arms. It suffered a disastrous fire in December 1970 and the site has now been redeveloped. By 1926 Pontrilas was a busy village with butcher, baker, grocer, coal merchant, motorcar proprietor, boot maker, stationer and post office, wheelwright, watchmaker, solicitor, motorcycle engineer. The doctor visited on Fridays from 11am to 12 noon. The dentist visited on Fridays from 10am to 3pm. Lloyds Bank sub branch visited on Fridays 11am to 2.30pm. and the National Provincial Bank visited on Fridays from 11am to 2.30pm. The local Auctioneers opened a small produce market.

November 1999 marked the end of an era when John Cole closed Pontrilas Stores after more than 40 years. It had become increasingly difficult to run a small grocery business in competition with the supermarkets. He was the third generation of the Cole family to keep this village shop started by his grandfather in Victorian times

The largest industry in Pontrilas today is the Pontrilas Saw Mill. Large quantities of timber are transported by huge lorries that travel along a road which runs parallel to the under used railway.

Pontrilas was the home of the Baskerville family from about 1500. Thomas Baskerville may have built or enlarged the first Pontrilas Court. His son Walter who also had three sons, inherited the house. The eldest son James inherited Pontrilas Court, and his brother William lived at Cwmaddoc in Garway. A third brother, Walter lived at Wormesley Grange. The Pontrilas Court that we see today was built about 1630. By 1700 Pontrilas Court was in the possession of Sir Philip Jackson, a merchant, in whose family it remained until 1815 when it was sold. After changing hands once again the property was bought by Colonel John Scudamore of Kentchurch Court. During the century that the Scudamore family owned the house it had several tenants. One of these tenants it is said to have been George Bentham (1800-1884) who was a renowned botanist. He was famous for his classification of seed plants (spermatophyte) and donated his herbarium of more than 10,000 specimens to the Royal Botanical Gardens at Kew. The Director, William Hooker invited Bentham to make a permanent base at Kew and he was very influential in the creation of Kew Gardens. I have been told that Bentham lived for several years at Pontrilas Court and was responsible for the planting of many of the specimen trees on the property.

In 1867 an advertisement appeared in the Hereford Commercial Prospectus for the

SCUDAMORE ARMS HOTEL, PONTRILAS NEAR HEREFORD.

The Hotel, formerly a Baronial Mansion is delightfully situated on the confines of the counties of Hereford and Monmouth, midway between Hereford and Abergavenny, and 200 yards from the Pontrilas Station. It is fitted for the reception of Gentlemen and Families of position, with extensive right of Fishing on the River Monnow, one of the best Trout streams in England.

W G Jones, Proprietor

The hotel closed around the mid 1870's.

At the end of the 19th century Benjamin St John Matthews, J P occupied Pontrilas Court. Over the next half century there were several occupants; Col. Richard Prescott-Decie, JP in 1905, Mrs M B E Lucas-Scudamore in 1926, William Stent JP in 1934 and Sir Alexander William Keown-Boyd K B E, in 1941. In 2003 the estate agents Knight Frank offered Pontrilas Court for sale at £1.45 million.

The river Dore and Dulas brook flowing under Pontrilas bridge.
This postcard was sent by Lettie Cole in 1908.

LLANGUA

Llangua is a rather small parish in the County of Monmouth of some 870 acres lying on the Monmouthshire bank of the river Monnow. In the late 19th century it had a population of about 90 people. In old records, Llangua appeared as Llangwym, the White Church. The original dedication of the church is to the 7th century saint Ciwa but St James was adopted as its patron in about the 14th century.

Lying on the bank of the river Monnow in a very beautiful and isolated position, the church is cut off from the rest of the parish by the wide, fast trunk road leading from Hereford to Abergavenny that evolved from the original toll road of the early 19th century. Further improvements took place during the 1960's and 70's to give the splendid road that we see today. Although lying so close to this busy road Llangua church remains unseen by the majority of motorists as they flash past oblivious to this interesting little gem which is perhaps more reminiscent of the Radnorshire style of church. (Plate 4) The earliest church at Llangua was held by Lire Abbey in Normandy to which it had been given in 1071 by William Fitz Osborne or his son Roger. It was known as Llanculan. Llangua church probably replaced this older foundation in the 13th or 14th centuries and contains a Norman font, possibly from the earlier church. By 1900 the church has been restored and Sir Joseph Bradney considered that there was of little interest in the building. The church has a simple plan of nave and chancel under separate roofs, which were probably built at different dates. There is a small, rather pretty timbered bell-tower with a pyramid roof at the west end, and the remains of whitewash on the exterior walls.

By 1952 the church was almost derelict and unsafe to use as the ceiling had fallen in and no services could be held. The plan was to dismantle all but the main walls. Fortunately, the chairman of the Historic Churches Preservation Trust, Mr Ivor Bulmer-Thomas offered to carry out the necessary repairs in memory of his first wife, Dilys who had died in childbirth in 1938. The Bishop of Hereford led the service of dedication at the re-opening in November 1955.

In 1886, Llangua church was removed from the jurisdiction of Llandaff and annexed to the diocese of Hereford and consolidated with the parish of Kentchurch. The living of Kentchurch with Llangua was a rectory in the gift of the executors of the late Col E. Lucas Scudamore.

William Fitz Osborne, Earl of Hereford, and the first Marcher Lord in the district, founded a Benedictine Abbey at Lire in Normandy in 1045. The Manor and church of Llangwym were given to the French Abbey by either William Fitz Osborne or his son and by the year 1183 a cell of monks had been established in the locality.

Although the cell was small, probably only consisting of three or four monks, it administered and collected rents from about 480 acres of good arable land. This money would have been sent back to the Mother House in Normandy until the outbreak of the Hundred Year's War when, like the Grandmontine Priory at Craswall, all alien houses were suspected of acting as conduits for money and intelligence and rigorously suppressed. Llangua Priory and the three other Lire Priories in England were bestowed by King Richard II on the Abbey of Montgrace in Yorkshire and then in 1413 once again transferred to the Carthusian Priory at Shere, Surrey. After the dissolution of the monasteries the Manor was 'granted' to John Scudamore of Kentchurch Court whose descendents still own it. Today, none of the Priory buildings survive but it is thought that Great House Farm is built of the materials from the monastic building and quite possibly on the actual site. Great House Farm is on the old Abergavenny Road as it climbs the steep hill from Monmouth Cap

The only 'village' at Llangua is centred round the 'Cap.' At one time, until the late 19th century, this was the Monmouth Cap Inn a noted coaching station between Abergavenny and Hereford. According to Mr Levett a popular drink enjoyed by the passengers as they awaited their coach was known as an 'Early Pearl' which consisted of half-pint of boiled ale, two pennyworth of gin, sugar, and a pinch of ginger. In a field opposite the Inn, cock fighting is known to have taken place and local men fought with bare fists for money.

In the 15th an 16th centuries Monmouth was renowned for its caps trade, a cottage industry encouraged by the laws of Edward IV, Henry VIII and Elizabeth I. The area known as Overmonnow is by tradition associated with this trade, and its church of St Thomas had a Capper's chapel, said to be 'better carved and gilded than any other part of the church'. In Shakespeare's Henry V, Fluellen refers to the wearing of leeks in Monmouth caps, but this is poetic licence, as such caps certainly did not exist at the time of Agincourt. These caps were made of wool in different colours with expensive linings and it would seem that Monmouth was the first place at which the continental art of knitting was applied to their manufacture. It is said that as a result of a great plague at the end of the 16th century the cap making industry migrated to Bewdley in Worcestershire. The Monmouth Cap Inn commemorated the trade for many years but lost its sign when it became a private house sometime at the end of the 19th century. The sign, showing a typical brown cap with a leek, on a red cushion was preserved in the hall of Cap house; I am not sure if it is still there.

Cap House the former Monmouth Cap Inn

In 1884 George Sayce was described as a farmer and shokeeper at the Monmouth Cap. By 1895 George Sayce was a farmer and shopkeeper at Cap Farm and E Lucas-Scudamore was living at Cap House. Mrs George Sayce was the farmer and shopkeeper in 1923 at Cap Farm and her daughter Miss Sayce was still there in 1934.

Edward Lucas Scudamore was the grandson of John Lucy Scudamore whose only child and heiress married Fitzherbert Dacre Lucas of Castle Shane, Ireland. Edward was her only child and owned almost all the land in Llangua. He died at Castle Shane in 1917 aged 64. In the early 20th century there was a grocer at Llangua Terrace.

The Monmouth Cap Inn was on the old road from Hereford to Abergavenny where it starts to climb up and over Campston Hill. This was a notoriously bad road that reaches a height of 600 feet and was a considerable obstacle to hauliers and coaches. The only roads near the Monnow were a few tracks and lanes leading to fields and farms.

The road improvement was closely linked to the building of the Hereford and Abergavenny Tramroad. By the early 1800's the need to have a regular supply of coal and other commodities to Hereford was becoming urgent. There were letters to the Hereford Times and groups were considering how to overcome the 'impassable barrier between the two counties, Campston Hill'. The cost of bringing coal from the Forest of Dean or the South Wales coal-fields was high, due to the difficulties of transportation. The cost would be almost halved if the coal could be transported by rail.

Three separate companies were formed to construct a tramroad from Abergavenny to Hereford. The first was constructed under an Act of 1811 and was from the Brecknock Canal at Govilon, around the north of Abergavenny to Llanvhiangel Crucorney, a length of 7 ¾ miles The second section, the Grosmont tramroad, was granted under an Act of 1812 and ran from the terminus at Llanivhangel to Monmouth Cap, a distance of 5 ½ miles. The final section, the Hereford tramroad from Monmouth Cap to Hereford followed at a much later date owing to much opposition from barge owners and other vested interests. It was not until September 1829 that the first consignment of coal travelled from Abergavenny to Hereford.

It was the Grosmont tramroad that had such an effect on the parish of Llangua. In addition to building this tramroad the Grosmont Railway Company built a Toll road and tolls were charged by the company for its use. There were toll-gates at Penissaplwdd and Monmouth Cap at the junction of the new road and the old Abergavenny road which went over Campston Hill. The length of the toll road was 4 miles. The old toll house at Penissaplwdd is now a private residence with its own private road, originally part of the toll road. The toll road between Penissaplwdd and Monmouth Cap is now almost entirely obliterated by the new trunk road.

The tramroad, which was built alongside the toll road, was of the simplest construction. Cast iron plate rails, each 3 foot long and 4 inches wide were laid on stone blocks of irregular shape, bedded into the earth. The gauge was 3 foot 6 inches. In addition to the tramway the Grosmont Railway Company built a cottage and garden at Pandy, stopgate cottages at Penissaplwdd, a cottage, wharf and weighing machine at Monmouth Cap. There was one private siding to a quarry near Pandy.

The evolution of steam locomotive meant the demise of these horse-drawn tramroads and in 1845 a new company was formed to construct a modern railway from Pontypool to Hereford under the title Newport Abergavenny and Hereford Railway and negotiations were begun to acquire the tramroads. The Grosmont tranroad was purchased for £16,250. It was reported that the length of track from

Govilon to Monmouth Cap was so neglected that it would soon be unfit for traffic. It had been in use for about 35 years.

The steam powered railway was constructed on a new line north of the river Monnow, but crossing the river three time just before reaching Pontrilas station. The Newport, Abergavenny and Hereford Railway sold out to the Midland Railway in 1860. This company now owned the toll road in addition to the tramway. In 1861 the toll road was conveyed to John Lucy Scudamore for the sum of £200. Very soon, in 1863, the Midland Railway line was absorbed into the Great Western Railway.

The following extract is from a newspaper cutting dated 27th July 1897

MONMOUTH CAP, LLANGUA
DEATH. Mrs Eliza Peglar, a very old inhabitant, died on Friday night last in the village, at her home, viz., the Level Crossing Cottage. The deceased was well known, and has attended to these gates for many years in the service of the G.W.R. Company, and her absence from this occupation will be sorrowfully observed by the many farmers who so frequently took her attention. The funeral was well attended on Wednesday evening, and was conducted by the Rev. MG. Watkins, MA Rector. There were a few choice wreaths and notes of sympathy from the surrounding villagers.

There is no indication on the modern O S map where this crossing may be, but the O S map of 1890 shows a track leaving the road by Cap Farm, crossing the railway and then the river Monnow and continuing to Rowlstone Park Farm and eventually to Rowlestone church.

Great House Farm c.1900

GROSMONT

Grosmont is situated, as its name implies, high on a river cliff, 200 feet above the river Monnow with the higher hills of the Graig and Garway nearby. It is a very large parish of some 6850 acres with the river Monnow forming the boundary to the north and east. The road to Grosmont from the south rises steeply after crossing the Tressenny brook and to the north the road dips steeply down Cupid's Hill to the bridge over the river Monnow and into Herefordshire. Grosmont has many natural advantages for defence and has been occupied from early times.

Grosmont village owes its existence to the building of the castle by Hubert de Burgh, possibly on the site of an earlier motte and bailey castle that in its turn may have been the site of a Celtic settlement. The name Grosmont is Norman French.

The site of the castle is a large more or less quadrangular earthwork surrounded by what has always been described as a deep dry moat. However, Dr Steven Pickford in his book *Hidden Grosmont*, describes how this moat was cleared of spoil in the 1920's by forty unemployed labourers. A spring emerges from the bank of the moat and a pipe was installed to divert this water out through the wood. Dr Pickford measured the outflow of the pipe and found it to be a considerable 360 gallons per hour. This must show that it was quite possible that at some time this moat did hold water. Suggestions have been made that this site may originally have been a Celtic stronghold. The castle on this mound is of an irregular shape. There is a large square keep on the west side and a great hall on the east side. An isolated chimney is still standing, its octagonal walls ending in an elegant pierced lantern, evidently part of the solar or private rooms of the castle. The castle as it now stands is the work of Edmund of Lancaster and his successors who often lived there until the marriage of Duchess Blanche to John of Gaunt, the third son of Edward III, in 1359. Blanche Plantagenent died of the plague leaving an infant son who was to become Henry IV. His son, Henry Prince of Wales, was born at Monmouth castle and inherited the throne as Henry V in 1413.

Long before this period, in the middle of the 13th century an incident occurred at Grosmont castle involving Henry III who was in dispute with the Marcher Lords, particularly Richard Marshall, Earl of Pembroke. In 1232 King Henry imprisoned Hubert de Burgh, who was not only Lord of Grosmont and Skenfrith castles but had the influential position of Justicar or Chief Minister of the Crown. He had been accused by the Bishop of Winchester of misappropriating public money. After managing to escape from Devizes castle, Hubert joined the forces of Llywelyn ap Iorwerth. The Marcher Lords were very much a law unto themselves and Henry declared that all the Lords of the Middle March had forfeited their estates and subsequently granted these estates, on paper only, to some of his foreign favourites. In 1233 Henry sent his royal army into Gwent and laid siege to Marshall's castle at Usk. This failed and Richard Marshall entered into an alliance with the Welsh prince, Llywelyn. So King Henry, unable to enter Hereford marched his half trained army of English and foreign mercenaries to Grosmont and installed himself with his entourage inside the castle whilst the army was encamped in tents outside the castle walls and along the banks of the river Monnow. Marshall and his allies staged a surprise night attack and overran the unprepared forces of the King. The royal army fled in disarray leaving behind many of their horses and much of their baggage, while Marshall went on to Monmouth where Baldwin de Guissnes had been given the command of a mixed force of Fleming and Poitevin mercenaries in Monmouth castle. There was a bitter battle on the castle fields and in the stampede to return to the castle, the bridge collapsed throwing many of the soldiers into the Monnow. Although Baldwin was wounded he managed to escape back to the castle. St Thomas's church at Overmonnow was set on fire during this attack and the new Cistercian Abbey of Grace Dieu which was destroyed by Richard Marshall's ally, Llywelyn ap Iorwerth. John, Lord of the Manor of Monmouth, had founded the Abbey of Grace Dieu three miles west of Monmouth in 1226 and staffed it with monks from Dore. After its destruction John had the Abbey rebuilt on a nearby site. Grosmont castle, meanwhile, was left in the charge of a garrison and the King and his retainers withdrew to Gloucester.

In the year 1405 Owain Glyndwr and his rebels were raiding up and down the Herefordshire border. He raised a great rebel army from among the peasants of South Wales and after attacking the castles of Caerleon and Usk marched on towards Grosmont. On March 11th the rabble army, estimated to be 8000 strong, attacked the town. Grosmont was burned and looted and the citizens either fled or sought sanctuary in the cathedral-like church. Prince Henry, who was at that time only 17 years of age, dispatched an army of royal forces, mobilized from four counties, under the command of his cousin Lord Gilbert Talbot. The royal cavalry were at an advantage over the rebel foot soldiers and it is said that their casualties were severe and that a Welsh chieftain whose name was not recorded was captured.

This attack had a devastating effect on the town of Grosmont from which it never really recovered. It was estimated that one hundred and fifty houses were razed to the ground never to be rebuilt and it's streets and causeways were to disappear under the turf of the surrounding fields. Prince Henry wrote to his father, King Henry IV, giving him a description of the battle.

Praised be He in all His works; for on Wednesday, the 11th day of March, your rebels of the parts of Glamorgan, Morgannwg, Usk, Netherwent, and Overwent, were assembled to the number of 8000 people, by their own account, and went the same Wednesday in the morning and burnt part of your town at Grosmont within your lordship of Monmouth. And I at once sent off by very dear cousin the Lord Talbot, and faithful knights, William Neuport and Johan Greindre, who were but a small force in all; but in the power of God and in the aid of the blessed Trinity, your people held the field and conquered the said rebels, and killed of them according to fair account in the field to the time of their return from the pursuit, some say eight hundred, some say a thousand, being questioned upon pain of death. Whether it be one or the other I will not contend. And in order to inform you fully of all that is done, I send you one worthy of credit, by loyal servant and bearer of these [dispatches] who was present at the engagement, and did his duty most faithfully as he has done on all occasions. And such amend has God granted to you for the burning of your houses in the above mentioned town. And of prisoners there was taken only one, and he was lately a great chieftain among them, and whom I would have sent but that he is not yet able to ride at his ease. And concerning the government which I propose to effect after these [events], may it please your Highness to vouchsafe full credit to the bearer of these dispatches in that he will show to your same Highness on my part. And I pray to God that He may preserve you always in joy and honour, and grant to me that I may [be able to] solace you speedily with other good news. Written at Hereford, the said Wednesday in the night. Your most humble and obedient son, Henry

Grosmont Church

Grosmont. Arthur 1907.

Grosmont was once an important town with status as a borough. The election of the Mayor took place in May each year and the new Mayor appointed his ale taster who was generally elected Mayor the following year. The last Mayor of Grosmont was elected in 1860 and no other officers ever seem to have existed. The original Town Hall in the market place was a timber framed building which, by the early 1800's was in a bad state of repair. The Town Hall now standing in the middle of Grosmont was built by the Duke of Beaufort in 1832 and is a smaller building than that it replaced. Mr Wyatt, Steward to the Duke of Beaufort said that the Duke would rebuild the market Hall if the Mayor and Corporation gave up all its claims to the Market Tolls. It was resolved *'To surrender to His Grace, The Duke of Beaufort and give up all claims to tolls arising at and from the several fairs held in this town, on condition the New Town Hall shall be made use of for the same purposes as at present, the use of J.P.'s for holding Turnpike Meetings, for keeping of public school, and for the annual celebration of the Mayor's election, provided they were exonerated from the annual fifteen shillings charged on said tolls.'* There is an upstairs room for public meetings with an outside staircase and an open market place beneath that was used for corn markets and fairs.

Lining the road through Grosmont are cottages on narrow rectangular strips of land known as burgage plots. These were marked out in the 13th century when Hubert de Burgh established his new town. When the town declined, the burgesses acquired land in the surrounding countryside and built themselves farmhouses, some of them very substantial. The village houses were left to the occupation of artisans and craftsmen which all contributed to making Grosmont a self-sufficient little town. The population during the 19th century varied between 550 and 700 people. Besides the usual trades there was a grocer and linen draper who also ran the post office; two clock and watch makers; two shoemakers; a baker and confectioner and Agnes Bevan who ran a ladies school. George Dale, MB, CM was surgeon, medical officer and public vaccinator. There were a number of public houses in Grosmont catering for the working population providing warmth and congenial company at the end of a hard day's work.

	1815	1824	1905
Duke of York	*	*	*
Angel Hotel	*	*	*
Cupid's Hill		*	*
Greyhound	*	*	
Hand	*	*	
Bush	*		
Cherry Tree			*
Red Lion			*

The Angel Hotel, which is the only public house still open, was always the main hostelry in Grosmont and was were the Court Leet was held. The other public house, which only closed on the death of the proprietor Joe Godding in 2001, was the Cupid's Hill Inn. (Plate 29) This was a quite extraordinary pub that had not changed for at least 50 years or more; it's one room with a single beer pump and oil-cloth on the bar. The first impression was that of entering a time-warp. Joe was the second generation Godding at the Cupid's Hill Inn. His father Vine Godding was a carpenter and wheelwright in addition to being an innkeeper and had a carpenters shop at Pontrilas which has now disappeared under the new road. His sons William and Joe also served their time as carpenters. After William married he went to live in Garway where he spent the rest of his life as a local builder and undertaker. Joe stayed in Grosmont and eventually took over the Inn in addition to continuing his work as an undertaker and coffin maker. It was a sad day when this anachronism of a bygone age finally closed.

The parish church of St Nicholas was built over a period spanning 1180 to 1300 with the porch and the bell-tower and spire being added later. The dedication of the church is to St Nicholas and does not, as is the case of so many local churches, have a Celtic dedication that was later altered. The church was built to serve the castle and the newly developing borough is of a cruciform plan with transepts, aisles and a surprisingly large nave. There is an octagonal tower with a spire at the intersection of the transepts. The size of the church is almost as big as a small cathedral, which shows that this was an important town.

By the mid 19th century the population of the town was declining and the castle was just a ruin. John Pollard Seddon, a partner in the firm of Pritchard and Seddon, architects to the Diocese of Llandaff, was appointed to restore the church. There were serious structural defects to be attended to and most of the chancel area had to be rebuilt. The very large nave was screened off from the rest of the church and cleared of all furniture. The entrance to the church is through the nave and to someone who has never visited this church before it comes as quite a surprise to enter this vast, rather dark, open space. There are two arcades of five bays, each twelve feet wide, with rounded piers supporting gothic arches typical of the mid-13th century. There are some interesting relics housed in the nave such as the unfinished effigy of unknown date but could possibly be Hubert de Burgh. There is also the trap belonging to Charles Wesley who was Rector of Grosmont from 1884 to 1914. He was decended from the Rev Charles Wesley whose brother John Wesley was the founder of Methodism in the early 18th century.

THE NAVE OF THE CHURCH, GROSMONT, HEREFORD.

KENTCHURCH

Kentchurch is a large parish of some 3,300 acres consisting of several farms, a few scattered dwellings, Kentchurch Court and the pub the Bridge Inn. Included in the ecclesiastical parish is the parish of Llangua in Monmouthshire which is held by the rector of Kentchurch.

The church of St Mary was rebuilt in 1858 at a cost of £1390. A memorial to John Scudamore who died in 1616 has survived from the previous church and is now in a side chapel. This memorial depicts two full-sized reclining figures with the smaller figures of their children at the base.

Memorial to John Scudamore and his wife in Kentchurch church

For the past 900 years Kentchurch Court has been the home of the Scudamore family. (Plates 5&6) In 1796 Nash updated the ancient house which was immortalized in a painting by James Wathen and recently by being featured in TV's Channel 4's "Regency House Party". The front lawns were used, in 1987, for the Garden Party scene in the film of Bruce Chatwin's novel 'On the Black Hill'. More restoration was completed in the 1830's under the direction of Thomas Tudor. The house is set among sweeping lawns with a deer park rising above up the steep slopes of Garway Hill. Members of the Scudamore family will feature quite often in the history of the Monnow Valley and most of them will be called John – which could be rather confusing.

Kentchurch Court

Not far from Kentchurch Court is the farm of Great Corras. In 1988, in the orchard opposite the farmhouse, Elizabeth Taylor and Mary Thomas excavated the remains of a chapel. Visible through the trees about 30 metres north of this chapel and very near the Monnow is a motte, now in the garden of a private house. At the time of the Domesday Book Ralph Scudamore, who was one of the nine knights of Ewyas Castle, owned the manor of Corras and it is still owned by the Scudamore family. The Scudamores moved from the castle at Corras sometime before 1386 to the moated site at Kentchurch.

The earliest record of the chapel at Corras is from a cartulary of the Abbey of St Peters in Gloucester. In 1100 Harold of Ewyas gave the chapel of Corras to the newly dedicated abbey. Its position, within the bailey of the castle would seem to indicate that it was the manor chapel. Excavation revealed the plan of the first building on the site with an apsidal east end that is typical of an early Norman chapel. Eventually, a squared east end replaced the apse. Sometime later the chapel was taken down and enlarged with the addition of a square stone tower. The chapel seems to have been finally demolished before 1400.

A famous character connected with Kentchurch Court is Owain Glyndwr. One of his daughters was married to a Scudamore and as an old man Owain lived at Kentchurch with this daughter Alice. It is thought that when he died sometime after 1415, he was buried at the home of his other daughter, Margaret at Monnington Court in the Golden Valley but this has never been proved.

A mysterious character that may have some claim to reality is John or Jack of Kent. A theory exists that this was a pseudonym used by Owain Glyndwr. John of Kent was very famous in the folk-lore of the counties of Hereford and Monmouth. As a boy he is reputed to have made a pact with the devil in exchange for his soul after death, whether his body was buried in or out of a church. Jack did not hesitate to trick the devil as the story of Grosmont bridge shows. Jack undertook to build this bridge overnight with the help of the devil who was to bring the stones from Garway Hill. When the bridge was finished, the devil claimed the soul of the first to cross. Jack threw some bread across the bridge and a little dog chased it. As animals have no souls the devil was outwitted. (The Bridge Inn, Kentchurch has an inn sign depicting this story). Jack's final outwitting of the devil came at his death when he was buried under the wall of Grosmont church – neither inside nor outside!

In May 1959 a very sudden and dramatic event occurred at Kentchurch Court. The county of Herefordshire was hit by one of the worst storms in living memory and late in the evening there was a cloudburst over Garway Hill. The stream, which flowed 30 yards from the Court became a raging torrent which brought down trees and debris which built up against the bridges diverting the flood water into the house. On May 15th the Hereford Times reported;

Thousands of pounds worth of damage was done to almost priceless furniture carpets and china; chairs were carried hundreds of yards into the fields; walls were swept away and windows were smashed. The owner of the house Mrs Sybil F. Scudamore narrowly escaped death. She had seen the water coming in under the library door, and within minutes was waist deep in the flooded room. She began climbing up the furniture with her two dogs before being rescued and carried to safety by her Italian servants Mr and Mrs Narciso Nicoletti and nanny Miss Daisy Rees. The flood itself lasted only hours. But for commander Lucas Scudamore and his wife, who arrived back from London at 11.30 p.m., the scene was horrific.

Massive antique furniture had been overturned, damaged and swept through the house to lie in mud-stained heaps. Inches deep mud covered the lawns and carpets; windows were smashed and doors were broken. A heavy Aga cooker was carried yards across the kitchen, a tarmac drive was ripped up, and chairs were found hundreds of yards away in the fields and broody hens and their coops disappeared

It was a combination of field walking and the recognition of crop marks from across the valley which were the first indication that there may be the remains of a Roman fort right on the parish boundary between Kentchurch and Garway. (Plate 7) During a dry summer in the early 1980's, some members of the Monmouth Archaeological Society were travelling by car from Grosmont to Skenfrith. They looked across the valley and saw distinct marks of a rectangle in a field of barley. Walking this field after it had been ploughed revealed large quantities of Roman pottery. The following year, after harvest, the farmer gave permission for the Society to dig a trial trench. This revealed that it was indeed a pre Flavian Roman auxiliary fort that had been occupied for about 20 years from approximately A.D.50. Auxiliary forts, known as castellum (the farm on which it was found is called Castlefield), varied in size from about 2 to 7 acres and would have held a unit of about 500 men.

A typical Roman fort is a permanent base for 500 soldiers often built in a fine position on a flat spur above a river with a road joining this fort to another fort a day's march away affording a supply and communications route.

The interior was set out in a very regular pattern. In the centre was the fort's headquarters, usually built of stone, which was the hub of the fort's activities and known as the 'principia'. On one side of the Principia would be the Praetorium or the residence of the commanding officer and on the other side a couple of stone built granaries where the food was stored.

In front of and behind these central buildings were the barrack blocks to house the infantry. There would be six in all each holding a century of 80 men. These buildings would be built of wood on stone foundations with wooden partitions. The centurion's headquarters that he shared with his second in command would be situated at one end of the barrack block and was larger than the soldier's accommodation. There would be ten compartments each of two rooms facing onto a verandah and shared by eight soldiers. The small room at the front would accommodate their weapons, equipment and personal belongings and the larger room behind was used for sleeping. There was no communal dining room so food was cooked in ovens built near the back of the rampart and eaten in the barrack. Other buildings may have included a workshop and stabling

The trench excavated at Castlefield cut through the rampart and ditch and into the interior of the fort. Post- holes for the barrack block were discovered and evidence of an oven behind the rampart. A large quantity of pottery including highly decorated Samian ware was recovered and the finding of coins helped the dating of the site. Excavation showed that in fact there had been two separate forts built and that they had both been destroyed by fire. Did the Romans fire the forts themselves as they left, or had the Silurians attacked them from across the river?

Starting to excavate the Roman Fort at Castlefield July 1986

GARWAY

Garway Church

Garway is a long narrow parish stretching seven miles from the top of Garway Hill to Pembridge Castle, which is just over the parish boundary in Welsh Newton. It is a parish of small hamlets but historically the centre was near the Church of St Michael at the Turning.

The first church in Garway was founded in the 6th century. According to the Book of Llandaff, land in Garway was given by Guorvodu, King of Ergyng to build a church and the living was given to his priest Guorvoe. These early churches were established, often in very isolated places, by Celtic missionaries in the 5th and 6th centuries and were the basis of the monastic movement. Their members adopted the religious life of a hermit or gathered together to form a religious community of a Celtic type and were housed in stone or timber cells clustered around a church and an enclosure known as a llan. Monastic schools were formed and missionaries preached the gospel to their countrymen. They founded daughter (clas) churches, each church taking the name of the founder of the monastery from which it had sprung. Garway was one of these clas churches. There is no evidence to show that this foundation was on the same site as the later church, but it is probable that the Templars used an already consecrated site for their new building.

The original Templar church consisted of the round nave, the chancel with its decorated Norman arch and the chapel all based on the design of the Temple in Jesusalem. The plan of the church (see page 105), with its circular nave, was almost identical to the design of the Templar church in London. (Plates 9,10,11) The Tower was built about 1200 and it is detached from the church. Its' rather odd position may be explained in relation to the round nave rather than to the nave as it is today. The present nave was built about 1400 when the Manor belonged to the Knights Hospitallers. It is not known for certain why the round nave was demolished, but as it was built on a slope subsidence may have caused a distortion that would have been difficult to repair on a circular building. Certainly, one side of the chancel arch is lower than the other, and it is still possible to see, on either side of the arch, the beginnings of the round nave. Although it had always been known that the church at Garway had belonged to the Knights Templars, it was not until 1927 that Mr G H Jack discovered the foundations of the round church and the existence of a round church proven beyond doubt.

The autumn Meeting of the Woolhope Naturalist's Field Club was held at Garway church on September 29th 1927. Explaining how he came to make the excavations, Mr Jack said that his friend Mr G E Chambers pointed out features inside the church of Garway which seemed to be indications of the existence there of one of the famous round churches of the Templars.

It so happened that I had not taken my annual holidays, so I decided to devote a week here. Once permission had been given, I started to work and was very delighted to be able to expose these remains of the church of the Templars. I believe that there are only five such churches in England, this being the sixth. Of course, there were other round churches, but not attributable to the Knights Templars. King Henry III so much admired the principles of the Templars that he was very anxious to be initiated into the Templar's church in London.

Mr Jack expressed appreciation of the assistance and encouragement given to him by Mr G E Chambers, who gave him the start; Mr G H Grocock, who made plans of the discovery; the Vicar, (the Rev J Collinson), who had given him every facility; and to Mr George Marshall. It was open to question whether it would be advisable to leave the discoveries uncovered. If it were decided that they should not again be covered, that would necessitate some expense.

Within the church are several reminders of the middle ages. Perhaps the most valuable is the large 'dug out' chest in the tower. It is 8 foot 6 inches long and dates from the late 12th or early 13th century. The sides and bottom are carefully squared; the top and the lid coped. The lid is in one piece, turning nearly the length of the chest, and there are three big strap hinges that are carried round the chest. Single straps bind the ends of the chest. This was almost certainly used by the Templars to hold their valuables and the revenue from the estates of Garway. Medieval gravestones have been reused in many places, for example as lintels over windows and on the chancel steps. The greatest mystery of all is the quantity of strange markings on the walls of the church both inside and out. There are many types of crosses, a pastoral lamb, a phoenix and strange fish and serpent like shapes over the piscine in the chapel. During the 19th century, before the village school was built, classes were held in the chapel (vestry) of the church

There is still a Baptist chapel at the Turning with its own schoolroom in the room above. The pub, the forge, the post office and the shop have long gone and are all now private houses. Another area of the village is the Common with the Garway Moon Inn and some old cottages facing onto the area that has been made into an excellent cricket and sports ground. All the houses except one, between the Garway Moon Inn and the new primary school have been built during the last 60 years and quite a few in the last 10 years.

Contrast this with the description given by Fred Hando in his book the *Pleasant Land of Gwent* written in 1944. After lunching at Broad Oak with a friend they "threaded narrow lanes to the great Common"

Soon we espied goats. Soon Dick was knocking at the door of a whitewashed cottage. To the tousled, frightened woman who opened the door my tall, handsome Scot raised his hat, and said, "Good Morning, Madame. Could you oblige two thirsty travellers with a glass of goat's milk? She asked us in. Dick's hair brushed the rafters in the tiny room as he raised his glass and in courtly fashion drank her health. He rewarded her generously, and we left her staring, open-mouthed.

A mile and half down the road towards Monmouth is Broad Oak, so named because of the old oak in front of what was the Broad Oak Inn, a very ancient hostelry that sadly closed around 1990 and became a private house. Opposite this was the little round toll-house that was demolished about 1950. There are several new houses in Broad Oak and a garage with workshop, fuel pumps and a small shop which is much valued by the local community.

The Broad Oak Inn, closed around 1990, now a private house.

Charles Harper, a gentleman from London who took walking holidays so that he could write books about his experiences, visited this area. This is was he wrote in 1893 about Broad Oak.

The place takes its name from an immense oak-tree standing where four roads meet and branch severally to Ross, Monmouth, Abergavenny and Pontrilas. This roadside settlement is not of ancient date, but already it has outlived whatever prosperous days conjured it up from the lonely crossroads, and is woebegone in the extreme and almost entirely deserted. The oak, now polled and shorn of something of its old-time majesty, remains, and beside it stands a lonely beerhouse. The empty cottages round about are all in different stages of decay, roofs sagging, or entirely fallen in, gardens long since grown wild, and windows smashed with the missiles of every passing urchin for years gone by. Even that old highway, the Abergavenny road that passed through the hamlet is shrunken. Originally of great breadth, it is now contracted between little lawns that have been allowed to grow from the hedgerows on each side, and only the crown of the highway is now in use.

Pembridge Castle is now just in the parish of Welsh Newton but historically it is connected with Garway. Its early history is somewhat obscure. The stone castle was built sometime just before 1219 and it is possible that the site used was the earthwork of a previous castle. (Plates 13,14,15)

Roger, Earl of Hereford and a powerful Marcher Lord, opposed the new King, Henry II when he came to the throne. In reprisal the king deprived Roger of the Earldom and confiscated his lands including Archenfield. King Henry was a great admirer of the Knights Templars and it is probable that he gave land in Garway to the Templars at this early date. In July 1199 King John confirmed to the Knights Templar "all the land of Langarewi with the castlry which was Herman's". No one has with certainty, been able to identify the site of Herman's castlry, but there is strong evidence to suggest that it was the site on which Pembridge castle was eventually built.

Pembridge Castle was built on lands called Newland that belonged to Garway until at least the 16th century. William de Braose, Lord of Radnor leased Newlands from the Knights Templar in the early 13th century, and handed it over to one of his tenants Ralphe de Pembridge. He had started to build the stone castle by the time he died in 1219, very likely on the site of the earthworks of Herman's castlery. His son Henry succeeded Ralphe, and it was not until 1375 that Newland passed out of Pembridge hands. In 1505 Pembridge Castle was in the hands of Margaret Beaufort as of the Manor of Garway, for £5 rent, suit of court and £10 in lieu of relief. She was the daughter of John, the first Earl of Somerset, the wife of Edmund Tudor and the mother of Henry VII. The name Pembridge Castle only seems to have been used after it passed out of the Pembridge family as it appears in Royal records as Newland or the castle of Newland.

At the Dissolution the castle was rented to Baynham of Newland. In the reign of Queen Elizabeth the castle was sold to David Baker who sold it to Sir Walter Pye. In 1630 a lease was granted by Sir Walter Pye of the Mynde, in the County of Hereford, to George Kemble and his wife Anne and their son and heir apparent Richard Kemble, of the castle of Pembridge, a conigrey (rabbit warren) and a total of 302 acres. This lease was renewed to Richard Kemble in 1660. It was at this time that the catholic priest Father John Kemble lived at the castle.

During the Civil Wars (1642-1651), the castle was an outpost of the Royalist garrison of Monmouth and in 1644 Colonel Massey and his troops besieged it. The steeply rising ground to the east of the castle gave the besieging troops the advantage of being able to fire over the castle walls. After a short time the supplies ran out and the castle was surrendered to Colonel Massey.

Pembridge Castle before renovation in 1912

Garden Party at Glanmonnow House in 1907

The castle and its land were surveyed in 1686 by W. Hill. The property was described as 'the manor house or castle and gardens, courts, folds and the warren adjoining containing 8 acres 2 roods 8 perches. In addition there was arable, pasture, meadow and woods amounting altogether to over 300 acres. By 1850 the castle belonged to the representatives of the late Sir Joseph Bailey, Bart who purchased it from the Townleys of Lancashire.

There is no ancient Manor House in Garway as the Lords of the Manor have always lived elsewhere on their estates. However, in the 1870's when Ambrose More O'Ferrall of County Kildare in Ireland was Lord of the Manor, he decided to build a 'Gentlemen's Residence' on land which had once been part of New House Farm. This house was called Glanmonnow and was built on an elevated position overlooking the river Monnow. It had ten bedrooms and dressings rooms, two bathrooms and four reception rooms.

On the death of Ambrose More O'Ferrall, his daughter Mabel inherited the Garway Estate. Jakeman and Carver's Gazetteer of Herefordshire for 1914 states that, Mrs Edmund J Dease of Rath, Ballybretlas, Queens County, whose husband Major Dease is resident magistrate, and resides at Yewston, Nenagh, North Tipperary, Ireland, is lady of the manor and owns two thirds of the parish of Garway. In 1918 the Garway Estate was offered for sale and was bought by Arthur Ernest Lawley, a Manchester businessman who had recently bought Hilston Park at Skenfrith. Mr Lawley died on 26th May 1920 just as the completion of the purchase of Glanmonnow was taking place. It was reported in the Monmouth Beacon that "the deceased, aged 45, was a keen angler. In fact it was only Thursday of last week that he caught a chill while fishing, and this set up the illness which resulted fatally, despite the best of medical attention. He leaves a widow and two daughters." The funeral took place at Alderley Edge and there was a memorial service at St Maughans church taken by the Rev. C de Labilliere.

The Hilston estate was sold at auction in May 1921. Lot 2 was Glanmonnow House, renamed the Dower House, with 1,130 acres of land and fishing in the River Monnow. However, the Lordship of the Manor of Garway was not sold and Mrs Lawley was referred to as Lady of the Manor in local Directories and in Parish Council Minutes up until 1945. Her daughter Francis Wright Lawley married Surgeon Lieut. Commander Claude de Labilliere and their son is General Sir Peter de la Billiere who was Commander of the British Forces, Middle East during the Gulf War of 1991. After the war he became Advisor to the Minister of Defence on middle eastern matters.

GARWAY HILL

At the other end of the parish of Garway, high on the slopes of Garway Hill is found the small settlement of White Rocks and the 200 acres of common land where sheep and ponies from surrounding small-holdings and farms are grazed. The summit of Garway Hill at 1206 feet is in the parish of Garway but much of the hill and the hamlet known as Garway Hill is in the parish of Orcop.

The higher slopes of the hill are bare of trees and covered with bracken and gorse bushes, except for the summit which is covered with short sheep cropped turf and from where the prospect is quite spectacular. The totally uninterrupted views of 360 degrees are unsurpassed by any other viewpoint in the county. On a clear day it is possible to see the counties of Brecknock, Radnorshire Shropshire, Worcestershire Gloucestershire, Herefordshire, Monmouthshire and if it is really clear Somerset. This position affords the only view that the casual observer can enjoy of the magnificent Kentchurch Court. There is a tolerably well preserved earthwork on the southern slope of the hill not too far from the summit. This more or less rectangular work with ramparts and ditch has never been excavated or dated.

It has been a long tradition that beacons have been lit on the summit of Garway Hill to celebrate events of national importance. I have attended celebrations of the Silver and Golden Jubilees of Queen Elizabeth II when beacons were lit on many hills and could be seen far into the distance. There was a very big celebration on the hill on Monday, 8th May 1995 on the fiftieth anniversary of the ending of World War Two, VE day. Many of the beacons on the surrounding hill were lit too early and therefore lost their impact. On Garway Hill, a very loud firework was let off to signify the start of the 2 minutes silence, at the end of which the beacon was lit.

Another memorable occasion on the summit was on Wednesday, 11th August 1999 when at about 11am, a hundred or so people gathered to witness the rare spectacle of the total eclipse of the sun. As the appointed hour drew near the daylight faded and darkness descended with the silhouettes of the Skirrid and Sugarloaf mountains fading away, the bird songs fell silent and an eerie darkness and stillness fell over the hill. Excited chatter become muted and was replaced by a tangible sense of awe. Unfortunately the cloudy weather obscured the sun apart from a brief moment as the eclipse approached. As the sky brightened there were large breaks in the cloud and people peered intently through special lenses until the shadow of the moon passed from the face of the sun.

Monday, May 6th 1935 was the day of the Silver Jubilee of King George V and Queen Mary and once again there was a beacon on Garway Hill. The Hereford Times reported that the proudest man in the merry crowd was the 77 year-old Mr Fred Gardiner, who had supervised the hauling of six lorry loads of faggots to the top of the hill for the Garway District fire.

Garway Hill, local people proclaim in spite of what the Ordnance Maps have to say, is over 1200 feet above sea level, and commands a view of the country around which cannot be surpassed by any other spot in the county. Thus it was that the watchers had an uninterrupted view on all sides, which took in so many beacons that it was impossible to count them with accuracy. Fires blazed merrily round the complete circle; there was only one spot where the view was in any way obstructed, for Garway Hill top is barren of trees, and that was where Graig Hill blocked the view down one of the valleys. Even here there was evidence of beacons and bonfires, for at one time a portion of the hill was silhouetted against the glow behind.

A very moderate estimate, says a Hereford Times *representative who was there, places the number of fires which could be definitely distinguished at well over 50. It was a magnificent sight; and so was Garway Hill beacon. General Bate, who provided the material, set it alight, and the well-built pile of about 400 faggots was quickly roaring away ignited on the stroke of ten as a rocket was sent hurtling into the air. It was an impressive scene as the many people present stood with bared heads in the flickering glare of the huge fire singing "God Save the King"*

When Garway Hill was chosen as one of the sites, the problem was how to get the material for the fire to the top. Mr F Gardiner solved it by offering to take it up on his motor-lorry! His son, Mr L Gardiner, did the driving, and in two days the task was completed. Certain it is that never before has a motor-lorry been on the summit of Garway Hill! The journey from the road was about three quarters of a mile, and in places it was very rough going.

The beacon-builders took good care of it when it was made. All Sunday night four men were on guard, and they were refreshed at intervals by hot tea.

Garway folk declare that of all the beacon fires theirs was the most successful (of course!) and that of all the views of other beacon fires, that to be secured from the heights of Garway Hill was the best (again of course!)

Hereford Times Photo.
Putting the finishing touches to the beacon on Garway Hill, the wood for which was conveyed right to the top of the hill by the motor lorry shown in the picture

The photograph that accompanied the article in the Hereford Times shows the famous lorry and members of the Gardiner family. The three men building the beacon, from the top down are, Walter Smith, Eric Arthur and Bill Smith. In front of the bonfire are two ladies and two boys, they are, left to right, Doris Gardiner, Pearl Gardiner, Robert Gardiner and Bill Gardiner. The small child is Stanley Gardiner. The two men in front of the lorry are the fathers of the small boys, Lewis Gardiner (who drove the lorry) and Bill Gardiner. Lewis's wife is standing by the old man, Fred (Wilfred) Gardiner.

In 1934 Fred Gardiner was living at The Dingle, Orcop (Kellys's Directory) but moved soon after to Sun Cottage, originally Sun Farm opposite the Rising Sun Inn. This Inn had ceased to be a public house around 1920 and became the local sub-post office and shop. A rough track up alongside the Rising Sun leading to Garway Hill was the route taken by Fred Gardiner's lorry with the faggots for the beacon. The parish boundary between Garway and Orcop follows the line of this lane.

In 1937 Herbert (Bert) Gardiner and his family moved into the old Sun to run the post office and shop and to carry on a business as a coal merchant and haulier after purchasing the lorry from Fred Gardiner in 1941.

Perched on the summit of Garway Hill is a low octagonal tower standing like some silent sentinel keeping a watchful eye over the Monnow Valley. This landmark can, on a clear day, be seen from about ten miles away and makes Garway Hill instantly recognisable to the observer with a keen eye. As memories fade and time takes its toll this little tower has become an enigma, with many well-meaning theories being espoused as to its previous function.

In the month of June 1941, three RAF personnel, a corporal and two airmen, arrived in an RAF Chevrolet radio control vehicle with an aerial mounted on its roof. They spent three weeks camped on Garway Hill, presumably making sure that it was a suitable place for sending and receiving radio signals. Shortly afterwards, six civilian men with a large load of building material from a company we believe was called the Ashphalt Public Works from Worcester, arrived to erect a structure on the summit of the hill. Two of these men, the Price brothers from Rhayader lodged with the Gardiners at the post office, the others in the surrounding district, one at least with Mrs Whistance at Little Garway Farm. The foreman was a man from Peterchurch. Sadly, it was heard that later in the war two of these men had been called up and were killed in action.

It was soon obvious that the lorry, which had delivered the building materials, could not get up the track to Garway Hill common. So once again, the famous Gardiner lorry, known as the first lorry to reach the summit of Garway Hill, was brought into action. The lorry was fully occupied during the working day but 12 year-old Les, son of Bert Gardiner came to the rescue by driving the lorry laden with bricks, timber and concrete blocks up the hill during the night. It is worth remembering that during the war years 'double summertime' was in force which meant advancing GMT by two hours instead of one, giving long evenings of daylight, enabling people to work until 11 p.m. However, it was a remarkable achievement for one so young, but if questioned, Les would now dismiss it with a smile and deny everything.

Many tales circulate as to the buildings' original purpose. I have contacted the Ministry of Defence and the Imperial War Museum without any success and the Herefordshire Sites and Monuments know nothing about it. However, I was fortunate enough to be put in contact with the boy who drove the lorry, Les Gardiner, and along with a photograph of the tower he was able to tell me the real story.

The tower was apparently built to house a type of radio antenna. An octagonal wooden tower, 25 foot high was built. It had a first floor in the middle and a second floor at the top with an eighteen-rung ladder for access. An aperture was left in the roof to accommodate an aerial/transmitter that was never installed. Around this was built a 7-foot high octagonal brick wall, 14 inches thick, as a defence, mainly against fire, a big hazard on bracken-clothed hillsides. The offset entrance fitted with an iron gate was a further fire precaution. Outside the brick wall were eight anchor points for the stanchions reaching down over the wall and supporting the tower. A further eight anchor points were located inside to secure the tower frame. Encircling the tower, about 40 yards out from the wall, a ditch was dug as a firebreak, three feet wide and two feet deep.

One hundred and fifty yards lower down the hillside an accommodation block was built of Broadmoor Cinderford bricks with single brick walls which were rendered This was divided into two rooms, one for living and one for housing instruments. Clearly visible are two 20mm cables each of 4 core and 8 strands projecting from the floor. Cables of this size were used to prevent a voltage reduction over a long distance and were dealing with 110 volts, direct current. This building could well have been to house a radio beam transmitter and receiver of signals. At one end was a concrete water tank to collect water from the roof. This building, which measured 21 feet by 15 feet, was also surrounded by a fire break that was just 15 yards outside the walls. A telephone cable was laid but a phone was never installed. There was no water laid on but there are springs just a little lower down the hill. The Black Pool which is fed by springs and which I have been told was deepened and enlarged in the 1940's, remains the main source of water for the sheep and ponies who graze the hill.

Even further down the hill, about 100 yards to the east of the modern radio mast and close to the boundary fence, was the engine house that was to supply the electrical energy to the tower. This was also of single brick thickness wall construction measuring 15 by 13 feet and appears to have had a corrugated asbestos roof. In here there were two diesel Lister Blackstone engines and generators, one to be used as a backup. Banks of big capacity accumulators would have been installed to store the generated electricity, each about two foot tall and nine inches square. Although the project was put on hold the engines were regularly started up.

The RAF Aerodrome at Madley was opened on August 27th 1941 and was for the training of ground and aircrew wireless operators. It is visible from the top of Garway Hill but I have found no evidence to suggest any connection between these two places.

There is however, the possibility that it was a satellite of RAF Defford in Worcestershire which was experimenting with aircraft radio-location beams and radar. So perhaps its original intended function was destined to be overtaken by fast moving technological innovations in a world at war. Consequently the station was never fully operational. This could also explain the involvement of a Worcester based construction company.

The three buildings are in alignment and about 40 yards on the tower side of the accommodation block is what appears to be a neatly shaped bomb crater about 15 yards in diameter. In 1948 the wooden tower was dismantled and taken away with presumably everything else that could be salvaged, leaving the strangely shaped brick wall as a source of speculation for years to come. The engine house and accommodation building survived for many years after the war and were still there in the mid 1970's. Now only the concrete bases and piles of scattered bricks are left to remind us of what would have been Garway's contribution to the War effort.

The Tower on Garway Hill in the mid-1940's and in 1999   photo: L. Gardiner

The former Sun Inn, Orcop and the tower on Garway Hill

SKENFRITH

Three castles fayre, are in a goodly ground,
Grosmont is one, on hill it builded was;
Skenfreth the next, in Valley is it found,
The Soyle about, for pleasure there doth passé.
Whit Castle is the third of worthie fame,
The countrey there, doth bear Whit Castles name,
A stately Seate, a loftie princely place,
Whose beautie gives the simple soyle some grace.

   Thomas Churchyard   The Worthiness of Wales 1587

Skenfrith in Welsh, Ynysgynwrraidd, The Water Meadows of St Bridget.

The little village of Skenfrith nestles at a point where three sweet valleys meet, not an important place now, it is true, but unique in its surroundings, and "girt about with Memories". Ten miles by high road from Ross, about eight from Pontrilas and Monmouth, it is out of the track of tourists and has few visitors. It is quite an event if there are guests at "The Bell" or strangers looking at the church and castle. Truly a change from the times it has known.

So wrote Mrs Jackson of Blackbrook seventy years ago. Nowadays many visitors come in cars and coaches to view the castle that is in the custodianship of the National Trust or stay at the splendidly refurbished "Bell". In 1893, Charles G Harper in his book, The Marches of Wales, described Skenfrith rather differently.

The first sign of Skenfrith was the ruinated keep-tower of its castle, ivy-covered and ragged with bushy shrubs that peeped problematically over the distant hedges. Then came the bridge and the Monnow, swiftly running in a deep stony bed between abruptly scarped banks. The Bell Inn, a comfortable-looking village hostelry, white-faced and quaintly gabled, the resort of anglers, faced the bridge; but fishermen filled the house to overflowing, and it was only in a humble cottage by the church that we were able to stay the night.

Skenfrith village was called into being only as a dependency of the castle, and ever since that fortress by the ford was deserted the place has dragged on a decrepit existence in this unhealthy sink between the hills, saturated with showers and melting snows of spring, scarcely dried by the heats of summer, inundated with the rains of autumn, and by the spates of the river; so the rheumatism, and bronchitis, diphtheria and whooping cough and agues are the commonest ailments of the inhabitants. The Monnow sends up clinging mists at night and in early morning, and not before the sun has performed half his daily round of a summer's day is the air clear and distant objects visible.

The village is merely one short, but broad and straggling street, traversed by strips and selvages of grass, grown where the scanty traffic rarely comes. It is a delight to the eye, haphazard and unconventional, frankly poor in general effect, but striving and utilitarian in detail, as where modern cottages, pigsties and a hideous modern flour mill are built on to and over against the castle ruins.

The late Fred J Hando of Newport recalled a visit he made to Skenfrith in the 1930's.

I have bathed in Lake Lucerne during a thunderstorm when the lilac light of the flashes made Pilatus and Rigi dantesque. I have bathed in midsummer seas by moonlight, but for perfect pleasure give me the Monnow on a hot summers day at Skenfrith, deep, inviting, charged with the upland air of its birthplace. When is Skenfrith most beautiful? In summer, autumn, winter, at twilight or by moonlight? To me it is most alluring on a May morning. The hillsides soft in outline, veiled in silver frame the lovely church. Fruit trees hold out the pearls of opals of their blossoms. The ancient yew breathes over it in its benediction; and the river sings its gay young song as it flows towards the mill

The site of Skenfrith at a ford over the river Monnow has been of strategic significance since the earliest times. The Celtic stronghold became a Norman Castle and archaeological excavations in the field west of the church have revealed the remains of houses burnt and destroyed by the raids of Owain Glyndwr (Plates 17,18,19,20).

The three castles of Skenfrith, Grosmont and White Castle are always thought of together as a unit; Skenfrith and Grosmont, both in the Monnow valley and White

Castle on a ridge overlooking the valley leading out from Abergavenny towards Monmouth.

The original castles were motte and bailey castles built by the compatriots of William FitzOsbern. They became part of the possessions of Hamlyn, the Conqueror of Over Gwent. Following his death without issue the castles belonged to Hamlyn's nephew Brian FitzCourt. Henry II (1154-1189) seized the administration of the three castles and in the reign of King John they were given to Hubert de Burgh who held them for many years until once again they were confiscated by the Crown. They remained Crown property until Henry III (1216-1272) gave the three castles together with Monmouth castle to his son Edmund of Lancaster. Edmund's grandson, Henry of Lancaster was born at Grosmont and was always known as Henry of Grosmont. At his death in 1345 the castle passed to his heiress, the Duchess Blanch and was absorbed into the vast holdings of her husband, John of Gaunt.

Skenfrith is the smallest of the three castles and the one that was least altered by its later owners. It lies in a very low position right on the banks of the river Monnow at a point where it was possible to ford the river. The river provided water for the moat or ditch. The castle is almost completely surrounded by hills and from the summit of the hill behind the Bell Inn it is possible to look down right into the castle. Its shape is that of a rectangular enclosure with a drum tower at each corner. There is a large circular keep standing on a motte in the centre of the court. The castle seems to have been neglected since the time of the Lancastrians, possibly because they had better castles at Monmouth and Grosmont. By Tudor times it was described as 'ruinous and decayed time out of mind'.

Skenfrith Castle and Village

A hundred years ago the castle was much overgrown and neglected with the walls covered with ivy and trees. The interior was an apple orchard and the keep a refuge for cows. Cottages were built up against the exterior walls and stone was pillaged to build cottages in the village. The castle is now owned by the National Trust and is in the guardianship of CADW. It is open free of charge to the public.

There is a story about a treasure supposedly buried in Skenfrith castle. In 1589, a Welshman imprisoned in the Tower of London wrote a letter, which is still in existence, to Lord Burghley offering to deliver this treasure to him if only he was given his freedom. He wrote, 'the voice of the country goes, there is a dyvill and his dam in the castel; one sets on a hogshead of gold and the other on a hogshead of silver'. He undertook to look for the treasure but his offer was not taken up! The devil and his dame were supposed to be seen dancing in Skenfrith castle when the moon was full.

In August 1983 a wonderful Son-et-Luniere cum Pageant was held in the castle as part of the Festival of Castles. On three consecutive nights in August, with perfect weather and a full moon, the village was filled with stalls and entertainment. When darkness fell the performance started inside the castle. Fifty local people mimed to the recorded voices from the Welsh College of Music and Drama and with professional lighting and sound, dramatised the history of the castle. Once again in 2000 the castle was host to the Centred Theatre Company who performed Merlin's Child, the legend of Arthur, to an appreciative audience, many of whom had brought picnics and bottles of wine

The church of St Bridget was built between 1228 and 1232 by Hugh de Burgh when he was lord of the Three Castles and Justicias of England. In recent years a great deal of work has been necessary to keep the building intact. Much of this work was completed by voluntary labour, especially by the Vicar, the late Bill McAdam who, although elderly and almost completely blind, re-roofed the church almost single-handed.

St Bridget's Church, Skenfrith

The most important estate in Skenfrith is that of Blackbrook which lies in a splendid position back off the road leading from Norton to Grosmont. The name is thought to have derived from the Benedictine monks who lived there before it became a possession of Dore Abbey. They wore black habits and cowls and gave their name to the house and stream – the Blackbrook.

For several hundred years the owners of Blackbrook had been Roman Catholics and being men of influence and standing were known to have sheltered priests from the Cwm. During the time of Sir Richard Morgan (died 1556), the estate was very extensive running from Upper Duffryn to Cross Vane and from Blackbrook Hill to just below Glanmonnow. Throughout the next two centuries the house continued to be occupied by Roman Catholic gentlemen.

Blackbrook House pre 1910

In 1797 Col. the Honourable John Lindsay bought the house which he rebuilt, enlarged the estate and planted many ornamental trees. He sold the estate in 1810 to John Briggs. By 1838 the mansion set in three hundred acres was up for auction at Mr Barretts' Royal Hotel in Ross. The sale catalogue described the mansion as-

A stone edifice, elegant and substantial in structure, built within the last thirty years by a gentleman of acknowledged taste at immense cost, timber throughout was oak and the house was embedded in shrubberies. The house had cost upwards of £8,000 and since the primary expense it had been improved by large additional outlay. The house contained an entrance hall, dining parlour, paved walk and gallery with columns 28' x 18', drawing rooms with folding doors, about 45'x15', breakfast room and billiard room, seven upper chambers, five best bedrooms, dressing room, kitchen, immense servants offices and outside, a courtyard with dairy and malt kiln, a wall and flower garden.

The property was sold to Mr John Crawfurd for £10,000. He was JP for the county and lived with his family at Blackbrook for nineteen years. In 1857 Blackbrook together with its estate of 1,864 acres was bought by Peter Rothwell Jackson. He added another 2,000 acres to the estate making his family the largest landowners in the district. Blackbrook employed the largest workforce in the parish. There was a staff of eight indoor servants, farm labourers, twelve gardeners, eleven teams of horses with four teamsters, gamekeeper, blacksmith, and in the 20th century, an electrician and a chauffeur who drove a Crossley car. The Jacksons were known as kindly and benevolent squires, concerned with the welfare of their workers and tenant farmers.

Jackson was a brilliant engineer who ran a factory in Salford. He pioneered many engineering techniques, such as producing steel tyres by precise dimensions and he was associated with the founding of the Institute of Mechanical Engineers. Peter had to commute between his house at Blackbrook and the Salford works. He travelled to Pontrilas station by horse and carriage to board the Great Western Railway Express trains which stopped there by request on Monday mornings and when he returned home on Thursdays. Peter and his wife Rebecca had five children, one son and four daughters. Rebecca died in 1863 at the young age of 47, but Peter lived on at Blackbrook with his second wife, until he died there in 1899 aged 86. He was buried at the Graig Methodist Chapel that he had built at Cross Ash. Robert Newton Jackson succeeded to the Estate on the death of his father. He carried on the Salford factory but was also keenly interested in farming and took many prizes for his Hereford cattle and pedigree stallions. In 1883 he bought the advowson of Skenfrith Church and in 1899 purchased the Castle.

Robert Newton married Wilhelmina Mary, nee Darby, who liked to be known as 'Mina'. She was a widow with one daughter Fritzie, who married Owen, later Brigadier General Sir Owen Thomas. They had four sons. Mrs Jackson researched extensively in the Public Records Office, British Museum and the Lambeth Library to find original documents relating to the district and just before she died in 1926 her book, 'Bygone Days in the March Wall of Wales' by M N J of Blackbrook, was published in a limited edition. The dedication is 'In Remembrance of many happy days, compiled before the war for my dear grandsons who have made the supreme sacrifice'. Her favourite grandson died aged 17 in 1906 and the lectern in Skenfrith Church is dedicated to the memory of Leyton Pershouse Thomas. In rapid succession came the news that Robert had been killed at Gaza in 1917 aged 27, and then Owen Vincent aged 25 whilst night flying; then Trevor at Neuve Chapelle aged 19. Tragically, her husband Robert Newton Jackson died in 1919. Her last years were spent in California where she had emigrated with her immediate family and Blackbrook was sold in 1920. She died on 20th November 1926 in her 80th year and was buried in the churchyard at Skenfrith. Her funeral was a distinguished affair and the night before her body had laid in the church at Skenfrith and a number of people 'of all classes' journeyed considerable distances to pay their last respects. After the hymns the Lord Bishop of Monmouth read the lesson. Mrs Jackson had chosen the bearers herself before she died and they were, Mr Reece, Demesne, Mr B Pugh, Mr C Williams, Mr Dance, Mr W Thomas, and Mr W Williams. Her gifts to Skenfrith Church included the oak reredos, lectern and organ and £3000 in trust for the maintenance of the fabric and other minor objects.

In 1920 Sir Alfred Fripp bought the Estate and he divided the land and sold it in lots including the farms. Walter Ralph Herring bought Blackbrook House in 1922 together with 275 acres of land. By the outbreak of the Second World War the house was being used as a private school for boys but in 1941 it was commandeered by the army for use by a searchlight unit and later as a camp for prisoners of war. After the war the house was occupied by a gang of Irish labourers and it was during this time that the fine avenue of trees lining the drive was cut down. By 1947 it was a school once again known as Beckett's School.

The property was bought in 1988 by Mr Adrian de Morgan and his family and they carried out considerable restoration of the house and farm buildings and planted many trees.

The Church & Castle, Skenfrith.   *Aerial photograph by Donovan C. Wilson*

LLANROTHAL

The next parish on the English bank of the river Monnow has a Welsh name, Llanrothal. The parish of Llanrothal lies in the south of the district once known as Archenfield or Ergyng. It has the river Monnow as one boundary and abuts to the parishes of Garway and Welsh Newton. In 1883 the parish boundary was changed to include the part of Dixton parish known as Llangunville. This addition to the south of the parish included Wern Farm, Broom Farm, Old Shop, Little Manston, Lower Buckholt Farm Llangunville, Lower Llangunville now Tump Farm and part of Buckholt Wood. A section of the old boundary of Llanrothal was part of Mansons Lane. This lane ran all the way from Dixton church to Moyles Cross and was thought to be the original road from Monmouth to Hereford before the present road through the Buckholt was built.

Somewhere in Llangunville was the church or chapel of St Michaels which was recorded in the ancient charters of the Llandaff diocese. The original dedication of the Celtic church was to Cynfall. At a later date the church was rededicated to St Michael and may have been rebuilt in stone. There is now no trace of this building but it is marked on old maps printed in the 17th and 18th centuries and was probably in the vicinity of Broom Farm which has been said to have fragments of the said church built into it.

The only way to visit this area is to take the very narrow and winding lanes either from Welsh Newton or Monmouth. The name Llanrothal is thought to derive from the British saint Ridol, in Welsh Rhyddol, who founded a church, or Llan, on the banks of the river Monnow. The Book of Llandaff names Llanridol amongst the Ergyng churches that were subject to the See of Llandaff under Bishop Herwald between the years 1056 and 1104. The Book of Llandaff describes the church as situated on the banks of the River Mynwy, 4 Miles north west of Monmouth. Little is known of St Ridol. It is reputed that he had a hermitage in the district before the time of St. Augustine. No record of his work survives but he is thought to have lived around the year 600 AD. In the 1291 Taxatio of Pope Nicholas IV, Llanrothal church was valued at £3. 6s. 8d. It belonged to Monmouth Priory. Some time after 1186, the church became dedicated to St, John the Baptist. The church is now unused and has been in the care of the Redundant Churches Fund since 1985. (Plate 16) In the middle ages there was a village near the church but this did not survive the Black Death in 1349. The parish now consists of farms and several private houses the most notable being Tregate Castle and the Cwm, which will feature later in this book

Today, Tregate Castle is a large house built on the site of a motte and bailey castle. It is high above the eastern bank of the river Monnow. Although it was not mentioned in the Domesday Book there was almost certainly a building there in 1086. Few places in Archenfield were detailed in the Domesday survey and Llanrothal was probably considered part of the manor of Monmouth. Evidence of a wooden keep has been discovered but it is not certain whether the keep was ever rebuilt in stone. It would seem that a stone manor house was built and this house most likely forms part of the foundations of the present house. In addition the church of St Roald at Llanrothal, there was a chapel at Tregate dedicated to St Thomas a Becket who had recently been martyred, and the chapel of St Michael at Llangunville. Both church and chapels were in the possession of Monmouth Priory in 1186.

In the reign of King John, Robert de Treget was Lord of the Manor. Subsequent Lords of the Manor have included Thomas le Rous and Sir William Mull who was unfortunate enough to be on the wrong side in the War of the Roses and whose property was seized and handed over to Thomas Herbert. In the middle of the 17th century Tregate belonged to the Barry family. During the Civil War, contemporary documents record "that in the spring of 1645 a peace conference was held at Tregate between Sir William Fleming, representing the King, and high ranking officers of the Scottish army." This meeting proved abortive.

After the Restoration, Martin Boothby of Bergan-op-Zoom, Holland, purchased Tregate. Mr Boothby's granddaughter married William Barry and the house once more belonged to the Barry family. It remained so until the death of their grandson, the Rev Martin Barry, Vicar of Llantrothal, in 1805.

Joseph Price, who died at the age of 82 in 1849, owned Little Castle House in Monmouth in addition to Tregate Castle. He had 24 children and was Deputy Lieutenant of the County and Justice of the Peace. Tregate Castle has been rebuilt and added to many times during the last 900 years. The motte is still quite distinctive and the outline of the bailey can still be seen.

At the end of the 17th century, Llanrothal Court, now a large farmhouse, was owned and occupied by Henry Milbourne Recorder of Monmouth and Agent to the Duke of Beaufort. Henry was killed in 1692 when his horses bolted into the river Monnow near his home. His body was never recovered and, according to local legend, his ghost was soon haunting the house. Twelve priests were sent for to exorcise this spirit, the oldest one being the Vicar of Raglan. The ghost appeared and all the priests fled except the Vicar of Raglan. The ghost asked the Vicar for how long he was to be laid and he was told, "until I next eat bread". The ghost disappeared into the river and was never seen again because, within hours, the Vicar of Raglan fell ill and died before he had the opportunity to eat any bread. A very deep pool in the river near Llanrothal Court is still known as Milbourne's Hole.

One of the few public bridges over the river Monnow is at Tregate. The two- arched structure that was built in 1741 was swept away in 1880 during a storm and the rebuilding of its replacement caused considerable controversy. The matter was brought before the Quarter Sessions for the Counties of Herefordshire and Monmouthshire and as both counties refused responsibility the situation remained deadlocked for six years. In 1887 legal advice was sought and the verdict was that it was the duty of both counties to repair the bridge. Not wishing to risk litigation, the Justices at the Quarter Sessions gave in and the bridge was opened in 1888

Sadly, in 2002 the powers that be felt it necessary to place hideous bollards and signs on each end of Tregate Bridge creating a blot on a lovely landscape. The bridge is little used and surely drivers would approach such a narrow bridge with caution. Many see it as another example of urban clutter in a rural environment.

ST MAUGHANS

On the Welsh bank of the river Monnow and north of Monmouth lies the parish of St Maughans. It is made up of the hamlets of St Maughans Green, the Maypole and Newcastle.

St. Maughans parish church is dedicated to St, Meugan, one of the Celtic Saints. In Welsh literature his name is spelt "Mawgan", which could be the source of the Anglicised name. The church is of a simple double nave plan with a square tower. Its most remarkable feature is the set of wooden pillars separating the nave and aisle. This arcade is made of three octagonal-shaped oak tree trunks. Mr J E W Rolls, the grandfather of the founder of Rolls Royce, restored St Maughans church in 1865 with J P Seddon as the architect and the church reopened in 1866.

The church is now rather isolated but before the turnpike road was constructed in the 1780's the lane on which it stands was the highway from Monmouth to Grosmont. Archdeacon William Coxe, cleric, scholar and traveller, author of "An Historical Tour in Monmouthshire" gives the following description of this lane.

The horse way to Skenfrith leaves the carriage road about five miles from Monmouth and after traversing St Maughan's common, proceeds through a narrow, steep and stony lane, overgrown with thickets and pitched with large stones, placed edgeways in the boggy soil, and horses not accustomed to such rugged ways continually stumble and flounder. By the side of this road a pleasant walk runs through the fields on the slopes overlooking the Vale of the Monnow. In the vicinity of lanes such footpaths are common in Monmouthshire, which those who are fond of walking will traverse with much delight, though the way is rugged, it is extremely cool and pleasant.

During the rebellion of Owain Glyndwr in 1402, the whole area round Monmouth including St Maughans was devastated. All economic life and civil administration ceased for several years. As late as 1420 it was reported that St Maughans was lying "wholly in decay"

Newcastle is a hamlet on the road from Monmouth to Cross Ash and Skenfrith. All that is left of the castle is a mound behind the farmhouse. It was called Castell Meirch (the castle of the war horses). According to Sir Joseph Bradney it was probably a fortified residence of a British chieftain that was improved by the Normans and became an outpost of Monmouth Castle. Further down the lane, which was once the main road, is the site of the famous Newcastle Oak that had the reputation of being a sacred tree. No one would attempt to fell or even lop this legendary tree because of the fairies that had this tree under their protection. Anyone who did try to cut the branches came to an untimely end or broke their limbs or some other misfortune befell them. When eventually the Newcastle oak did fall down, probably from old age, those who collected the kindling wood managed to set their houses on fire The Wellington Inn, one time a pub is now a private house. It was originally called the

King's Head and the name was changed "when Colonel Evans came back after Waterloo". It was one of three inns in the village, the others were, the Castle and the Old Boot. The petty sessions were held in a room at the Wellington Inn until at least 1897 when the Petty Sessional division of Skenfrith was moved to Monmouth. A visitor to the district in the 1940's described the Inn thus.

The Inn itself is of uncertain antiquity and in the spring it has a beauty unexpected even among such beautiful surroundings. It is built as three sides of a square, and might not attract a great deal of notice at any other time of the year, but in the spring, about May, the whole building is hidden in a haze of wisteria, the most wonderful wisteria I have ever seen. It is known to be over two hundred years old, and it was not a new plant then. It has a huge trunk on the one wall, and the branches spread right round the three sides until the whole building is covered; the branches are even beginning to creep round the corners, and will soon be around the back as well.

By 1950 when Fred Hando visited the Inn the wisteria measured 150 feet from tip to tip of its branches and the open top of its trunk was from time to time carefully filled with cement.

The Wellington Arms, Newcastle   *Fred Hando*

The main estate in St Maughan's parish is Hilston Park. The family who owned the original house on this site were Catholics, mentioned frequently in the Recusant Rolls from 1679 onwards. Sebastian Needham came to Skenfrith in about 1660 and before the end of the 17th century his descendants had acquired the estate of Upper Hillstone in the parish of St Maughans. It remained in this family until 1803 when John Needham sold it to Sir William Pilkington, who in turn sold to Sir Robert Brownrigg. Sir Robert was responsible for founding Newcastle school and for the building of the stables at Hilston at a cost of £4000. They were described in the sale particulars as 'containing overhead, five capital bedrooms for servants, a hay loft, three store rooms, a Bailiff's room and two carpenters workshops'.

In 1838 George Cave JP, a Bristol Banker bought the property and began building the house that we see today. He planted many trees and created a beautiful wooded park of 500 acres. John Hamilton the younger of Liverpool became the owner in 1861. During his ownership he completed the building that he then passed to his son, Captain Pryce Hamilton. By 1873, James Graham owned the estate. His son had the oak panelling removed from the hall at Lower Duffryn and installed in the hall at Hilston. He was also responsible for building the two lodges, new cottages and the reservoir.

Before the First World War Arthur Ernest Lawley a businessman from Manchester bought the Estate which was let to a tenant until after the war. He died on the 26th May 1920 aged 45, just as he was completing the purchase of the Garway Estate that added considerably to his holding of land in the area. Consequently his widow, Elizabeth Wright Lawley put the whole property up for auction.

John D Wood and Co., of Grosvenor Square, London, offer for sale on Thursday, May 19th 1921, Hilston Park in the Wye Valley District, one of the finest domains in this glorious country. The estate comprises 3,372 acres of beautifully disposed, wood-capped hills and broad vales with six miles of trout fishing in the river Monnow and unrivalled shooting (575 acres coverts). The Mansion, in fine condition, situated 500 feet up, has glorious southern views for 30 miles. Hilston House has twenty bedrooms and dressing rooms, five bathrooms, five reception rooms, panelled halls, electric light, central heating, telephone, and is a most comfortable home, economical to run, with splendid model cottages, lodges, Home Farm and a richly wooded park of 475 acres. Also, all in good order and let to a good tenantry, on short tenancies, 21 farms, one with original Tudor house, numerous cottages, small holdings etc, with the Dower House, in a beautiful situation, with ten bed and dressing rooms, two bath and four reception rooms.

The Dower House, which was sold with 1,130 acres as Lot Two, was Glanmonnow House in Garway that had only been bought the previous year. A total of fifty-six lots were needed to sell this very large estate and the total sales amounted to £53,000. Mrs Lawley left the house in February 1922 and Mr Edmund Henry Bevan JP of Wadhurst Castle, Sussex, who had bought Hilston Park and 1000 acres, moved in.

Mr and Mrs Bevan, who had one son and four daughters, lived in some style. They were the largest employers in the St Maughans and Skenfrith district. There was a chauffeur, gamekeeper, cowman, other farm workers, a blacksmith, forester, head and under gardeners, a woodman, and a general maintenance man. The indoor staff comprised, a butler, footman, pantry boy, lady's maid, housemaid, cook, parlour maid, kitchen maid and laundry maid. Mrs Bevan died in 1942 followed by Mr Bevan in 1945 at the age of 83. They are both buried in Skenfrith churchyard.

By 1957 Hilston Park was up for sale again. This time Monmouthshire Education Sites and Buildings Sub-Committee decided to purchase the Mansion and about 15 acres of land for use as a special school for the teaching of sub-normal children. In 1968 Gwent Education Authority opened a school of Environmental Studies and Outdoor Pursuits Centre that still provides courses for students throughout the county.

ROCKFIELD

Rockfield is a parish just north of Monmouth lying on the Welsh side of the river Monnow. It is quite a small parish with just 1848 acres and the population during the last 200 years has never risen above 270. The church at Rockfield is dedicated to St Cenedlan, a 5th century saint who was one of the daughters of Brychan who gave his name to Breconshire. The present church, which is on the site of a much older foundation, was restored and much of it rebuilt in 1884. Inside the church, under the communion table lies a slab measuring 6 feet long by 3 foot 6 inches broad which is the burial place of Father Matthew Pritchard, the catholic bishop and priest who resided at Perthir until his death on 22nd May 1750. (See chapter on Matthew Pritchard in part three).

Rockfield has always been a small village. In 1884 Kelly's Directory records a population of 227. There were two crosses, one in the churchyard and one at the entrance to the village, both having lately been restored. There was a shopkeeper, a butcher, a carpenter and wheelwright and two blacksmiths. The three inns do not seem to have survived into the 20th century. They were the Red Lion which was opposite the stables of Rockfield House, the Horse and Jockey at the end of a row of cottages and the White Hart at the entrance to the bridge leading over the Monnow to Rockfield Park, (which despite its name, is actually in the parish of Monmouth). There are also some grand houses; Rockfield House which was the principal residence of the parish, Pentwyn meaning 'top of the tump' and Newbolds. Perthir, the most historic house in the parish is now no more.

The ancient manor house of Perthir was close to the river Monnow. It was originally called Plas-yn-y-barth-hir, the mansion within the long fence, and was for many years one of the chief seats and estates in this part of the county. In 1904 the site of the mansion was barely visible with a modern farmhouse built nearby. A hundred years earlier Perthir was visited by William Coxe on his Historical Tour of Monmouthshire and his description, published in 1801 is worth quoting in full.

The family of Herbert, which seems to have been first established at Werndee, was remarkable for its multifarious branches, and occupied, under the names of Herbert, Jones, Powell and Proger, numerous seats in this country. In the vicinity of Monmouth several places are distinguished, which once formed the residence of these various branches; most of which, from various causes, particularly from the extinction of the male line, have been conveyed to other families, but still retain traces of their former distinction.

In company with the Rev. William Roberts, who resides at Perthir, and to whom I was indebted for various communications, I walked to this ancient place, which is situated two miles from Monmouth, in a fertile plain, to the right of the road leading to Grosmont, not far from the banks of the Monnow. He introduced me to John Powell Lorimer the present proprietor, who favoured me with a friendly reception, permitted me to inspect his pedigree, and gave me all the information concerning his family, which the scanty documents in his possession enabled him to afford.

Perthir, which once vied with Werndee as the most ancient seat of the Herbert family, appears to have been the residence of Swillim, son of Jenkin, lord of Werndee. His grandson Howell ap Thomas was lord of Perthir, and ancestor of the line who resided at this mansion. His son William, (called in the Welsh pedigrees, ap Howell ap Thomas ap Gwillim) first adopted a surname after the English custom, and changed his patronymic ap Howell into Powell, by which name this branch has since been distinguished; he was killed at the battle of Banbury, under the standard of his cousin the earl of Pembroke, His lineal descendant John Powell, dying without issue male towards the beginning of this century, left four daughters, who were unmarried, and the estate came to the family of Lorimer seated at Newbolds in the vicinity, one of whose ancestors had espoused a Powell of Perthir.

'Perthir'.   **'Werndee'.**

A few remains of ancient magnificence appear in a gothic window of four compartments, with stone mouldings, which seems to be at least as early as the reign of Henry V; in the hall or passage, thirty-seven feet in length and nine in breadth; in the wooden rafters, which contain timber sufficient for four modern roofs; and particularly in the long and lofty hall, with a curious vaulted ceiling, and a music gallery at one extremity, the windows of which are emblazoned with the Herbert arms. There are a few family portraits; Mary, wife of John Powell, the last male of the family, and their four daughters, Mary, Bridget, Catherine and Winifred, who died unmarried. There is also a head of the Rev Matthew Pritchard, a friar of the order of Recollets, and Roman Catholic bishop, long resident at Perthir, where he died in 1750, aged 81; he was buried at Rockfield church, under a sepulchral stone with a Latin inscription, commemorating his profound learning, extensive benevolence, and great attention to the duties of his pastoral office.

The mansion is now considerably reduced from its former size and magnificence which were equal to the ancient estates of the family, which were once so large, that according to tradition, they stretched from Perthir to Ross. The present proprietor took down a part of the house, which was much too large for his family, containing thirteen bed chambers, and other offices. The mansion was formerly surrounded by a moat, which was provided with two draw-bridges. The family being Catholics, there was likewise an elegant gothic chapel, dedicated to St Catherine, which was demolished in 1745. A whole length portrait of St Catherine, not ill executed, was the altar-piece, and is now used for the same purpose in an apartment of the house.

Ruins of Windows of Perth-hir Mansion.

By the end of the 19th century the house had become a ruin and the splendid stone gateway that had adorned the garden was removed to Clytha Park where it makes a grand entrance to the estate and is still known as the Perthir Gate. (Plate 27) It is thought that the window in the north wall of Llanrothal church may have come originally from Perthir. There are now very few remains left of this historical house. When Sir Joseph Bradney visited in the early 20th century the ruins of two windows were still standing. When I visited in 2002, there were just a few ornamental stones lying hidden in the grass and weeds.

There were two mills at Rockfield. Pentwyn Mill was on the Nant-y-Gern brook that flowed into the river Monnow. A large dam had been provided to supply water to this mill which was shown on the tithe map as a tuck mill. It was recorded as disused by 1880. Perthir Mill on the river Monnow was a large mill with quite a complex of buildings. In 1700 the records show that it was a paper mill in addition to being a corn mill. Later in the 18th century the records show that there was also a fulling mill operating but that this was only for a few decades. There are now no remains of Perthir mill as it was burned down in 1890. (Fulling or tucking was a processes in the production of cloth).

A little known commercial success is the rural Rockfield Studios which are the world's first residential recording studios. This was the inspiration of two brothers, Charles and Kingsley Ward. Throughout the last 40 years the legends of Rock have recorded here and in 1997 had no less that five number one albums. They claim to be the world's most successful Rock and Roll studio.

Post Office & Cross, Rockfield.

The remains of the ornamental window at Perthir

St. Mary's Church, Monmouth.    *Monnow Gate, Monmouth.*

The Wye Valley, Monnow Bridge, Monmouth.

MONMOUTH

The ancient borough of Monmouth, as its name suggests, lies in the Monnow Basin where the river Monnow flows into the river Wye. The Welsh name for the town is Abermynwy, meaning the mouth of the Monnow. It is on the extreme eastern edge of the county of Monmouthshire and is surrounded by beautiful scenery.

As it nears Monmouth the river Monnow enters the geological area known as the Monmouth basin; a spread of terrace gravel and alluvium that appears to have been excavated during the Ice Age. Most of the town of Monmouth was built on a terrace where it was safe from flooding well above the flood plain. Monmouth is almost enclosed by its two rivers. The Monnow makes a semicircle around two sides of the town and the river Wye flows along the third side. These rivers dictate the whole character of Monmouth. The castle was built on a good defensible position on high ground with the advantage of good river communication. The size of the town that developed around it was limited by the flood plain that surrounded the town on three sides. Because of the danger of flooding there has never been any development on the fields at Vauxhall, (previously known as the castle fields), on Chippenham or along the banks of the Wye towards Dixton. The only part of the town, which was liable to flooding, was the lower end of Monnow Street and at Overmonnow.

Monmouth is an ancient town with a history that spans at least 2000 years. Since the period of the Roman occupation when a small military fort was built in about 55 AD, there has been a continuous occupation of the town. The original fort developed into the Roman town of Blestium. Following the departure of the Romans the Anglo Saxons occupied Monmouth which was in the most southerly part of Archenfield.

As at Ewyas Harold, the Normans very soon occupied Monmouth and William Fitz Osbern had established a castle there by the year 1067. A Benedictine monastery under the control of St Florent de Samur was established by 1075 and during the 11th century Monmouth was the home of Geoffrey of Monmouth, the writer of the romantic Historium Britonum.

Thanks to the meticulous archaeological work undertaken in Monnow Street during the 1990's by the Monmouth Archaeological Society, led by Steve Clarke, there is now confirmation that there has been continuous occupation of the town since the 11th century. The foundations of the medieval houses and burgesses in Monnow Street proved to have been totally undisturbed over the centuries. As this area was regularly flooded slag from the local iron industry was used to build up the street level. The residents built up the floors of their houses and all the rubbish and deposits became sealed under these layers leaving valuable evidence for future historians.

In medieval times Monmouth was a walled and moated town with fortified gates and bridges. The earliest bridge over the river Wye would have been constructed in timber and then at a later date, in stone. It was known as the Monmouth Bridge and like the more famous Monnow Bridge had a fortified gatehouse that shows up on John Speed's map of 1611. No exact date can be given for the gatehouse bridge over the river Monnow giving access to the town. The original bridge over the Monnow would have been of timber construction and was replaced sometime about 1270, by a stone bridge of three arches about 160 feet long and 27 feet wide. The gatehouse built to guard the bridge was constructed above the stone bridge about 1300. It is one of only two such bridges surviving in Europe and one of the most important monuments in South Wales. It has served many functions during its long existence apart from its original role as a guard to the entrance of the town. In the 18th century it was converted into a house where the porter lived and more room was created by heightening the structure and creating an attic floor. An extension was also built which hung over the river and is often seen in old paintings of the bridge. Its next use was as a storehouse and the pedestrian passageways in use today were pierced through the tower. In 1900 the 9th Duke of Beaufort presented the gatehouse to the Monmouthshire County Council and a plaque was erected on the gatehouse to commemorate the gift. However, the Somerset family had only owned the lock up house on the bridge since 1830 when the Town Council exchanged it for a piece of land on which they wanted to build a watchtower. By the twentieth century the increase of traffic over the bridge had become a real problem and the bridge was quite often damaged. The terrace of houses just south of the bridge was demolished in 1925 in an effort to improve the flow of traffic. (Plate 29)

The lower part of the town of Monmouth and Overmonnow has always been subject to flooding and various schemes over the years have been adopted in an attempt to alleviate this problem. The confluence of the Monnow with the river Wye has changed at least twice, once naturally and once artificially.

Early maps show the last few hundred yards of the river Monnow flowing a different course from that which it does today. After passing under the old Monnow Bridge the river turned north and then meandered south before entering the river Wye, leaving a small spit of land between the Monnow and the Wye. Morris's map of 1800 shows the layout. By 1835 a map of Monmouth shows that the river had broken through this small spit of land and entered the Wye upstream from the original confluence, leaving the small spit of land as an island in the river Wye. The land between the Monnow and the Wye was the location of the Chippenham Racecourse and the land south of the Monnow was owned by the Duke of Beaufort.

The Paving Act for Monmouth was given Royal Assent on 3rd June 1818. It was 'an Act for paving the footpaths and cleansing lighting and watching the streets of the Town of Monmouth'. A committee was formed with members from each of the wards of Monmouth. Almost immediately, at a meeting on 3rd August 1818, the committee applied themselves to the problem of flooding in Overmonnow. Two of the Paving Commissioners were delegated to meet Mr Wyatt, the agent to the Duke of Beaufort, who lived at Troy House, with a request that the town ditch should be reopened as a watercourse to discharge the floods also the channel of the Monnow from the bottom of Monnow street to the Cinderhill should be cleaned and straightened so as to raise material from the bed of the river for the repair of the streets and roads of the town

On 7th September 1818 the following letter was sent to the Duke of Beaufort at Badminton.

Jury Room, Monmouth, 7th September 1818

My Lord Duke,

As Commissioners for the Improvement of the Town under the recent Acts of Parliament, we request permission to trouble you with this letter. Your Grace is appraised that the floods have of late years been extremely injurious and inconvenient to the lower part of the Town which is now overflowed to a good depth thro' the whole of Overmonnow and up Monnow Street to Mr John Hughes', which there is much reason to think did not happen in ancient times by means to the same extent as many houses were considered to be built above the floods which are now inundated four or five feet.

The causes in a good measure seem to be that the Town Ditch from Drybridge to the Cinderhill which is now let by the Corporation into your Graces' fields (formerly a very considerable watercourse) is now so much filled up as to be almost useless and sends the water by Drybridge Turnpike down the street in which the flood is sometimes eight feet deep. That the channel of the Monnow below the Bridge downwards is very much filled up by shoals of sand and gravel and that the channel itself having taken a circuitous turn near the bottom of Chippenham the current becomes obstructed and retarded the effect of which is to delay the flood of the Monnow until that of the Wye (in general three of fours hours later in its decent) comes down which holds up the Monnow and throws it back upon the Town.
A flood not long since lasted a week thro' which most persons were supplied thro' their upstairs windows.

It has long been the general opinion that much of this calamity may be prevented and we beg leave to state the means which have been suggested to Your Grace.

1.The Cleansing of the Town Ditch by sloping it gradually to its intent depth, replacing the turf and by placing rails for fences between Your Graces' fields instead of hedges and ditches recently run cross them. The soil will be good manure which such of those occupying may have who will pay for the excavating and cleaning. And if any refuse permission is requested for Your Grace to deposit the mud upon the ground until it can be sold. A culvert under the road near the Cinderhill Turnpike Gate the expense of which the Turnpike Trust and parish would perhaps divide.

2 Cleaning the channel of the Monnow from the Bridge downwards which it is considered would not cost more than the Gravel raised would be worth for the Highways.

3 Making a new channel from the river across Your Graces' meadow as marked on the plan which appears from the surface of the ground to have been its course in ancient times, which persons offer to execute upon consideration of having the land which will be separated from the meadow and lie on the Chippenham side of the new channel and also for the proposed bed of the river which would be laid dry by a new channel – a considerable part of the isthmus has accumulated from Chippenham and the present bed of the river in time of memory and it appears from the surface that the course of the river was anciently near if not within the line now sketched for the alteration.

PLAN OF MONMOUTH

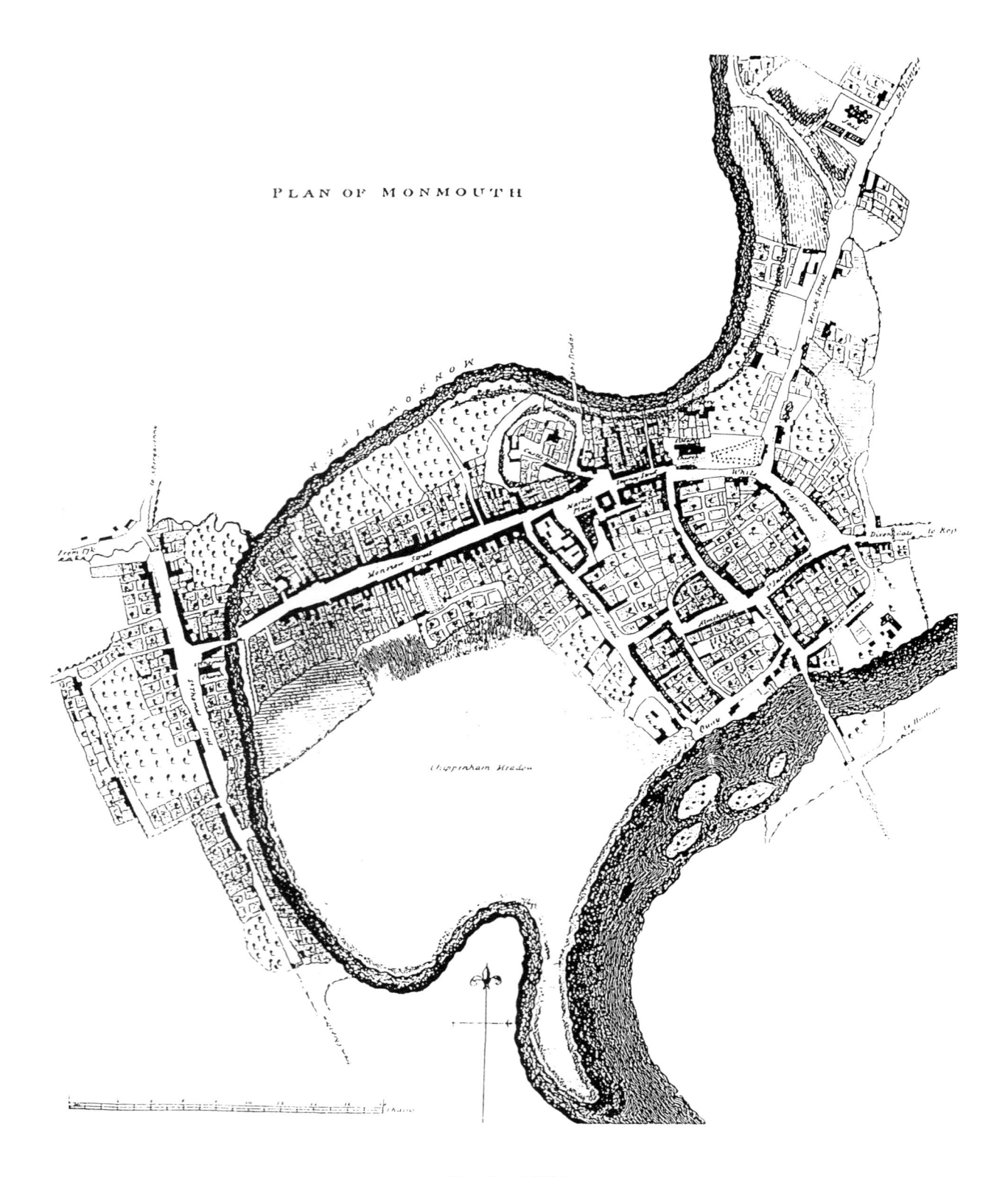

Monmouth Museum

Morrises' 1800

Monmouth Museum

Mr W F Powell and Mr Wanklyn proprietors of the part of Chippenham opposite, from whose land the whole of the present channel is taken will consent to this as will the corporation to any claim they may have to the bed of the river.

When Your Grace favours us with an answer we will meet Mr Wyatt to enter into the particulars of executing the work and if it can commence without delay the work may be finished before the expected deep flood after to long a dry season with great respect

Your Graces' obedient and humble servants

Signed by all the Commissioners present.

To the Mayor.

Badminton Gloucestershire September 11th 1818

Dear Sir,

Upon my return home the evening before last, after an absence of some four days, I received a letter signed by yourself and several other gentlemen acting as Commissioners for the Improvement of the Town of Monmouth, upon the subject of the Floods which frequently take place in Monnow Street and parts adjacent. I trust I need not assure you I am ever ready to concur in any measure that may tend to the improvement of the Town and convenience of its inhabitants, but as I am not sufficiently well acquainted with the situation of the places named in your letter I must beg to refer you to Mr Wyatt to whom I have written on the subject.

I am sir, your most obedient and very humble servant, Beaufort.

Troy House, Monmouth.

Flooding continued to be a serious matter for those living at the lower end of Monnow Street and at Overmonnow. The early 19th century saw flooding most years with the floods of 1847 being particularly bad. The Paving commissioners who blamed the flooding on the fact that the Monnow entered the Wye against the current first discussed the realignment of the river Monnow in 1818. As can be imagined, when the Monnow is in flood, so is the Wye making it almost impossible for the water in the Monnow to enter the Wye. The river Trothy which enters the Wye just a short distance downstream, has the same problem. All the water pouring down the rivers Monnow and Trothy then spreads out over the flood plain providing wonderful silt for the farmers on the water meadows but great damage and suffering to those whose homes are inundated with water.

No action had been taken in 1818 and it was almost 40 years before the problem of flooding was addressed again. The Minute Books of the Paving Commissioners show that they were inundated with drainage problems and did not seem to have the money to carry out all the work needed. (Unfortunately I have only been able to track down the first two Minute books covering the dates 1818 to 1848).

Flooding re-occurred in the years 1824,1827,1835,1836,1837,1838,1846,1847,1848. In 1847 the floods were particularly bad owing to the spoil from the Troy railway tunnel having been spread over the Troy meadows. The floods of 1852 were disastrous. 250 houses being flooded in February, 300 in November and 100 in December.

On 13th November 1852 a public meeting was held with the Mayor of Monmouth as chairman. A Treasurer was appointed to collect subscriptions 'for the relief of those poor persons who are at present deprived of the means of subsistence in consequence of the very great flood in the rivers Wye and Monnow which will be promptly undertaken by gentlemen knowing the necessities of persons in the locality'. The list was published in the Monmouthshire Beacon and started with three subscriptions for £5, quite a few for £1 and ending with 'two poor persons 4d'. A concert was held with the proceeds going to the Relief fund.

Another public meeting was held on 6th December 1852 to issue further orders as to the distribution of coal. Questions were asked about whether the coal should to given to people whose houses had not actually had water in them. Someone suggested that if they deviated from the rules there would be no end to it until they reached the top of the Kymin and up the Buckholt! It was decided that for some, although the water was not in their houses, as they were surrounded with water and were in great need a discretionary power should be given. The meeting arranged that one tram of coal at a time should be deposited in each district and that one or more gentlemen should be present to see to its proper distribution and that each family whose house had been flooded should have 2 cwt of coal to help them dry out their houses.

After the severe winter of 1855 when both the Wye and the Monnow froze and there was skating on the rivers for a fortnight, the thaw caused considerable flooding and the races had to be postponed. The fact that the gentry were inconvenienced may have had some bearing on the fact that a decision was finally taken to realign the Monnow. The Duke of Beaufort agreed to give the land and preparations were made to commence the excavation of a new channel

A notice appeared in the Monmouthshire Beacon on 27th July 1856 as follows.

PROPOSED ALTERATION OF THE COURSE OF THE RIVER MONNOW.

At the Meeting of the Committee for carrying out the above object, held on the 9th day of May, 1856 in the Jury Room, in the Town of Monmouth, W M Davis, Esq, Mayor in the Chair.

It was resolved –
That an appeal be made to the owners and occupiers of Property in flood-way and to the inhabitants of the Town of Monmouth and the neighbourhood for Subscriptions to carry out the contemplated improvement. Subscriptions will be received by Messrs. Bailey and Co.'s; and Messrs Bromage and Co.'s, Monmouth.

There followed a list of 148 names with amounts ranging from 5 shillings to £10.

At a meeting on 1st August the Monnow Cutting Committee was formed. It was resolved that –
Mr Nicholas, Mr Watkins, Mr Vaughan, The Mayor and Mr Probyn form a Committee to superintend the works of the Monnow Cutting and they are empowered to render such orders as to them shall seem expedient.

It would seem that the digging of the cutting proceeded as had been planned way back in 1818 and was completed in just a few months. Unfortunately the Minutes Book of the Paving Commissioners for this period cannot be found and the minutes of Monmouth Town Council do not mention the matter until February 1857 when 'it was unanimously resolved that the thanks of the Town council are due to Mr Thomas Maddocks for the very able and efficient services rendered by him gratuitously in completing the Monnow cutting, and that the Town Clerk enter this resolution on the Minute Book and forward a copy to Mr Maddocks'. There is no indication as to who Mr Maddocks was but there is always the possibility that the Clerk spelt the name incorrectly and that he was one of the Maddox family. G V Maddox who died in 1850 was the Architect who built the new market, Priory Street and the Methodist Church.

Excavation of the cutting commenced in July 1856 and the work was contracted to Messrs. Day and Heat who had been working on the Coleford, Monmouth Usk and Pontypool Railway. The line had reached Usk by June 1856 and was opened to Monmouth Troy Station on 12th June 1857. This must have seemed an opportune time to use the men who had been working on the railway cuttings and tunnels for the excavation of the new river bed. The spoil from the new bed was to be used to fill the channel of the diverted river. Flooding still occurred but it was reported as alleviating much of the former damage and disruption.

Naturally the Duke of Beaufort had to be thanked and the following resolution was presented to him by the Mayor.

That this meeting is of the opinion that the absence of floods in the streets and dwelling houses in the lower part of the Town of Monmouth is mainly to be attributed to the improvement made in the course of the River Monnow by the New Monnow Cutting. That the absence of floods has rendered the dwelling houses of the poorer classes much more healthy and a great source of sickness and distress has been removed. That the Duke of Beaufort having most generously given to the public the land through which the Cutting passes the Committee were enabled to carry out an object so beneficial to the Town of Monmouth.

Chippenham had always been an open space of common fields used for grazing. It was the custom 'immemorial' for the tacking (grazing) of horses and cattle on a mead called Chippenham to commence on the Monday after the 24th August yearly. It was decided at a meeting of the common council on 11th August 1721 that as there was a race meeting recently established which was found to be 'advantageous and beneficial to the Town' that it was ordered that the mead be turned to tack on Monday 14th August. The two-day race meetings on Chippenham were grand affairs and were usually held to coincide with the Assizes. This was a great social occasion for Monmouth with balls and assemblies and all the principal families including the Somersets would attend. A grandstand would be erected near Cornwall House for the Duke and Duchess of Beaufort. The Hereford Journal for 25th September 1869 reported that the races had brought to Chippenham Mead a large and fashionable company. It was not however, quite as fashionable as it had been 100 years previously when a journalist of the day wrote *'of the public dinners held daily at the Beaufort Arms, the King's Head and Angel Hotels and the ladies had a special ordinary of their own every day, at which all the beauty and fashion of the county of Monmouth were to be seen. An assembly was also held every night at the Town Hall, and the result of such grand proceedings was to draw to the borough a company "brilliant, fashionable, and polite in the extreme". The residents of Monmouth, too, for the whole time gave themselves up to pleasure seeking and enjoyment, and it is not too much to say that Monmouth, in the 18th century and the beginning of the 19th, bore on these occasions a much gayer appearance than has been witnessed latterly.'*

These races were not universally popular as some of the religious moralists considered that they attracted 'the dregs of society'. The Beacon frequently published letters condemning the racecourse. The incumbent of St Thomas's Church, Overmonnow, in a long letter starts –

I suppose that no one, who lives in the lower parts of the town of Monmouth, can forget the flood with which we were visited in the year 1852. Many persons were pleased with the fine sheet of water which was spread over Chippenham; but when the waters retired, and even some weeks after their disappearance, our cellars were filled with mud, and our houses were damp, and we had to endure bad smells. The races, I believe are hurtful to the best interests of our fellow men, as the flood was hurtful to health and property. It may, no doubt be pleasant for some persons to attend the races at Chippenham, but if they would attend on some days, and even weeks after the races, the public houses, and beer houses, and lodging houses, and many other houses they would find in them something worse than the mud which the flood leaves behind. In some houses they would see men fearfully changed from what man ought to be. And that change, in part, effected by strong drink, and gambling, and quarrelling, and indulgence of the grosser passions. And they would meet some women, not at all resembling Milton's fine description of Eve.

Another correspondent gave a list of reasons (much abbreviated) why he should not go the races –

1. *I cannot go to the races because I have an immortal soul and have been taught to pray 'lead us not into temptation.*
2. *I cannot go to the races because I feel I am a sinner, and I know that I must die.*
3. *I cannot go to the races because I know those who go to the races are people who live without God.*
4. *I cannot go to the races because I have placed my soul under the care of the great physician*

> 5. *I cannot go to the races because it is first on the Race Course that many young persons have their Christian principles first shaken.*

The race meetings were held on Chippenham fields from the early 18th century until the end of the 19th century then they were moved to Vauxhall where there were plans to build a Grandstand and Luncheon Rooms but in fact only a Members Stand was built. The races continued, with disappointing attendances until the First World War.

The river Wye offered an important means of communication for Monmouth. It provided a highway for trade with Hereford and Bristol, bringing in goods for a wide area of surrounding country. Until 1815 most of the merchandise reaching Monmouth arrived via the river using barges hauled by men

One of the chief problems with the navigation of the Wye above Monmouth was the considerable number of mills and forges that depended on weirs for their water supply. These weirs, of course, disrupted the natural flow of the river. Apart from being an essential part of the water supply to the mills and forges, these weirs had also been erected for the purpose of catching salmon and they were in the ownership of various people. There was constant disagreement between the barge owners and merchants who wished to remove the obstruction and the millers and fishermen who wished to preserve them.

In 1622 an unsuccessful attempt was made to remove the weir at Monmouth, which had been built in the reign of Mary Tudor just below the Wye Bridge, so that barges could sail upstream beyond it. The weir was 11 feet high on a foundation of loose stones and was said to be impassable to boats which had to be hauled ashore and then dragged by oxen a hundred yards upstream. The verdict of the commissioners was that the weir should be removed but the owner appealed and it was not until the 18th century that the weir was removed. Some of the goods arriving by boat were landed in Chippenham below the weir at Monmouth and carried on to Hereford by road. Goods from Bristol could be brought on the tide to Brockweir and transferred to barges then hauled up to Monmouth.

Coxe (1801) described his journey from Ross to Monmouth.

We passed several barges towed by 10 or 11 men, which by great exertion are towed towards Hereford in two days. The inhabitants of Monmouth are principally supported by the navigation of the Wye, trade with Hereford and Bristol, the supply of neighbouring districts with varying shop goods, and the influx of company.

Bark was brought down from the Forest of Dean, pared and cleaned at Monmouth, and then exported through Chepstow. There would be as much as 50-100 tons piled on the wharves at Monmouth. These flat bottomed barges did not draw more than 5 or 6 inches of water and were anything up to 50 feet long and 10 feet broad and could carry up to 20 tons. They were propelled downstream by the current but were hauled upstream by the bowhaulers, one man to each 2 tons at a speed of three miles per hour. Above Monmouth the boats had to be much smaller loading about 4 tons and had a draught of 16 inch.

During the late 18th and early 19th centuries the Wye Tour was a very fashionable pursuit and a great tourist attraction for the 'well-to-do' who because of the wars with France could not go on the Grand Tour. The 40 miles from Ross to Chepstow were of great scenic beauty. After embarking at Ross the tourists visited Goodrich Castle and climbed up Symonds Yat. The most spectacular scenery was through the gorge past the Seven Sisters Rock and the Iron forge at New Weir. The first day's journey ended at Monmouth where the passengers would find accommodation for the night.

The advent of the railways in the 1850's virtually ended the Wye trade. The pleasure traffic continued until the early 20th century when road improvement and motor transport became more convenient for the tourists.

The river banks at Monmouth were busy places with wharves, warehouses and cottages of the boatmen with inlets to allow boats to lie near the cottages. Wyebridge Street led down to the bridge over the Wye and Weir Street to the river bank. The people of Monmouth had access to the river which had played such an important part in their prosperity. All of this was to change in the 1960's when the need for fast modern roads meant that Monmouth acquired a by-pass and a connection to the new Motorway system. Unfortunately, the new road was to cut the town of Monmouth off from the river Wye. Much of the history of the river trade vanished. All the buildings, the wharves, the boatmens' cottages and the warehouses were destroyed along with some important houses and farms between Monmouth and Dixton. The new road cut across Chippenham meadows and crosses the Monnow before entering the new tunnel cut through Gibraltar hill near where it had been planned to cut a railway tunnel way back in the 1860's for the ill-fated Monnow Valley Railway. It is difficult to believe now that Monmouth relied so much on it's river traffic. The schools and the Rowing Club still use the river but commercial traffic is just a distant memory.

A new crossing of the river Monnow at Monmouth was discussed and planned as long ago as the 1920's and again in the 1930's. The ancient Monnow Bridge carried the A40 trunk road and a by-pass was seriously considered in 1941. Due to cost and the considerable number of houses that would have to be demolished this scheme was delayed for several years until the Monmouth by-pass was built. The road over the ancient bridge was then demoted to the B4293. During the 1960's and 1970's the Monmouth Borough council had started demolishing buildings in Cinderhill Street in anticipation of the building of a new bridge.

The first call for this new modern Monnow Bridge was in a document prepared by the Monmouth District Council in 1981 but it was not until 2000 that two options were put forward for consideration. The first option was just 70 meters downstream from the ancient bridge and this was the cheapest and easiest option. The second option was 140 meters from the old bridge and fortunately, this was the one that finally was chosen and work started on the new bridge in May 2003. The cost was estimated to be 4 million pounds but the work turned out to be considerably more expensive. The new bridge is very modern in appearance and not to everyone's taste. However, it has relieved the traffic problems in Monnow Street and Priory Street and hopefully the old bridge, now used for pedestrians only, will last another 500 years.

Monmouth

Flooding in Drybridge Street, Monmouth   Monmouth Museum

Part Two

The Knights Templars and Hospitallers In the Parish of Garway

ST. JOHN'S GATE, ST. JOHN'S LANE
CLERKENWELL, LONDON EC1
Headquarters of the Most Venerable Order of St. John

St John's Gate, Clerkenwell

ARCHENFIELD

O Land of Erging! Land of Archenfield
In dark oblivion is thy story sealed;
No chronicle records nor tongue can tell,
Where Roman conquered or Briton fell.

The Bold Marauder from Deheubarth shows
The Skenchill's slopes when manned by Erging's sons,
And flees the beacon fire on Orcop's crest,
The signal to the Marches and the West.

For soon from castle, cot and moated hall,
Responding to the balefires' warning call,
Footmen and bowmen, knight with spear and shield,
Flock to the gate of strength to safeguard Archenfield.

Reverend W D Barber, Rector of Tretire with Michaelchurch, 1914

THE KNIGHTS TEMPLAR AND HOSPITALLER

It has been known for a very long time that the Knights Templar built Garway church. The question is often asked, who were these people and why did they come to Garway? In 1187 King Henry II granted 2000 acres of land in the woodland of Archenfield at Llangarwy to the Knights Templar with the right to clear the woods. It is believed that the Templars built their Preceptory on the site where Church House now stands very close to their church which they built with a round nave and a detached tower, the plan being almost identical to the Templar church in London.

Land could not be cleared without Royal permission and the granting of a pardon to the Templars for such large clearances at Garway was exceptional. The land, when farmed would have provided income for the Order that helped to finance the Crusades.

The idea of the medieval knight developed out of the feudal system in Western Europe and several factors led to the presence of knights in the Holy Land. The concept of penance was very strong and a pilgrimage to the Holy Land as a penance was very popular. The idea behind the first crusade in 1095 was that the knights should devote their energies to repossessing the holy places. By 1099 Jerusalem and the Church of the Holy Sepulchre had been freed from Islam and were once more in Christian hands.

It was within this climate of knighthood and religion that the Templars and the Hospitallers were formed. Near the church of the Holy sepulchre in Jerusalem was a monastery of Benedictine monks with their church of St Mary ad Latinos. Attached to this monastery was a hospital that had been founded in the first half of the eleventh century by some merchants from Almalfi. The increase in the number of pilgrims travelling to Jerusalem at this time meant that the hospital became very busy and so it was reconstituted as a brotherhood separate from the Benedictine monastery. This new foundation was known as the Brothers of the Hospital of St John. Because the hospital was in the charge of a Hospitaller or Infirmarius who supervised the medical staff and distributed the alms, they became the Order of St John of Jerusalem and known as the Hospitallers. Other Hospitals were set up along the pilgrim routes and the brotherhood acquired more and more property. Gifts of property were given in Western Europe and the Holy Land. The Order became large, influential and wealthy and from 1136 when it was given a castle in the Holy Land it became a military order, the members taking monastic vows of poverty, chastity and obedience and giving over their worldly good to the common stock. The arms of the Order were a plain white cross on red and its habit black with the badge of a white 'Maltese' cross on the shoulder.

Not long after the capture of Jerusalem by the Crusaders in 1099 nine knights formed a holy brotherhood in arms and made a solemn compact to aid one another in clearing the Palestinian highways of infidels and robbers and protecting pilgrims on their journey to the Holy City in the Kingdom, of Jerusalem or "Outremer", the Land Beyond the Sea as it came to be known. Baudouin I, King of Jerusalem considered the protection given by these knights so worthy a cause that he placed an entire wing of the royal palace at the their disposal. According to tradition these quarters were built on the foundations of the ancient Temple of Solomon. And so it came about that the

Order was known as the Knights Templar. At a church council held at Troyes in 1128, the Templars were officially recognised and incorporated as a religious-military order. Hugh de Payen was given the title of Grand Master. The Templars were to combine austere discipline with martial zeal. They were sworn to poverty, chastity and obedience and were obliged to cut their hair but forbidden to cut their beards. They had to wear white habits or surcoats with a red cross of eight points worn on the left shoulder and these white garments came to have a symbolic significance. Their behaviour on the battlefield was strictly controlled and they were not to ask for mercy but must fight to the death.

One of the most significant privileges granted to both the Hospitallers and the Templars was their exemption from all allegiance to anyone but the Pope. They were totally independent of all Kings, Princes and Prelates, and from all interference from both political and religious authorities. This independence would have repercussions, even in an insignificant place such as Garway.

For the next two hundred years the Templars and the Hospitallers continued fighting crusades, acquiring much wealth and influence and many properties throughout the western world. The idea of supporting the fight against the infidel was very popular and men willingly gave money and lands and also gifts of tithes, tolls, houses and even slaves. The Templars also acted as international bankers and almost as 'tour operators' getting knights and pilgrims to and from the Holy Land.

In 1185, the year of the consecration of the Temple church in London, Geoffrey Grand Master of the Order in England had an inquisition taken of all the manors, farms, churches, villages, wind and water mills, land and all kinds of property belonging to the Templars in England. The total was considerable.

On great estates Priory houses had been erected. On smaller manors a Preceptory was built for a Knight Templar, some serving brothers and a priest. They would manage the farms of this manor producing rent and produce which would add to the Templar wealth and help finance the occupation of the Holy Land.

All Templar property had various powers and immunities that put them beyond the jurisdiction of the church and absolved them from any taxes. Every acre of their land had the right of sanctuary. No fugitive, debtor or criminal could be taken once he had set foot within the limits of the territory of the Knights. All these rights and privileges were held equally by both the Hospitallers and the Templars

As the years went on these two Orders became even more firmly entrenched in Papal favour and had their privileges still further strengthened. For example, neither Hospitallers nor Templars could be prevented by the Bishop from converting churches and tithes to their own use. This was the cause of much ill feeling between the brethren and the secular clergy. Henry II and his successor Richard I were lavish in their gifts and favours to the Orders. These included the privileges of being free of tolls and the requirement to do service in the army. They could not be tried except in the Courts of the Order even for crimes such as larceny, rape, arson and murder.

From their modest beginnings these two military orders became very powerful organizations. There was a permanent garrison in the Holy Land behind which lay long lines of supply, the estates back in England and throughout Europe being a source of revenue expended in the Holy War.

The downfall of the Templars was sudden and dramatic. Whilst increasing its wealth and influence in Europe, the Order had also become increasingly arrogant, brutal and corrupt. The situation in the Holy Land had become desperate and by 1291 nearly the whole of the Holy Land was under Muslim control. Only Acre remained, and in May 1291 this last fortress was lost. A heroic stand by the Templars was

JACQUES DE MOLAY, chef des Templiers.
(XIIIe SIÈCLE)

defeated and the Grand Master, although wounded, fought on till his death. The Templars established themselves in Cyprus, but the real reason for their existence, to keep the Holy Land free of Infidels had now ceased to exist.

The person considered most responsible for the destruction of the Templars was King Philippe IV of France. The professional military force of the Templars was much stronger than any that the King of France could muster. He owed them money and coveted their immense wealth. When it was time for the election of a new Pope, King Phillipe put forward his own candidate, the Bishop of Bordeaux whom he persuaded to issue orders for the suppression of the Templars. Secret orders were sent out which were to be opened everywhere simultaneously and implemented at once. At dawn on Friday 13th October 1307, all the Templars in France were to be seized and placed under arrest on the grounds of alleged heresy, sorcery, sodomy and corruption. Within 24 hours this order had been carried out. The Inquisition examined the Templars and many were tortured and made to confess to a range of crimes, most of which were quite untrue. Sixty-seven Templars were burned at the stake. Grand Master, Jacques de Molay was tortured by the Inquisition and eventually in 1314 he was burned to death in front of Notre Dame Paris. In England, Phillipe's son-in-law Edward II, at first rallied to the support of the Templars but under pressure from the Pope had them arrested and imprisoned in the Tower of London where they were tortured in an effort to make them deny their vows. Eventually, many were released and reconciled to the church.

At the trial of the Templars in London, Brother John de Stoke, who had visited Garway in 1294, gave a strange confession. He was giving evidence against Brother Jacques de Molay who was Grand Master of England from 1293-1295. They both visited Garway in 1294 and while there Brother John was summoned to the bed-chamber of the Grand Master. The Master said he wanted John to make proof of his obedience and commanded him to sit at the bottom of the bed on a small stool. The Master then sent into the church for a crucifix and two serving brothers stationed themselves on either side of the door with drawn swords. Being told that he must deny Him whom the image represents, he said 'Far be it for me to deny my Saviour', but the Grand Master ordered him to do so or he would be put into a sack and be carried to a place which he would find by no means agreeable. For fear of instant death, he then denied Christ with his tongue but not with his heart.

When the Order was suppressed in 1308 there were two knights seized at Garway by the sheriffs' officers. They were Phillip de Mews, Preceptor of Garway and William de Pokelington.

The Hospitallers escaped this suppression. They continued to be just as powerful and wealthy. In the mid-thirteenth century they were reported as having nineteen thousand manors throughout Europe. On the suppression of the Templars it was decreed that all their possessions should be handed over to the Hospitallers. This hand-over was not altogether straightforward. The King himself had treated the Templar estates, upon the dissolution of the Order, as if they were his own, despite the protest of the Pope. Many of the original donors of land and property given to the Templars thought that it should be returned to them. In 1333, Bishop Thomas de Charlton received a letter from the King asking for a return to the Treasurer and Barons of the Exchequer of the churches, pensions and portions which the Prior of the Hospital of St John of Jesusalem had to his own use in the diocese of Hereford, and what went to the Hospital itself, and of what used to belong to the Master and bretheren of the Military Order of the Temple in England. Also a return of the actual value of these churches pensions and portions.

Woolhope Transactions 1927

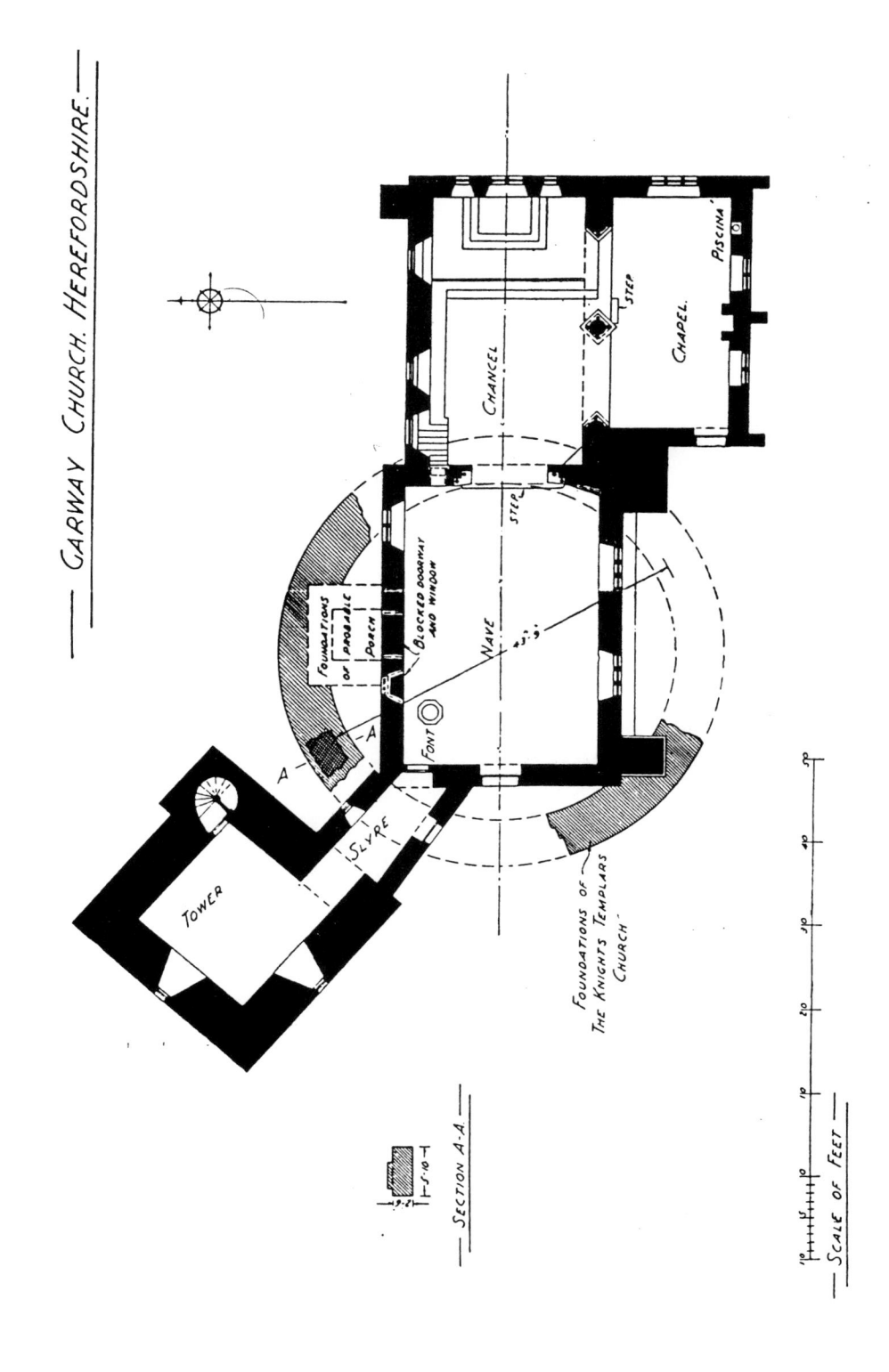

14th Century Chapel in the grounds of Dinmore Manor

Late 12th Century Chest in Garway Church

The Bishop made a return as follows:-

Ecclesia de Suttone Michaelis	*v marc.*
Ecclesia de Oxenhale	*viii marc*
Capella de Rolstone	*xx marc*
Ecclesia de Wombrugge	*v marc*
Capella de Clya sancta Margarete	*di marc*
Caella de Calewe	*x marc*
Pensio in ecclesia de Brampton	*xx marc*
Capella de Harewood	*nichil valet*
Ad Magistrum et Fratres Milicie Templi:	
Ecclesia de Cardynton	*xx marc*
Ecclesia de Garewy cum capella de Stantone	*x marc*

The Hospitallers were involved in many years of litigation and it was not until 1334 that an Act of Parliament legalised their claim. They were now wealthier than many of the sovereign states of Europe and their Grand Master one of Europe's most powerful men. All the estates belonging to the Templars in Garway were handed over to the Knights of the Hospital of St John of Jerusalem, known as the Hospitallers, at their Commandery at Dinmore six miles north of Hereford. A Jacobean Manor House stands on part of the domestic buildings of the Commandery with the ancient chapel of the Hospitallers very close. Dinmore ranked as third or fourth in importance among the fifty or so Commanderies in England and Wales. These estates were usually staffed by a small complement of knights with a chaplain and servants. They enjoyed certain privileges one being that the Commandery at Dinmore was entirely free of tithe. Dinmore is known as an ex-parochial or peculiar parish for, although it possess a parish church, (one of only four dedicated to St John of Jerusalem), it forms no part of a diocese neither do the bishop or the ecclesiastical authorities have any jurisdiction there; indeed until the mid-nineteenth century the parishioners were exempt from paying local rates. This transfer of property did not happen immediately and for a time, Garway remained in the Kings' hands. John de la Haye was appointed to be Custodian of the Manor of Garway for one year from the Feast of St Michael in the sixth year of the reign of King Edward II (29th September 1312). Included in the Manor of Garway was land at Harewood, St Wolston in Welsh Newton and Llanrothal. The Accounts left by John de la Haye give a glimpse of life in the village of Garway during that year.

In the five years after the Knights Templars were arrested there must have been some confusion in the village. It is unlikely that there was anyone living in the Preceptory until John de la Haye was sent there. The social structure of the village was probably unaffected by the change of ownership of the manor. There were several free tenants and customary tenants and for the manor as a whole their rents amounted to £30 4s 4d. Originally these tenants would have been obliged to perform certain services for the Lord of the Manor, but these had become converted to money payments.

The villein tenants were un-free tenants who had to share in the agricultural system of the Manor. They performed work for the Lord of the Manor in lieu of rent. The Villein's holding was at the will of the Lord and he could be deposed from it. His daughter could not marry without payment of a fine, and his heirs would pay a heriot when he died which was usually the best beast. The holding of the villein would be about 30 acres. The amount received in works by the villeins in Garway was 40 shillings and in Harewood 2 shillings which gives some indication of the relative sizes of the villages.

The next social group in the village is not mentioned in the Account because they would not be paying rent. They were bordars or cottars and were the labouring classes of the village. They were allowed to cultivate some land, up to about 5 acres, which would give them subsistence, and in return they worked for the Lord of the Manor either free or for a fixed sum.

There were various official jobs in the village. The Account mentions carter, drivers, shepherds, cook, woodward and the reeve. The reeve was one of the most important men in the village. He was responsible for organising the daily business of the Manor. To him fell the task of enforcing the rules for the organisation of the fieldwork, collecting the fines and chivvying the work-shy. He was often the spokesman of the village in negotiations with the Lord or his steward. The reeve was elected annually by his fellow villagers and possibly the post was held in rotation and there was no escaping from it except by the payment of a fine. The woodward was responsible for the woods and forests.

John de la Hayes' Account records that several houses in Garway were roofed in stone. The work was paid by piecework and cost 6s.7d. Other roofs thatched with straw were also repaired at a cost of 3s.1d. It is almost certain that the important houses in the village would have had a stone roof. Adjoining the manor house would be the grange or granary, stable, ox house and wain house all surrounding a yard containing ricks of hay and straw. There would be a garden or paddock and be used for grazing and growing fruit trees, apples and pears, and for growing vegetables such as leeks, cabbage and beans.

Another feature of the manors of the time was the dovecote that had been introduced into England by the Normans. They were the prerogative of the Lord of the Manor and tenants were usually forbidden to build their own in case the birds fed from the manor crops. Doves were an important source of winter meat and their droppings were used for manure. In 1312 the Account reported that the dovecote at Garway was yielding nothing as it was broken down. When the Hospitallers took possession of the manor in about 1324 a new dovecote was erected under the supervision of Brother Richard de Bire with the assistance of Gilbert the Mason. The record of this event in 1326 can still be seen on the tympanum over the dovecote door.

Columbarium, Garway.

This dovecote is the earliest example in Herefordshire and probably the finest in England. The walls are 3ft 10 inches thick and are lined from floor to arch with tiers of nesting holes, 666 in all. The openings of the holes are about 6 inches square, and they recede about 14 inches into the wall. If the cavity were the same throughout, the bird would not have room to sit on her nest; it therefore enlarges right or left about 10 inches in width. The holes are twenty inches apart in rows, each row being ten inches above the one below, and an alighting ledge of stone projects underneath each alternate tier of holes.

There were two fishponds very near the dovecote with the evidence still visible of a dam between them, one being higher than the other. These ponds are fed by a spring that rises at the South East corner of the churchyard.

One of the most important buildings in the village would have been the mill. In 1213 the Account values the issues from Garway mill at 65 shillings, those of Ryd-d-car mill in St Weonards 10 shillings and of Harewood mill nothing for it was broken down. Garway mill could not have been in very good order because a new mill-stone was bought costing 5 shillings and also iron and steel was bought costing 10 pence. The villagers were compelled to use the mill and forbidden to grind their own corn at home using a hand-operated quern. The tolls paid to the miller were part of the manorial revenue. Garway mill obviously produced more corn than was needed in the village as there is an account of corn, hay and beans sold, although no details are given about quantities. Other crops mentioned that were sold were fruits from the gardens of Garway for 5 shillings and 6 pence and fruits from the gardens of Harewood and St Wolstans for 3 shillings.

Oxen pulled the ploughs and one ox sold for 11 shillings because it was weak. The hide of one ox that died was sold for 2 shillings. Three new pairs of plough wheels were bought made from the lord's timber and cost 4 shillings and 6 pence. Two bags were bought for carrying seed into various fields where it was sown by broadcasting and they cost 18 pence. Two new fans were bought for winnowing costing 2 shillings and 6 pence. A cow, which was not as valuable as an ox, sold because it was weak, made 6 shillings and three calves sold for the same reason sold for 3 shillings and 6 pence. The hide of one calf that died was valued at 2 pence and the skins of 42 sheep sold before shearing made 10 shillings and 6 pence. There are no details of the wool sold, but at that time the weight of an average fleece was a little over a pound and the price of wool was about 4 shillings a stone (14 pounds).

A very interesting item in the Account is as follows

Ointment for the sheep. Milk for the lambs. Lights bought for watching the sheep and lambs when they were anointed. Expenses for shearing. Also linen cloth bought for wrapping cheeses when they were made 7 pence.

During the lambing season the ewes were separated from the rest of the flock and placed under the care of a hired shepherd. If milk were bought for the lambs it would seem likely that the ewe's milk was used for making cheeses, which were then wrapped in linen cloth. The sheep suffered from scab and possible death from a disease called murrain. They were anointed with ointment made from tar, or pitch and hog's grease and even verdigris and quicksilver were used. Two gallons of hog's grease cost 1 shilling and 10 pence.

Keeping livestock through the winter was a problem. Many of the animals were killed and salted down to provide food. Fine salt was bought for the dairy costing 6 pence and salt was bought for 'the households in all the places 7 shillings and 6 pence'. As salt cost 6 pence a bushel then 15 bushels would have been bought for the village. It is interesting to speculate who would wear the pair of gilt spurs that were bought and if the white leather bought for making and repairing various harnesses were for his horse.

A section of the Account deals with the church. The amount received in oblations and obventions (donations for pious uses), of the altar of Garway church was 49 shillings and 6 pence. Of Harewood chapel only 6 pence, but the tithes from Welsh Newton church amount to 106 shillings and 8 pence. The expenses of Garway church were-

Wine for mass and against Easter 13 pence
Four pounds of wax for candles for Christmas and Easter 3 shillings
Oil for lamps in the church 6 pence
Incense for the church 2 pence
Blessed bread for Easter 2 bushels
Stipend of one clerk serving the church for one year 5 shillings
Stipend of one carter to carry the tithes of the church in the autumn 3 shillings
A boy helping him 20 pence
Stipend of one chaplain serving Harewood chapel for the year 6 shillings and 8 pence
In livery of one clerk serving Garway church 4 quarters 2 bushels of wheat.
The roof of the chancel was repaired with tiles by piecework costing 9 pence.

By 1338 Garway had become an extensive manor belonging to the Knights Hospitallers of Dinmore. There were in demesne, 720 acres of arable land with 60 acres of meadow, the works and customs of the villeins were assessed at 60 shillings yearly. Although attached to Dinmore, Garway continued as a separate unit of administration, functioning as a local hospice and preceptory.

In 1388 Garway was in charge of Brother William Dallnaly who was in receipt of the usual robe and mantle of the Order of St John. He was the chaplain. The officials included the chamberlain, the bailiff and the seneschal (steward). The numerous servants included a cook, a baker, the porter and personal servants of the keeper and two attendant pages. The reeve of the manor was responsible for the allocation of labouring services of the villeins. All the servants were in receipt of wages ranging from 3 shillings to 13 shillings and 4 pence a year. Three other men living at the preceptory in 1388 were holders of corrodies. These men, in return for substantial donations, were lodged and maintained by the preceptory and received from its funds an annual pension. This was a method of insurance against old age that was common in the middle-ages. Gilbert de Pembridge could dine at the table of the brothers and receive a pension of 20 shillings. Hugh Despencer and Stephen le Port could dine at the table of the free servants and receive a pension of 10 shillings each.

The travellers who frequented the borders of Wales made heavy demands on the Preceptory of Garway as can be seen from the annual consumption of food

60 quarters of wheat   £9
20 quarters of corn malt)
80 quarters of oat malt   )   £11
Meat and fish for the kitchen at 4 shillings a week.

Garway was responsible for the upkeep of its own buildings and supplied the wine, wax and holy oil used in the services in the church.

Like the Templars, the Hospitallers were free from all the feudal and pecuniary obligations imposed by the State. In such veneration were they held and so great were their privileges, that every acre of their land and possessions had the right of sanctuary. No fugitive, debtor or criminal could be taken once he had set foot within the limits of the territory of the Knights. Stone crosses marked these boundaries.

In the year 1485, William Bongam of Garway, labourer, was imprisoned for burglary at the house of Isabel Cutta of Penbleyth from whom he stole a brass pot and other household goods to the value of £3, a horse value 6 shillings and eight pence, and six shillings in money. He pleaded guilty but stated that he had taken refuge in a house in Wormelowebrugge, a possession of the Knights Hosptiallers, from which he was forcibly removed by Roger Bodenham, Sheriff of the County, and he demanded to be restored to the same house.

John Stokes, on behalf of the Hospital of St John, said, "that the house in question was a parcel of the preceptory of Dinmore and that from time immemorial the Hospitallers have always had and still possess this privilege and liberty, to wit, that any man or woman coming to any house belonging to them to take refuge after felony committed, and demanding this privilege, shall have safety and protection for their life without disturbance from any officer of the King of England or of any other person." The jury found that the house belonged to the Hospital and the Hospitallers had the privilege of this claim.

Those who safely claimed sanctuary had the option of standing trial or leaving the realm. In the latter choice they were afforded safe conduct to the nearest port, with heavy penalties against anyone who dare interfere. There were however, a few sanctuaries of a special character where those interred might remain indefinitely. The law of sanctuary was inviolate, regardless of the gravity of the crime.

(ii) PRECEPTORY OF GARWAY (ORDER OF THE TEMPLARS).

PROPERTY.	DESCRIPTION.	DONOR.	DATE.	REFERENCE.
Garway.	Assart of 2,000 acres of land at Garway. All land of Llangarewi and Castlery which belonged to Herman. Church of Garway (with Chapel of Stanton)	Henry II. Richard I.	c. 1173-1189. Confirmed 1189.	Cartae Antiquae Chanc. Misc. Bundle 12/4 (Lees 142). Cartae Antiquae Chanc. Misc. Bundle 12/5 (Lees 141). Episcopal Return of 1333. Episcopal Return of 1347.
Harewood.	Manor. Chapel (? Church).	Godescallus.	1199-1216.	Book of Fees, 1251-1252, p. 1273. Plac. q.w. 271. Larking, 196. Episcopal Return of 1333. Episcopal Return of 1536.
Pembroke.	Mill on arm of sea at the bridge of the Castle.	Richard I.	1189.	Cartae Antiq. Chanc. Misc. 12/5. Monasticon, VI, ii, 838.
Lundy Island.		Richard I.	1189.	Cartae Antiq. C. Misc. 12/5.
Hereford.	One house.	Donor unknown to Jurors of 1212.	Before 1212.	Book of Fees, 1198-1212, pt. 1, p. 101.
St. Wulstan.	Manor.		Before 1308.	Larking, 197.
Pencarn. Cogan.	Manor.		Before 1308.	Ancient Correspondence, XLIX, No. 143. Larking, 213.

The Grand Prior Thomas Docwwra, 1501–1527

THE BISHOPS VISITATIONS

Ever since the sixth century, the Bishop had made inspections of the temporal and spiritual affairs of the parishes in his diocese. These ecclesiastical visitations by the Bishop occurred every three or four years and the archdeacon visited annually. Groups of laymen from each parish were summoned to answer questions concerning the conduct of the clergy and the morals of the laity. They would also have to answer questions about the condition of their church and the vestments, books and equipment.

By special decree the Templars and Hospitallers enjoyed the privilege of being exempt from visitations by the Bishop of Hereford though their tenants were not exempt from parochial dues. In March 1290 Richard de Swinfield, Bishop of Hereford, on his journey round the diocese visited Garway. Although the Templars permitted no Episcopal interference with their establishments and maintained one of their own brethren as resident priest, the Bishop seems to have been received favourably. Bishop Swinfield lived to see the suppression of the Templars in 1308. When the Hospitallers took possession, Garway was let to tenants subject to their maintaining a chaplain. The smaller churches were summoned to Garway church to attend the Bishop's visitation.

The church of Garway is not recorded in the Taxation of 1291, possibly because it was exempt from ecclesiastical and secular contributions. It doubtless served as the church of the parish for it is recorded in the 'survey' of 1338 that there was a private chapel in the preceptory at which the chaplain in residence officiated. By the time of the Reformation the parish church of Garway had been reduced to the status of a chapel, served by Hugh Rees as curate and the revenue was much reduced.

In 1397 the following visitation returns were made for these parishes in the Monnow Valley.

Garway
The parishioners say that Meuric Pengryche and Rys Duy have laid violent hands upon Sir William Watkyn and Thomas Pengryche, father of Mauric, aided and abetted them. Sir Thomas Folyot visits taverns over-much and excessively to the great scandal of the clergy, and had revealed the confession of Robert Scheppert his parishioner in public. John Smyth is committing adultery with Alice Willcok, his concubine, and ill-treats his wife. Richard the chaplain there celebrates mass twice a day, viz at Garway and Wormbridge, and gets two salaries. The priest is incapable of maintaining the care of souls there, as he cannot speak Welsh and most of parishioners have no English. Llewellyn ap Jevan ap Madoc and Gwladus Bach swore a bond for their marriage, but have not married. Jankyn, servant to Peter Smyth is committing fornication with Joan Shepphert, Hugh Wells is ill-treating his wife, often threatening to kill her and treating her cruelly.

Kentchurch
The parishioners there say that Howel ap John is fornicating with Gladys, whom he keeps. Also the Cadwgan Webbe is fornicating with Janet whom he keeps. Also that Jevan Webbe is fornicating with Eva Elvael. Also that Roger ap Watkyn is fornicating with Gwellian, whom he keeps.

Llanrothal

The parishioners there say the chapel is unroofed in default of the Rector and Vicar. Also that the chancel windows are broken, in default of the same. Also that the Rector is obliged to find one portable breviary for taking divine service, he does not. Also the Rector rents out the tithes without seeking or obtaining permission. Also they say that the Prior of Monmouth has violated the sequestration imposed on the same tithes of the church by the Rev Father Bishop of Hereford. Also that Perwar, wife of Thomas Jerwerth is committing adultery with Nicholas Game. Also that Sir David, Vicar, administered the sacred sacraments on Easter Day to Meuric Pengryche and Rys Duy excommunicants because they assaulted violently Sir William Watkyn, chaplain, as Sir David himself knows this.

St Weonards

The chaplain Sir John frequents the pub and in there gossips shamefully, causing great scandal, etc. Also the same Sir John is incontinent with a certain Margaret whose surname they do not know. Also, according as the common talk has it, the same Sir John is unfitted and ignorant of the care of souls.

The custom of the Bishop of Hereford's triennial visitation of the parish church of Garway where he received 53 shillings and 4 pence in respect of the customary dues continued until about 1500 when there started a long dispute between the Bishop and the Prior of St John of Jerusalem. On 15th March 1505, Richard Mynors and Richard Plomer, bailiffs of the Prior of St John of Jerusalem at Garway, refused to pay the usual tax to the Bishop on his visitation of Garway church, claiming that as an estate of the Manor of Dinmore they were exempt. The bailiffs were cited to appear in the Archbishop's court in Canterbury. As extra evidence an Inquisition was taken, which can still be read, written in English, in the Rental of the Knights Hospitallers in Dinmore and Garway. This is kept in the Hereford County Record Office.

An Inquisition taken at Garway in the yere of our Lord God 1504 as touching the Jurisdiction within the Lordship of Garway being in varience between the Bishop of the diocese of Hereford upon the one part and the Lord of Saint John and his bretheren upon the other part. And whereas the said Bishop pretends his title and right to have correction of all special causes and matters, the tenants and inhabitants there do say as hereafter followeth.

Jankin ap Howell about the age of 66 years, John ap Richard Thomas about the age of 100 years, William Hughs about the age of 90 years, John ap Philpot Jolif about the age of 70 years, Hugh ap Rice about the age of 60 years, John ap Philpot Kyte about the age of 96 years, Phillip ap Thomas David about the age of 50 years, Morgan ap Rice about the age of 85 years, William ap Phillip about the age of 50 years, Thomas David Lloyd about the age of 50 years, Morgan ap Richard about the age of 85 years, William Here of Cwmaddoc about the age of 66 years, David Here about the age of 53 years, Philip Foude about the age of 90 years, Jenkin ap Jevan Colly about the age of 90 years, Thomas ap Jevan about the age of 75 years, William John ap Jenkin about the age of 60 years, Phillip Griffiths about the age of 60 years, Howell Jolif about the age of 56 years, William Marshall about the age of 60 years, Thomas Tyler about the age of 76 years.

And many others born and bred in that Lordship of Garway do say and be ready to depose upon the book if they be required that their fathers and elders did know Mr Beth, Mr Pitt and Mr Rode Commanders of Dinmore and Garway which had three commissioners under them within the Commandery of Dinmore to minister and execute the correction with the Lordship of Garway yearly as their elders and fathers did say and show them. And in their days, that now be tenants, they know Sir William Dawney Knight and Commander that he had to his commissionary one Mr David Stephens which did sit within the Lordship of Garway upon correction of sin done within the said Lordship. And the said tenants do say that to their knowing they never knew none of the Bishop's Officers that sat within the Lordship of Garway during the time of the said Sir William Dawney Knight and Commander there to admonish nor to correct any sin done within the Lordship of Garway. For in that time Thomas ap Tomlin was Summoner of the Lordship and when that any sin was committed he would shortly summon the parties for his advantage.

The Bill of the Bishop of Hereford against the bailiffs of Garway contained 16 propositions or arguments addressed to the Court of Canterbury.

In March 1507 Bishop Mayhew visited Garway and demanded the same dues that had been paid to his predecessor. The bailiffs, by command they said, of the Prior of the Order himself, refused to pay. They were once again summoned before the Archbishops' Court. Evidence was given that Bishop Audley had on three triennial visitations received from Garway four marks though it was said that they had been refused to his predecessor Bishop Myllyng. One of the bailiffs confessed that he had paid the Bishop but only so as not to incur his displeasure. The suit dragged on for three years at great expense. A complaint was made to the Pope by the prelates of the province of Canterbury against the Knight of St John urging him to control their privileges as being injurious to the rest of the Church.

Bishop Mayhew seems to have met with no further opposition at Garway but his successor was again refused payment of dues. This time the Prior of the Order of St John offered to pay six shillings and eight pence yearly 'or else I stand by my defence, which is to pay nothing at all'. Bishop Bothe declined to accept this offer, and at his next visitation in 1523 instead of being received with ringing of bells he found the doors of Garway church bolted and barred against him. He therefore placed the parish under an interdict and excommunicated all those who by their ill-will had prevented his visitation. This meant that everyone in the parish was excluded from all matters spiritual and that people from other parishes would be discouraged from having any social contact with them. However, within 15 years this conflict would have little relevance when the Reformation brought an end to the power of the Knights Hositallers.

PEOPLE AND PLACES

The lack of suitable documentary evidence makes it difficult to assess with any a degree of accuracy the size of medieval populations. Census returns were unknown but some tax returns survive which give details of numbers of people in a village and their names.

The effect of the Black Death in the area can only be guessed at. By March 1349 the Black Death had taken a firm grip on the whole lordship of Abergavenny and the adjoining lordships of White Castle, Grosmont and Skenfrith and the plague was travelling northwards through the border counties of Herefordshire, Shropshire and Cheshire. It is estimated that a quarter, a third or even in some places up to a half of the population died. The disease broke out again periodically throughout the second half of the 14th century.

The immediate effect was agricultural neglect, harvests un-gathered and animals straying over pasture and fallow. The gradual changes that had been taking place in the organisation of the manor were hastened by the death of so many of the population. Customary workings were being commuted into wages and more labour was being hired. In the reign of Edward I (1272-1307), a Statute had been introduced limiting the wages of labourers and artificers and from time to time workers were fined in the courts for breaking this law. This extract is from the Hereford Assize Roll, 1355 –6 and shows that 22 men and women in Garway were fined for overpayment of wages.

Pleas before the Juries at 'Lanwaren' (Tueday before the feast of St Gregary, 30 Edward III.
The sheriff was ordered to summon 20 proud and lawful men of the vills of 'Garewy, Wylton' and 'Lanwaren'

The jurors present that;
Walter Crokker (fine 6d), Nicholas Lewley (6d),
Robert Baronn (6d), John Brugge (6d), Hugh Shepherd (6d)
Nicholas Coyseil (6d), David Midrych (6d), Cradok Key (12d),
Hugh le Hunte (6d), John Kemp (6d), Richard Wat (6d),
Jenn Bagg (12d), Crystina Dewe (6d), Jenn le Smyth,
Geoffrey Braas, Himych Bryan (6d), William Endyn,
John Grundy (6d) Nichloas Cogh (6d), Thomas son of John (6d)
Howelus Wytkyn and David Vaus (12d),
Threshers, mowers and reapers, servants and workmen of the vil of 'Garewy' took more for their service and work than they were accustomed.

The Poll Tax of 1377 for Garewy with hamlets was valued at £5 4s. 4d and the collector of the tax was Maurice ap Henry. The tax was levied on every man and woman over the age of fourteen, medicants (beggars) were exempt. This means there was a taxable population of 313. It is interesting to note that this is the largest amount of tax paid in the Wormelow hundred, Ross being valued at £4. 6s 8d.

In 1524, a tax system was introduced based on the value of each man's estate. All persons having salaried, land, moveable goods, (i.e. Coin, plate, stock, merchandise, grain, household stuff or money owing), over the value of £1 were liable to the tax, paying on whichever brought in the greatest income to the exchequer. The rate was 1/40th or 6d in the pound for goods. The tax on wages was 4d in the pound and on land 1 shilling in the pound.

The Lay subsidy 15th 16th Henry VIII (1523-4) for Lytyll Garreway, (Little Garway, now a farm at White Rocks).

John Waythen	In goods	£6	3s Tax
Ap Powell		£10	5s
Ap Haly		£4	2s
William Phelip		60s	18d
Henry Prosser		60s	18d
William Seysilt		60s	18d
Ric ap Loell		40s	12d
John ap Rosser		40s	12d
Edward ap Rosser	Profit for wages	20s	4d

The Rental of the lands of the Knights Hospitallers in Dinmore and Garway, which is held at the Hereford County Record Office, gives details of all the land in Herefordshire owned by the Knights of St John. The two main Preceptories were at Dinmore and Garway. The Rental, dated 1504, is written on parchment and mostly in Latin. It is the earliest known comprehensive survey of the Manor of Garway. It lists each property with its land and gives the name of the tenant and the previous tenant.

Item Hugh ap Rees holds 1 messuage with 2 parcels of customary land late in the tenure of John Tornour by rent of 12s per annum, suit of court and heriot.

There are 52 items like this for Garway, 4 for Corras (now in the parish of Kentchurch) and includes Pembridge Castle, St Woolson in Welsh Newton, land in Penros and Whitchurch, all belonging to the Manor of Garway at that time. There are 22 messuages mentioned, that is a house with its outbuildings and yards. Some fields are given names such as Cowarneland, Craghesland, Newbolts, Tuffesland, Frogland, and Le Longmeadow. The only identifiable farms mentioned are Trollway, Commadoc, le Oldfield, Little Garway, Corras, Penros alias Trepenkennok, all of which are still farms today. The capital messuage was held by Richard Maynours Esq, (Richard Mynors of Treago in St Weonards).

Item Richard Meynours esq holds the capital messuage of the manor there with all demesne lands, meadows, feeding grounds and pastures adjacent to the said capital messuage or manor, together with a water mill and the profits of the mill as Jenkyn ap Howell later farmer there had and occupied it for rent of £8 6s 8d per annum as after by an indenture made concerning the agreements

The value of the properties varied from £8 6s 8d down to 4 pence halfpenny for one close of land. The sum of the rents for the Manor of Garway was £40 per annum. Just before the Renal was written in 1504, a grant was made to John ap Phillpott of Garway by Brother John Kendall of the Hospitallers of St John of Jerusalem of land in Garway called Tenorfield. John Kendall was Prior of England from 1489 –1501 so the document, which is undated must have been written sometime between these dates.

To all faithfully Christians to whom this present writing shall come Brother John Kendall Prior of the Hospital of St John of Jerusalem in England and his Brothers send Greeting. Know ye that we the said Prior and Bretheren with the assent consent and approbation of our Abbott have given and granted and by this our present Deed to confirm unto John ap Philpott of Garway and to his Heirs and Assigns one field within the said Manor and Liberty of Garway called Tenors Field between Meers and Bounds there being contained in the whole (blank) acres of land between a field of St Magdalen and the Oldfield near Honscross and a meadow within the said Manor of Garway called Long Meadow. To have and to hold the said Field and Meadow with its appurtances unto the said John Philpott his Heirs and Assigns forever rendering therefore yearly to us the said Prior and our succesors or the (blank) of Dynmore for the time being 20 shillings at the Feast of the Nativity of St John the Baptist and the Purification of the Virgin Mary in equal proportions and paying and bearing all other ordinary and extra burdens and charges due in respect of the said Field and Meadow likewise yielding and paying to the said Prior and our Successors on the (blank) of Dynmore for the time being.

From this one field developed the large farm that is still called Tennersfield.

By the 16th century the strong Welsh influence on the names of the inhabitants of this part of South Herefordshire was beginning to wane. The use of 'ap'- meaning 'son of', was disappearing. If the surname began with R or H then the P of ap would stick as in Probert, Pritchard and Prosser. Ap Rice became Price, ap Hugh became Pugh and ap Harry became Parry. If the name began with a vowel the 'p' changed to 'b' and so ap Evan changed to Bevan and ap Owen to Bowen. Very often the ap was dropped altogether and a genitive 's' added instead, as in 'Williams'.

The Reformation was a violent act of state that led to Henry VIII disowning all Papal authority in England and to a series of Acts of Parliament which, in 1534 cut off all financial, judicial and administrative links with Rome. This was followed by legislation that would, in Thomas Cromwell's words, make Henry 'the richest Prince in Christendom'. The following Act of Supremacy gave Henry and his successors the title of, 'the only supreme head on earth of the Church in England'. In 1538 began the Dissolution of the Monasteries when the religious shrines were dismantled, the relics destroyed and their treasures confiscated.

In 1535 an official inventory was taken, the Valor Ecclesiasticus, of all monastic and ecclesiastical properties. In 1536 all religious houses with less than twelve monks or nuns that had an annual value of less than £200 were stripped of their possessions. In 1538 the houses of the friars were dissolved and in 1539 the larger monasteries. In 1540 an Act was given royal assent for the dissolution of the Order of St John. The Prior of each Preceptory was required to draw up an inventory of the property, including money, plate and landed estates and the members of the Order were forbidden to use the titles and dress of the Order.

All monastic buildings were to be destroyed and all lead and other materials were to be removed. All gold, silver plate, vestments and money were seized. The instrument for carrying out this work of destruction was the Court of Augmentation created in 1535. It administered all the lands, possessions and revenues of the dissolved houses and succeeded in augmenting the royal income by £32,000 a year.

To all faithful Christians to whom this present writing shall come Brother John Kendall Prior of the Hospital of St. John of Jerusalem in England & his Bretheren send Greeting. Know ye that we the s[ai]d Prior & Bretheren with the assent consent & approb[ation] of our Abbott have given & granted & by their present Deed have Do Confirm unto John ap Philpott of Garway & to his Heirs & Ass[igns] One Field within the said Manor & Liberty of Garway called Senores field between certain Meers & Bounds there being cont[aining] in the whole Acres of Land betw[een] a field of St Magdalen & the old field near Honeonake & a field Meadow within the s[ai]d Manor of Garway called Long Meadow To have & to hold the s[ai]d Field & Meadow with its app[ur]t[enances] unto the s[ai]d John ap Philpott his Heirs & Ass[igns] forever Rendering therefore yearly to us the s[ai]d Prior & our Successors or the   of Dynmore for the time being 20[s] at the Feast of the Nativity of St. John the Baptist & the Purific[atio]n of the Virgin Mary in equal p[ro]port[io]n & paying & bearing all other ordinary & extra[ordinary] Burthens & Charges due in respect of the s[ai]d Field & Meadow likewise yield[ing] & paying to us the s[ai]d Prior & our Success[o]rs or the   of Dynmore for the time being

Letter from John Kendall, Prior of England

John Scudamore of Kentchuch Court was one of the Particular Receivers of the Court of Augmentation for the County of Hereford. He was concerned with the Monastery of Dore, Monmouth Priory and of Clifford, a Cluniac Priory. The Account for the year of 1536 lists all the goods, grain, cattle, money and jewels, debts, lead, and bells appertaining to the late religious houses at the time of their suppression. At Monmouth Priory the value of the rents and farms amounted to £49 16s 2d; moveable goods and silver-plate to £16 6s 11d; debts due to the house £30 15s 2d; lead and bells £11 6s.

At the Monastery of Dore the rents and farms were valued at £100 7s, moveable goods and silver plate, £71 9s 8d, debts £5 15s 8d. The superfluous buildings were sold by the commissioners to John Scudamore included 'the old house by the wayside next to the bridge', and for £2 the roof, slates and timber of the refectory. For the sum of 64s, Scudamore together with Thomas Baskerville and Miles ap Harry purchased the old infirmary and all the glass and iron of the dorter, the frater and the chapter house. The lead and bells at Dore were valued at £24 1s 8d. The lead remaining on the steeples of Monmouth and Dore Priories was valued at 30s and the bells remaining, £32 2s.

The King's Commissioners were paid expenses. John Scudamore claimed 60 shillings expenses for riding from his house in the County of Hereford, including the carriage of gold plate from Monmouth, Dore, Clifford and Aconbury to London and delivering it to the Treasurer of the Court of Augmentation. These valuable goods delivered to London included gold plate from Clifford, 3oz parcel gilt, 5 oz white plate worth a total of £36 10s 4d. Also 'a certain ornament of the church delivered to the aforesaid Treasurer from the Priory of Monmouth, together with a velvet cope of crimson colour and a pallium of the colour of Baudekn crimson, valued at 100 shillings.

Before the Dissolution, William Weston, the Grand Prior of England had leased the estate of Dinmore including the Manor of Garway, to a widow called Margaret Rotsey and her son Edward at an annual rent of £96 10shillings, a lease that seems to have continued after the dissolution.

There are no more details until 1585 when an enquiry into the estate describes Garway as consisting of a manor house, with outbuildings, dovecote, orchard, demesne, meads and pastures and one water-mill called Garway mill, the whole being let to Richard Mynours who had sublet the manor to Jankyn ap Howell as farmer at a rent of 6s 8d yearly. There were 27 tenants, mostly customary tenants, living on the manor paying rents ranging from 1d to 12s 6d a year. A house called Landmore in Garway, with demesnes attached, formerly let to Thomas ap Ieuan, was now the occupation of John ap Ieuan at a rent of 10s yearly. The total proceeds from the Garway manor, including the rents of free and customary tenants amounted to only £19 13s 1d.

Plates 1 and 2. Llanveynoe Church and Ancient Cross in the Churchyard

Plate 3. The Olchon Valley with a blanket of cloud on Hatterrall Ridge

Plate 4. Llangua Church

Plate 5. Kentchurch Court

Plate 6. Kentchurch Court, Glyndwr's Tower

Plate 7. The ploughed field shows the site of the Roman fort on the slopes of Garway Hill looking from Wales across the Monnow into England

Plate 8. Llanvihangel Court, home of John Arnold

Plate 9. Garway Church with wild daffodils in the churchyard

Plate 10. The interior of Garway Church looking towards the Norman Arch

Plate 11. Garway Church, Agnus Dei or Paschal Lamb over the door of the chapel

*Plate 12.
The Dovecote, Church Farm
Garway*

Plate 13. Pembridge Castle, Welsh Newton

Plate 14. Pembridge Castle, the gatehouse

Plate 15. Pembridge Castle, the chapel

Plate 16. Llanrothal Church *(Christopher Dalton)*

Plate 17 and 18. The Bell, Skenfrith in 1902 and 2002

Plate 19. Blackbrook Manor, Skenfrith

Plate 20. The village of Skenfrith (*John Gapp*)

Plate 21.
The grave of Saint John Kemble in Welsh Newton churchyard

Plate 22.
The grave of Saint David Lewis in Usk churchyard

Plate 23. The remains of Coed Anghred churchyard

Plate 24. The ruined steps into the churchyard at Coed Anghred

Plate 25 and 26. Dan-y-Graig chapel, Grosmont

Plate 27. The Perthir Gate, Clytha Park

Plate 28. Rockfield Church

Plate 29. Monnow Bridge, Monmouth

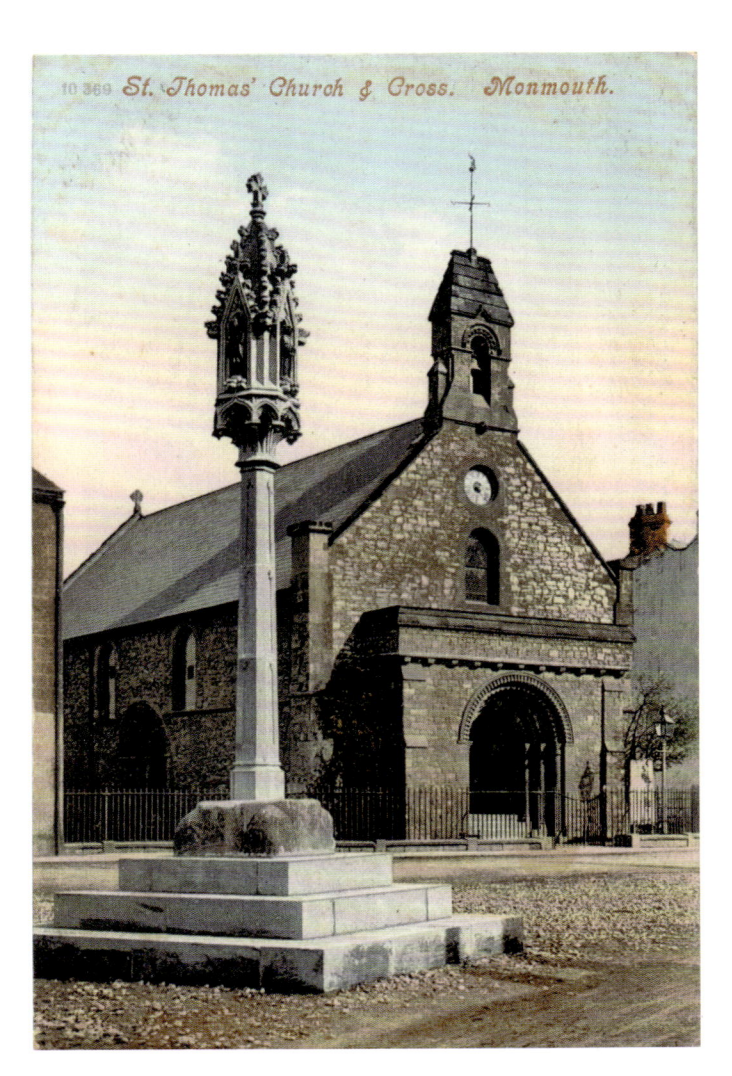

Plate 30. St Thomas' Church and Cross, Overmonnow

Plate 31. Grosmont Castle

Plate 32. Cupid's Hill Inn, Grosmont

Part Three

The Catholic Martyrs

Father David Lewis, one-time Rector of the Cwm

CAVALIER SONG

Come draw us some wine
Or we'll pull down the sign,
For we are all jovial compounders.
We'll make the house ring
With healths to our King
And confusion light on his confounders.

Since former committee
Afforded no pity
Our sorrows in wine we will steep 'em.
They force us to take
Two oaths but we'll make
A third that we ne'er meant to keep 'em

RECUSANCY

Recusancy was the term used to describe the failure or refusal to attend church in accordance with the Act of Uniformity. This was a term used mainly about Roman Catholics. The upheaval in the religious life of this country lasted for several centuries and had great relevance to the people living in the Monnow Valley. The geographical situation of the Monnow Valley with the river Monnow not only being the border between England and Wales but also the boundary between the Diocese of Hereford and that of Llandaff, together with its remoteness and difficult terrain, fostered a spirit of independence and conservatism amongst the inhabitants. The traditions of the old Marcher Lordships with their feudalism still lingered on and made it easy to ignore the Statutes that distant London tried to impose upon them. The very hilly and thickly wooded countryside made it easy to hide or find refuge.

The political reformation under Henry VIII when he broke irrevocably away from the jurisdiction of Rome changed the church in England and Wales forever. This change continued during his son Edward's short reign. Henry's daughter, Mary Tudor returned to the Catholic Church of Rome and for the five years of her reign there were extreme penalties against both Protestants and Puritans.

When Elizabeth I came to the throne in 1558 you can imagine how confused most of the population would have been. Would Elizabeth carry on as her sister Mary had done or would she return to the religion of her father Henry VIII? Opinion was divided on this subject. On one side there were those who supported Mary and these included all the bishops who had been appointed by her. The remainder of the bishops had either been burned at the stake or had fled overseas. The majority of the people in the country wanted a Catholic church of England without the servility to Rome and a church which was reformed from the abuses which had gathered round it during the Middle Ages. During the first years of her reign, Elizabeth re-established the Church of England and the Acts of Uniformity and Supremacy were passed. These Acts established Elizabeth as head of the Church and required a uniform service for all churches and there were stiff penalties for anyone who refused to conform to this one establishment. The Queen's subjects were bound to attend church every Sunday unless they had a lawful excuse to absent themselves. A fine of 12 pence was to be levied by the churchwardens on each occasion of absence and the money would be used for the benefit of the poor of the parish.

At first, Elizabeth was quite tolerant of those who refused to accept the new regime. It was sufficient if Papists, as the recusants were called, stood in the porch of the Protestant church during the sermon and many Roman Catholics conformed to this extent. This was accepted as a denial of their religion. The stauncher Catholics called this practice schismatic. However, the determination of the Pope to humiliate Elizabeth caused the atmosphere between the government and the recusants to deteriorate.

In 1570 there was a formal trial of Queen Elizabeth in Rome, witnesses being found from among the recusants who had fled from England. Elizabeth was found guilty and excommunicated and deposed, and all her subjects were dispensed from their oath of allegiance to her. The verdict was smuggled to England and nailed to the door of the Bishop of London's Palace by a man called John Felton. This was a disaster for the recusants. With the passage to time, Elizabeth's anti-catholic legislation became increasingly severe. The threat to the security of the throne and the physical safety of the Queen was blamed on the Jesuit Mission, Spanish interference and the intrigues of Mary Queen of Scots. Roman Catholic men were leaving England for the continent where they were training at Catholic and Jesuit Colleges as priests and missionaries and returning secretly to England and Wales to preach and convert.

In 1571 an Act was passed against bringing in and putting in execution Bulls and other instructions from the See of Rome, or importing any crosses, religious emblems such as pictures, beads or suchlike superstitious items. Anyone singing Mass was to be fined £133 and imprisoned for a year. Ten pounds a month was to be paid by anyone keeping a recusant schoolmaster. In 1581 another Act was passed which imposed a penalty of £20 a month for anyone over the age of 16 who refused to attend church.

In 1585 there was an Act against Jesuits and Priests. Anyone who helped them was condemned to death. A further Act against recusants was passed in 1587 stating that anyone in default of paying the £20 a month fine would result in the seizing of two thirds of their land and property. This Act set the pattern for the next hundred years. In 1593 another Act forbade recusants to stray more than 5 miles from their homes without a licence. The fines from recusants had become an important contribution to the national exchequer.

On the death of Elizabeth and the accession of James I in 1603, hopes were high that the Catholics would be treated with more toleration, as James had expressed no desire to persecute them and he genuinely hoped that reconciliation with Rome might be possible. This greatly encouraged the recusants and priests poured into the country hoping for a mass movement toward Rome. However, by the beginning of 1604 James publicly announced "his utter detestation" of the Papist religion that he condemned as superstitious. Three days later a proclamation ordered all the Jesuits and priests to leave the country with fines for recusancy once again being imposed. So all hopes of tolerance were dashed when the King protested most vehemently "that he would take it as an extreme insult if anyone imagined that either then or at any time in the past he had entertained the slightest intention of tolerating their religion". By 1605 it was reported to Rome that the Catholics in England had reached a state of desperation and were very resentful of the commands by the Jesuits to hold back from violence. The new Pope, Paul V who had been elected on 29th May, was asked to issue a brief against the used of armed force probably as a result of the troubles amongst the recusants on the Welsh borders who were notorious for their turbulence. The Gunpowder Plot of 1605 finally shattered any lingering hopes of tolerance.

Following this unfortunate event, the severity of the legislation increased. All recusants were to receive the sacrament of the Lord's Supper. The financial penalties for failing to do so were £20 a month for the first year, £40 for the second year and £60 a month each subsequent year. The Crown could refuse the £20 monthly fine and instead seize two thirds of the land of a rich recusant. After the Gunpowder Plot, James I imposed an Oath of Allegiance which denied that the Pope had any power to depose the King. Some English Catholics took the Oath on the grounds that the Act was political rather than religious. By the Acts of 1610 and 1611 recusants who refused to take the Oath of Allegiance were to be imprisoned, while recusant wives were forced to pay £10 a month, forfeit one third of their husbands lands or go to prison. It was forbidden to send children to be educated overseas or to support foreign colleges.

After the Civil War, during the Commonwealth period some toleration was given to Catholics. The Cavalier Parliament, however, in 1661 pressed for laws against dissenters and passed four Acts known as the Clarenden Code. All magistrates were to take the Oath of Allegiance (1661), the Church of England was to be the only form of worship tolerated (1662), all dissenting ministers were forbidden to come within five miles of any corporate town neither were they allowed to teach (1665), and not more that five persons, unless of the same household or the established church, were allowed to assemble for worship in houses (1670). The Test Acts stipulated that anyone holding a position of trust under the Crown must take the Oath of Allegiance and receive the sacrament of the Church of England. Anyone who refused was ineligible for other offices and fined £500. They were also debarred from prosecuting suits in Law and Equity and from becoming guardians or executors.

On the death of Charles II in 1685, James II, his brother became King. James and his wife Mary of Modena were Roman Catholics. His first wife, Anne Hyde, was the mother of his two daughters Mary, the wife of William of Orange and her sister Anne, both of whom succeeded to the English throne. Churchmen were worried as to how James, a Catholic head of the established church, would use his power.

James lacked prudence and his dearest wish was to restore the Catholic faith to England. He might have succeeded if he had not been so impatient. His enthusiasm and lack of tact caused great anxiety among his opponents. It was now five generations since the passing of the Penal Laws in Elizabeth's reign and James was determined to relax them. He insisted that all Catholics should be free to serve him both in the army and state regardless of the Test Act, and demanded that a Declaration of Indulgence be read in all churches

This was almost unbelievable for all those who had been in hiding and for years had paid crushing taxes and seen members of their family carried off to prison. Suddenly, they could see Catholic priests openly carrying out their religious duties. Both church and state were convinced that the foundation of political life was in jeopardy.

One thing James did achieve during his short reign was the setting up of a system of Catholic Church government in this country. Ever since the death of Queen Mary, no Catholic Bishop had exercised his office in England. This meant that there was no Bishop to give the sacrament of confirmation or to direct the efforts of the missionary priests who were risking their lives to minister to their flocks. Although a Bishop had long been requested, the authorities in Rome feared that such an appointment would lead to increased problems with the English government. There was a controversy as to whether the appointment should be a Bishop in Ordinary or a Vicar Apostolic.

The storm broke with the revolution of 1688 ending the Catholic revival of 1685-88, a brief respite from persecution. The one thing that remained amidst the ruin of all Catholic hopes and plans was the establishments of the Vicars Apostolic. James' daughter Mary and her husband, William of Orange were invited to take the throne. This opened up a new period in the history of Catholicism in England and Wales. E Watkins, in his book *Roman Catholicism in England* (Oxford 1957) had called it "the most dispiriting period of their history, of persecution without heroism of martyrdom, of exclusion from the government, a period of defections and diminishing numbers."

In 1696 an Act forbade Catholics from becoming members of the legal profession or to inherit or purchase land. Another Act of 1715 required every papist to register his name and real estate with the Clerk of the Peace for his county. The document they had to sign read as follows.

Oath of Allegiance

I A B do sincerely promise and swear that I will be faithful and bear true allegiance to his majesty King George. So help me God.

Oath of Supremacy

I A B do swear that I do from my heart abhor detest and abjure, as impious and heretical, that damnable doctrine and position, that princes, excommunicated, or deprived by the pope or any authority of the See of Rome, may be deposed or murdered by their subjects, or any other whatsoever and I do declare that no foreign prince person prelate, State or potentate hath or ought to have any jurisdiction power superiority pre-eminence or authority Ecclesiastical or Spiritual within this realm. So help me God.

Declaration against Popery

I A B I do solemnly and sincerely in the presence of God profess testify and declare that I do believe that in the Sacrament of the Lords Supper there is not any transubstantiation of the elements of bread and wine into the body and blood of Christ; at or after the consecration thereof by any person whatsoever and that the invocation or adoration of the Virgin Mary or any other saint, and the sacrifice of the mass as they are now used in the church of Rome, are superstitious and idolatrous and I do solemnly in the presence of God profess testify and declare that I do make this declaration and every part thereof in the plain and ordinary sense of the words read unto me as they are commonly understood by Protestants without any evasion, equivocation or mental reservation whatsoever and without any dispensation already granted me for this purpose by the Pope or any other authority or person whatsoever, or without any hope of dispensation from any person or authority whatsoever or without believing that I am or can be acquitted before God or man or absolved of this declaration or any part thereof although the Pope or any other person or persons whatsoever shall dispense with or annul the same or declare that it was null and void from the beginning.

Declaration of Christian Faith

I A B do solemnly declare in the presence of Almighty God that I am a Christian and a Protestant, and as such that I believe the Scriptures of the Old and New Testament, as commonly received among Protestant Churches, do contain the revealed will of God and that I do receive the same as the rule of my doctrine and practice.

Eventually, the Catholic Relief Act of 1791 enabled Catholics to worship freely in their own churches and in 1817 commissions of every rank in the army and navy were open to Catholics. At last, in 1829 the Catholic Emancipation Act was passed.

It is against this background that the events that took place over a period of 300 years in the Monnow Valley must be viewed.

With so much oppressive legislation, maintaining faith in the Roman Catholic Church was not easy. How well or conscientiously these Acts were carried out varied throughout the country. There were many land-owning Catholic families with wealth and influence and not all Bishops regarded recusancy with any urgency. It was easy to support the persecution of 'Papists' in general but not so easy when it came to prosecuting neighbours, friends or members of the family. All large groups of recusants included at least one member of the gentry whose houses formed the base of operations for itinerant priests.

Many recusant families lived in South Herefordshire and Monmouthshire. Catholics crossed and re-crossed the river Monnow that flowed through well-wooded country. Priests from Herefordshire frequently moved into Monmouthshire in times of danger. It was easy for squire, tenant and priest to conspire together against the government in distant London. The area was remote, hilly and the dense woodland made it easy to hide. Recusancy in Wales was almost exclusively confined to the counties formed out of the Marches of Wales.

During the reigns of Elizabeth and James I, about two per cent of the population aged 16 and over were convicted recusants. Monmouthshire had the most convicted recusants in the country with 117 recusant households per thousand of the population; Lancashire was second with 112, Durham third with 31 and Herefordshire fourth with 25. Seventeen English counties scored less than 10.

The local administration of the Penal Laws was the responsibility of the churchwardens who were considered by the ecclesiastical authorities as the proper guardians of the parish church. The office of churchwarden, originally known as Oeconmus, came into being early in the 12th century. The wardens were chosen by the minister and the parishioners and were elected by the vestry, usually on Easter Tuesday. After being sworn in, the churchwarden had no power to refuse the appointment. If he did refuse he was fined heavily. The office carried great responsibility and included the following duties.

The custodian of the parish property and income.
Representing the parishioners in matters of collective obligations and any action they may wish to take.
The upkeep of the church fabric
Providing the facilities.
Ensuring that parishioners attended church regularly and brought their children for baptism.
Attending the Archdeacon's court.
Accounting for the expenditure of the church rate.
Helping to keep the parish register.
Reporting, if necessary, on any failing in the duty of the incumbent.
Supervising the education and relief of the poor.
Arranging for the burial of unknown strangers and the baptism of foundlings.
Responsibility for the parish army and paying soldiers.
Presenting offences with the cognisance of the church courts.

Parishes appointed at least two and sometimes four churchwardens. They were obliged to answer the questions in the detailed returns made to the Archdeacon. These returns are often called the "Bill of Detection" and accusations could be made upon a proved or provable fact, upon a 'fame' or rumour, or merely upon 'vehement suspicion'. The accused had to appear in court on a given day. Many matters now regarded as purely secular remained as the responsibility of the ecclesiastical courts until a century ago. The church and state were in alliance to punish wickedness and vice and maintain the true religion and virtue. The church courts were there to achieve this state and the punishment of excommunication was the last and most

Garway

ARTICLES OF ENQUIRY

Exhibited to the

MINISTERS, CHURCH-WARDENS, And SIDE-MEN

OF EVERY

PARISH

WITHIN THE

Diocese of HEREFORD,

To be Return'd at the

PRIMARY-VISITATION

Of the Right Reverend Father in GOD,

PHILIP,

Lord Bishop of that Diocese,
M. DCC. XVI.

LONDON:

Printed by W. BOWYER in the Year M. DCC. XVI.

ARTICLES, &c.

Articles of Enquiry.

IS your Church or Chapel, with the Chancel and Tower, in good and sufficient Repair? Particularly,

1. Is the Roof both of the Church and Chancel cover'd?

2. Are the Windows well glazed?

3. Is the Floor paved? Is it kept plain and even?

4. Are the inside Walls white and clean?

5. Is there a convenient Reading Desk and Pulpit?

6. Is the Communion Table cover'd in time of Divine Service with a Carpet of Silk, or other decent Stuff, and with a fair Linen Cloth at the time of the Administration of the Holy Sacrament?

7. Is there a fair Chalice, a Paten, and a Flagon proper for that Service? Are they kept for this Use only?

Here you are to write distinct *Answers* to every *Question.*

Garway

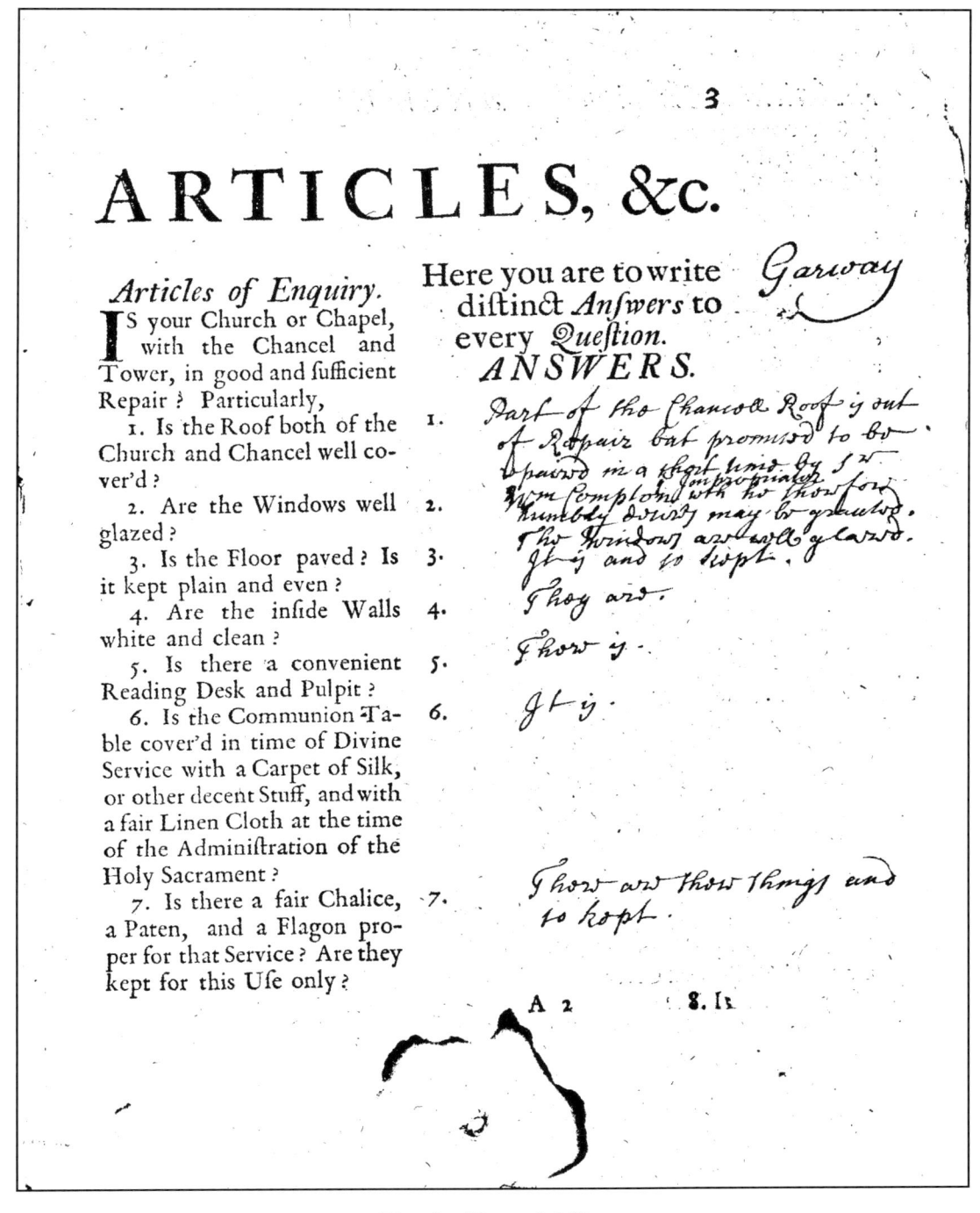

ANSWERS.

1. Part of the Chancell Roof is out of Repair but promised to be repaired in a short time by Sr Wm Compton wth he therefore humbly desirs may be granted.

2. The Windows are well glazed.

3. It is and so kept.

4. They are.

5. There is.

6. It is.

7. There are these things and so kept.

A 2

8. Is

Hereford Record Office

129

dreadful weapon they administered. Any irregularity in the parish such as adultery, whoredom, incest, drunkenness, swearing, ribaldry, disturbing divine service by behaving rudely, defending Popish doctrine or not attending church on Sundays would be presented by the churchwarden to the Archdeacon at his visitation.

The Archdeacon's Court for the Archenfield Deanery for the years 1673-1681 contained examples of many of the activities considered sinful that were reported (presented) by the churchwardens. These examples come mainly from the Parishes of Garway, Welsh Newton and Llanrothal.

> For being unlawfully begotten with child
> For committing fornication and unlawfully begetting with child one Maria Watkins
> For abusing the clergyman with vile language.
> For executing the office of midwife without licence and delivering one Mary Meyride of a bastard child.
> For suffering Anne Helman to be buried in the churchyard being an undesirable person.
> For not receiving the Holy Sacrament according to the ordinance of the church.
> For absenting himself from church and parish at the time of divine service
> For reputed papacy and absenting himself from church and lying under examination.
> For keeping a set of ninepins in the churchyard and playing with them himself and inviting others to do likewise upon Sundays and other days.
> For hedging on the Lord's Day.
> For suffering Joan Haybrook who stood long excommunicated to be buried in the churchyard and suffering her to be brought into the church and a popish rite to be performed.

The records for the parish of Garway for the year 1675 give a glimpse of deep trouble between the minister and two of the churchwardens. The minister was Jeremiah Jackson who was incumbent from 1664 until his death in 1677. The churchwardens were Edward Robinson who lived at Church farm, just a few yards away from the church and Richard Hughes.

Early in the year 1675, the churchwardens Hughes and Robinson were presented to the Archdeacon's Court for neglecting their duties. Their names crop up several times for not exhibiting the church accounts at the visitation and for not repairing the seats and bells in the church. They, in turn presented the minister, Jeremiah Jackson for not wearing his surplice on Sundays and for endeavouring to set his neighbours at variance with one another.

On March 25th, Jeremiah Jackson wrote to the Chancellor of the diocese, Sir Timothy Baldwyn, on behalf of several of his parishioners.

May it please your Worship to understand that some of the persons whose names are underwritten are not papists, but frequenters of the church, but their wives do not, and how they came to be presented at first I know not, yet now they ly under excommunication and being poor men; day labourers, that having nothing to spare, scarce enough to maintain their families by, they rather ly under it than stir to prove their absolution. Besides for all of them if are papists have repaired to Captain Scudamore, (through my persuasion with them to come to church) who hath presented them, that if they do so, they shall come off freely with charges, upon oath. They are very willing, and I conceive many now will follow them on the same account. But as for Elianor Philpott who lyes under the same lash, for professing the part of midwife, she is a poor woman, and what she doth is amongst the poorer sort of people, yet her gain is very small indeed, and many of them will be in danger to perish if she be restrained. She being not able to come to Leominster herself nor yet to prove neither lycense nor absolution. Therefore I beseech your worship to consider their presentments and grant them their absolution that we may not be deprived of their company that are willing to come to our Assemblies and shall now remain Sir your Worships Remembrance to the Throne of Grace.

Garway 25 March 1675   *Jere Jackson*

Thomas Rawlins and wife
William Williams and wife
Richard Morgan
Elianor Philpott
John Davis of Little Garway, Jeffrreys son in law
Richard Jenkins
Richard Rogers.

I humbly desire your Worship to reason of their age and inability to come to Leominster to send your commission to Mr Tylor and myself to absolve them as soon as maybe that they may receive the sacrament.

On 30th April 1675 Jeremiah Jackson sent a long reports to the Archdeacon that starts "Several abuses neglects and offences done and suffered by Edward Robinson and Richard Hughes before and in the time they were churchwardens, some presented upon common fame and some upon by own knowledge sight and hearing", and continues;

1. Hughes and Robinson by entreaties, promises and threats to me and my wife and others tried to persuade me to preach but once a month at least and when I did not to mention anything I saw or heard about them or any of their friends, papists and others.
2. Robinson allowed his pigs, ducks and poultry in the churchyard and several times in the church, chapel and chancel, so much so that of late when assembled in prayer we had to shut the door to keep them out.
3. Hughes and Robinson seldom come to church and when they do seldom or never stay to hear the sermon, or but very little and then go out to the great disturbance of me and the whole congregation.
4. Upon Easter day last in the morning according to our custom having prayer and sacrament before the sermon for those who are not able to fast so long, the whole congregation had to wait for bread an hour because neither Robinson or Hughes were there to see what was needed and bring it.
5. Neither Hughes nor any of his household have received the sacrament to the best of my knowledge for 10 years, not Robinson but once this 4 or 5 years.
6. Hughes and Robinson have both incensed the Papists and other people against me by informing them it was me not them, the churchwardens that did present them and that I do nothing but preach against papists.

7. Robinson did several times give out that he might easily be and er long should make as good a preacher as any minister in Herefordshire.
8. Robinson by telling untruths had persuaded many people to sign a petition to my Patron to out me. In it are most notorious untruths.
9. Robinson one Sunday all day and a great part of the night gathered a company of people to ring the bells and that in the church he made them all drunk. This was revenge against me for excommunicating him.
10. Lastly Robinson had baptised all his children in the Roman way and at the time of divine service and sermon causes a great stir by going in and out of his house by his own people and strangers which I think are papists. I can see and hear out of the pulpit through the church windows with great disturbance to my self and the congregation. Having a house with papists so close to the church and with such a stir with in has terrified many of the congregation and stopped them from coming to church

I have not found any record of the outcome of this quarrel but Jeremiah Jackson died two years later in 1677. He did not leave a will but his wife Margaret was granted probate and an inventory was taken of his goods and chattels. His wearing apparel was valued at £2 and there was a small study of books that shows he was reasonably literate. There were beds and furniture, brass and pewter and a table and stools, some jugs, earthenware and candlesticks. It would seem that Jeremiah Jackson apart from being a curate was a farmer in a small way. He owned 4 cows and a calf, 32 sheep and 5 lambs, 10 small pigs, corn of several sorts in the barn, hay and some poultry. There was also a bridle and saddle but no mention of a horse. The total value was £26.

Attached to the probate papers is a list of people to whom he owned money. Fifteen people are listed and include Edward Robinson to whom he owed £4 9s 6d. There is a debt for hearth tax of 9s. By 1677 Jeremiah Jackson occupied a house with 3 hearths (the largest house in Garway had 7 hearths) but unfortunately we do not know where it was. Hearth tax was introduced in 1662 and lasted until 1689. It was payable on every hearth and stove within every house at the rate of 2s per hearth per year. There was double duty for stopping up or concealing a hearth.

Throughout the 17th century there are certain names that crop up time and again as persistent recusants. William Baskerville, gent and his wife lived at Cwmaddoc in Garway, a large farm of more than 300 acres with a rather grand farmhouse of 7 hearths. By the late 17th century it was already an old farm being mentioned by name in the Rental of the Knights Hospitallers written in 1503. It was (and still is), situated at Broad Oak, on the borders of Llanrothal and nearer to Llanrothal church than Garway church.

William Baskerville came from a prominent Herefordshire family. In 1650 he married Mary, youngest daughter of John Powell of Perhir. (Mary's brother Edward had four daughters, all of whom who died unmarried. Her sister Catherine married Thomas Lorymer and it was their son Michael who inherited Perthir). William's name heads the list of Jurors sworn in at the Court Baron held at Garway on Thursday 3rd May 1678 before Henry Milbourne Esq, Steward of Sir William Compton, Bart, Lord of the Manor. The Baskervilles were persistent recusants, their names appearing regularly over the years in the Consistory Court books and they were always fined. Along with other gentlemen in Garway, William Baskerville had supported the Monarchy during the Civil Wars and in 1650 the Commonwealth confiscated two-thirds of his estate. William died in 1687.

George Loope also had his property confiscated by the commonwealth. At least three generations of George Loope lived in Garway. The family originated in Orcop. George Loope and his wife Elizabeth Alice were included in the lists of recusants for more than 40 years. His son, George Loope and his wife Winifred also lived in Garway. He was a chirurgion. When he died in 1679 the inventory of his goods and chattels included 'Books for chirurgerie and implements for chirurgerie'. This word is the old form of surgeon. The third generation George Loope was born in 1648 the son of George and Winifred. He was sent to Flanders for his education (an illegal and punishable offence), and by the time he was 19 he had joined an order of Discalced (barefooted) Carmelite friars at their Priory at Louvain taking the name of 'Edmund of S. Joseph'. He continued his studies at Louvain and at the Missionary College of St. Pancras in Rome.

Edmund returned to England in 1677 and was sent to minister in his native county of Herefordshire. It was an inopportune time as the country was beginning to panic over the alleged 'Titus Oates plot.' Local magistrate, John Scudamore of Kentchurch Court, who must have known Edmund's father, George Loope, instigated a search for Edmund. He hid in woods and outhouses and once in a haystack into which the searchers plunged their swords without detecting or injuring him. Eventually Edmund fled to London in disguise where the search for him continued and where he had several narrow escapes.

In 1680 Edmund moved to Worcester where there had been no priest for over a year. There he led a very austere lifestyle, dressing in the rags of a beggar and giving away to the poor all the alms given to him for his own sustenance. Eventually his health broke down under these harsh conditions and he was given an assistant, Father Francis to help share the mission. By 1686, in the new climate of tolerance engendered by James II, a public Catholic Chapel was opened in Worcester in a house in Forgate Street, but when James II fled in 1688, the fathers also had to leave as the mob prepared to attack and wreck the chapel.

Father Edmund became the English Vicar Provincial in succession to Father Lucian of St. Teresa who died in 1691. He held this office for at least 12 years. During his years as Provincial he wrote *The Queen of Heaven's Livery* subtitled, *A Short Treatise of the Institution, Excellency, Privileges and Indulgencies of the Most Famous Confraternity of Our Blessed Lady of Mount Carmel, commonly called the Scapular: Together with a brief Relation of the Antiquity and Never-interrupted Succession of the Religious Order of the Carmelites, to whom the Blessed Virgin Mary gave this her Sacred Livery.* The book was printed in Antwerp in 1709.

Father Edmund of St Joseph died in London on 6th February 1716 aged 68 in the forty-ninth year of his profession.

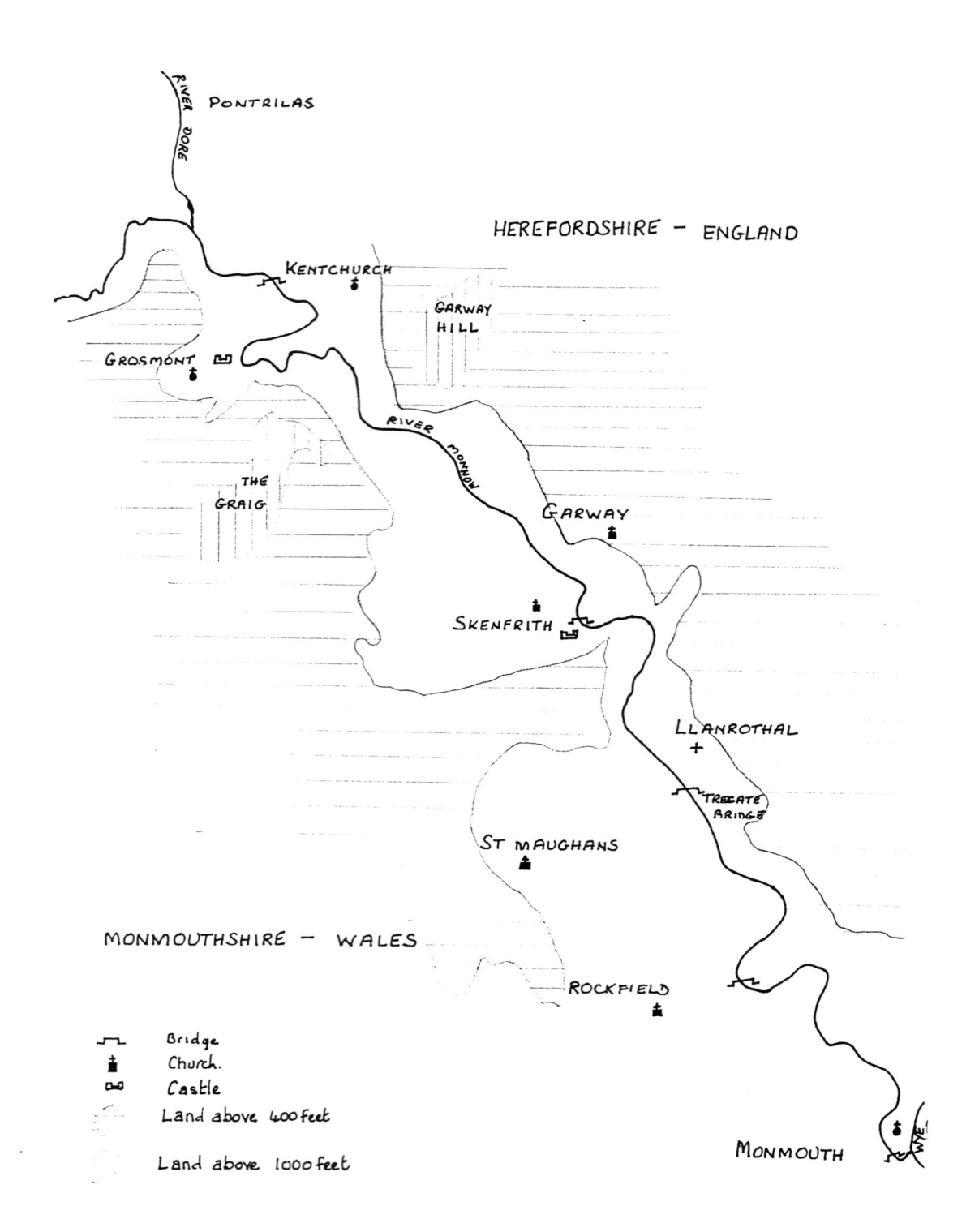

THE RIOT

The non-attendance at church caused serious problems apart from the danger of being fined and excommunicated. Church was necessary for what was known as the 'rites of passage', baptism, marriage and burial. At birth, not to have been baptised meant eternal damnation. A marriage if conducted by a catholic priest was illegal. At death, the matter became even more serious – there was a body to be disposed of. It was an illegal burial that started all the trouble. We are all familiar with the Gunpowder Plot of November 1605 but how many people realise that here in Herefordshire, earlier that same year there was an uprising of Catholics that was of national importance. For a period of six weeks from the Tuesday after Whitsunday until the month of July, a state of lawlessness persisted in the area surrounding the Monnow Valley.

It all started in the village of Allensmore, five miles southwest of Hereford. Alice Wellington, the recusant wife of Thomas Wellington a yeoman died excommunicate and was refused burial by Richard Heyns the Vicar of Allensmore. The Catholic community in the area were furious and very early on the morning of Tuesday 21st May 1605 Alice was buried in the churchyard by torchlight, with all the Catholic ceremonies including candles and bells. Richard Heyns immediately went to Hereford to the Bishop's Palace and gave the names of all those in the burial party whom he had recognised. A list of 25 names was given to Bishop Robert Bennett including James Coles, from Hungerstone, a weaver, together with his wife and daughter. He was known to act a massing clerk to Roger Cadwallader, a Priest. Also named was Phillip Giles who 'bare the crosse'.

Three days later the High Constable of Hereford visited the district with a warrant issued by the Bishop of Hereford and arrested three men who had participated in the burial. They first went to the hamlet of Hungerstone where they arrested James Coles and William Chandor, both weavers who worked in adjoining rooms. They both struggled and Chandor was chased for some distance but escaped. Coles grabbed a knife and wounded two of the constables. Leonard Marsh, another man named in the warrant, joined in the struggle. Coles managed to escape but Leonard Marsh was taken prisoner. Then William Marsh, brother of the prisoner appeared. He shouted to the constable to wait until William Morgan of Treville Park had had a word with him. This was refused and William shouted to his brother to resist. Suddenly, 40 or 50 men, armed with bows and arrows, staves, bills and swords surrounded the Constable and his party. These armed men demanded that the Constable tell them where he was taking the prisoner. Outnumbered, the Constable released the prisoner warning the men as to the consequences of their rebellion. He went straight to the Bishop who at once dispatched the news of the riot to the Privy Council in London.

The Privy Council's first reaction was to deal with this violence with stern repression. The King, James I in a speech made to the Judges at the Court of Greenwich made it plain that there was no longer any need to spare the blood of recusants and that Herefordshire men would do well enough to set an example to the rest of the country. However, the Privy Council was reluctant to use force in the King's name for fear of provoking an even more serious uprising. They thought the best solution was to try to capture several of the rebel leaders and that the Herefordshire magistrates were the people best equipped to deal with this matter.

By the beginning of June, Bishop Bennet had decided to arrest William Morgan of Whitfield in Treville Park. Today, Whitfield is an early 18th century house up a two-mile drive from the Hereford/Abergavenny road. In the early 17th century it was probably not much more than a rather grand farmhouse. Mass was said there by Roger Cadwallader, a seminary priest who was martyred at Leominster in 1610.

A little after midnight on 5th June the Bishop's party arrived at Treville. The Bishop was accompanied by Sir James Scudamore of Holme Lacy who was Member of Parliament for Herefordshire. Also in the party was Sir Roger Bodenham of Rotherwas whose wife, Lady Bridget, was the daughter of Sir Humphrey Baskerville of Eardisly, (a man described by the Bishop as 'countenancing all priests and recusants'). Sir James Scudamore was known to be a papist but he acted with discretion. The Bishop's party was expected.

Near the house were at least sixty men, maybe as many a hundred armed with bows, pikes, bills, swords and javelins. Twenty or thirty were in a dell called the Cockett. It was not planned that there should be a direct attack on the Bishop's party, but to wait for William Morgan to be arrested and then rescue him. The ambush had been ready since the Bishop's party had left Hereford. James Cole, William Chandor and Leonard Marsh were among the waiting men. Reinforcements were expected from the recusants in the Monnow Valley. The leader of this ambush was a man called Thomas Pritchard of the Grange, Skenfrith. The magistrates arrived and searched the house taking away a number of incriminating letters written by Morgan himself. Morgan was arrested and eventually sent to London. For some unexplained reason the ambush was called off. Maybe William Morgan felt he had enough influential friends to speak for him. Sir Roger Bodenham was known to have some sympathy with the recusants and that he had some influence over Thomas Pritchard. Most of the men in the ambush party went into hiding.

So where did these men escape to? Not very far from Allensmore and Treville Park are the River Monnow and Monmouthshire which was 'almost wholly corrupted' according to the Bishop. Monmouthshire was also out of his jurisdiction being in the diocese of Llandaff.

On the Sunday following the fiasco at Treville Park, three hundred people, with weapons in their hands, had assembled for Mass at the Darren Chapel on the bank of the river Monnow in the Herefordshire parish of Garway. Expecting trouble, many of them lingered on over the Monday and Tuesday. Among them were William Hugh of Monmouthshire and the servants of William Vaughan of Llanrothal including James, his shepherd carrying a forest bill and a long hanger. One of the Bishop's men who ventured too close was roughly handled but no one else put in an appearance. The Bishop had a problem. As he put it, "if we go out with a few we shall be beaten home; if we levy any strength we are descried and they are all fled into the woods and there they will lurk until the assizes be past".

On Wednesday June 19th the Justices made their biggest effort yet. Sir James Scudamore, William Rushall, Rowland Vaughan and Thomas Kyrle of Walford with a strong force searched the Darren and villages adjoining, house-by-house, all that night and the day following, making a thirty-mile sweep along the borders of Monmouthshire. They found altars, images and books of superstition, relics of idolatry but hardly a living soul apart from an occasional child or old woman. The villages were deserted. The entire population had fled westwards and southwards into the comparative safety of Wales.

According to the Bishop only one man was caught. There is a strong local tradition in this area that this man was an outlawed priest called Ainsworth. The Justices are supposed to have caught this man in the Darren woods and beheaded him on the spot. According to the legend, this took place by a spring of water and that the rocks around this spring are still stained with his blood, the marks being especially bright when the stones are wet. There is no proof that this violent act happened in 1605, but there is strong evidence that it could have happened much later in 1679 at the time of the Titus Oates allegations.

The Justices returned to Hereford with no positive results from their intensive search. A report reached the King on Sunday, June 23rd, that the Bishop of Hereford had not only been resisted but had fled for his life. A thousand Catholics were reported to be in arms at one spot alone and a full-scale rebellion was feared. Dr Bennet sent his own report of the situation to London, but many believed he was only trying to make excuses for his own incompetence.

The Privy Council were very undecided as how to deal with the insurrection in the Monnow Valley. They tried putting the blame on the magistrates who 'failed to carry out their orders with that dexterity which was contemplated by the King and Council'. Some, including the King, were all for sending an armed posse against the Catholics but others feared that force would fail in so recusant a county with the danger that the revolt would spread.

Eventually it was decided that the Earl of Worcester, by reputation a Papist, would be sent to calm the situation. He was a personal favourite of the King and as his seat was Raglan Castle he was the natural overlord of the area. He was to talk to the recusant leaders and to quell the revolt. Hopefully, as a Catholic himself, they would trust him and defer to his authority.

Edward, the 4th Earl of Worcester was an interesting character. He was directly descended from John of Gaunt and his third wife, Katherine Swynford. John of Gaunt was the third son of Henry III. His first wife was Blanche of Lancaster and their eldest son became Henry VI. After 10 happy years, Blanche died and John married Constance of Castile. One of Blanche's favourite ladies had been Katherine Swynford, wife of Sir Hugh Swynford and when he was killed in Aquitaine, Katherine became the mistress of John of Gaunt. Their eldest son, John Beaufort, was born in about 1373 to be followed by three more illegitimate children, Henry, Thomas and Joan.

Constance of Castile died in 1394 and John married Katherine. John was determined to have his children legitimised and eventually in 1397 Parliament granted the Beauforts letters patent of legitimation and the eldest son John Beaufort was created Earl of Somerset. His son John, the first Duke of Somerset, was the father of Margaret Beaufort who was the mother of Henry VII. The male line then continued through John's brother Edmund whose grandson Charles Somerset was created the Earl of Worcester. It was through his marriage to Elizabeth Herbert, the daughter of the Earl of Pembroke, that he acquired vast possessions in Wales, among them the Castle of Raglan. During the final years of the reign of Queen Elizabeth Edward was made a Privy Councillor and Lord Lieutenant of Monmouthshire and Glamorgan. When King James came to the throne in 1603 the Earl of Worcester became a firm favourite often acting as the King's private secretary. Although a 'stiff papist' in his youth he had married Elizabeth Hastings, the daughter of the Earl of Huntingdon, a strong Protestant family. Many of their children were brought up in the Protestant faith they but eventually married back into Catholic families. Edward was known for his easy nature and benevolent spirit despite being one of the wealthiest men in the country.

Raglan Castle at the beginning of the 17th century was a magnificent structure surrounded by its deer park, orchards barns and stables. It was built round two courtyards, the Stone Court and the Fountain Court, divided by the Great Hall which had windows looking into both. Battlement towers contained arched rooms, one containing a library that housed a renowned collection of rare Welsh manuscripts. The most impressive room in the castle was the great hall with its rare roof of Irish oak incorporating a large cupola for light. A windowless stone enclosure projecting into the basement kitchen of the Yellow Tower may have been the Earl of Worcester's strong room and used as a priest-hole.

The Earl of Worcester arrived at Raglan Castle on Saturday, June 29th 1605 and this was the beginning of the end of the rebellion. The Earl decided that the affair should be played down. The first six days after his arrival were spent contacting the leaders. The priests and others who might suffer serious punishment were quietly got away and out of reach, warned well in advance. The Earl had 'a few fellows of the baser sort' put in prison more to show he had done something than because they deserved punishment. The tumult in the Monnow Valley was at an end.

Not however, the strong presence of the Catholics. Several rich and influential families lived in the valley including families from other parts of the country who had moved there because of its remoteness which enabled them to practice their chosen faith in relative safety and obscurity.

CADW   **Raglan Castle**   **Reconstructed drawing by Alan Sorrell**

THE CWM

The Cwm, sometimes known as Coombe, means wooded valley, shelter or hollow. The present house was rebuilt in about 1830 on the foundations of an old house that had been pulled down. Originally the old house was known as the Upper Cwm, while the present Upper Cwm farm was known as Lower Cwm. The Cwm is in the parish Llanrothal three miles north of Monmouth. A line of hills rise above the river Monnow and the Cwm rests in a slight hollow about a mile and a half along a quiet lane that leads off the main Hereford to Monmouth road at Welsh Newton.

During the 17th century the area was densely wooded and the lane was a stone track that led past the Cwm to Llanrothal church. A branch off this lane leads to the manor house of Tregate and on over the Monnow to St. Maughans. About two miles further upstream are the Darren woods and Skenfrith. A mile uphill from the Cwm is Pembridge Castle.

The Society of Jesus, or the Jesuits were associated with the Cwm for more than 100 years. The Jesuits were a company of ordained priests who, in 1540, took vows of obedience calling themselves the Company of Jesus. The Jesuit organisation was military and trained as an elite corps to carry out the wishes of the Pope. They were very privileged, paying no taxes and were exempt from all other Catholic Orders. Their aim was to educate, to preach and to hear confession. Wherever there was educational work to be done, the Jesuit Colleges were important instruments for Catholic influence and propaganda. The two men associated with the foundation of the Society of Jesus were Ignatius Loyola and Francis Xavier.

At the time of the disturbances in 1605 William Griffiths and his wife lived in the Cwm. William was an important Glamorgan landowner and despite the fact that he had forfeited two thirds of his estate he was still able to settle his family at the Cwm. He was a prominent Catholic layman and had travelled many times to the continent and was in touch with the Prefect of the English Jesuit Mission. He was the eldest of six brothers. Close by in Llanrothal lived his sister Jane Griffiths who had resumed her maiden name after the death of her husband John Watson. Her son John and his wife Sara were also rich, staunch Catholics. It is also probable that another brother John or James, a doctor of medicine, was residing at the Cwm with his wife Mary.

The exact date of the earliest Jesuit connection can only be guessed at but it is probable that there was a Jesuit Training College established at the Cwm as early as 1595. During 1605, Father Jones, known as 'the fyerbrande of all', who had said Mass at the Darren, was a frequent visitor. When he became Superior of the English Jesuits in 1609 he made his headquarters at the Cwm where he remained, dying in office in 1615. Father Salisbury, who was chaplain to Lady Frances Somerset at Raglan Castle, succeeded Father Jones in charge of the Mission of North and South Wales in 1615. He took a lease of the Cwm and surrounding land as a Jesuit Headquarters. The Earl of Worcester, who owned the property, was obviously aware of the Catholic activity there.

In 1622 the English Mission had been created a vice-province by Rome and the Cwm was made the College of St. Xavier. The other colleges were St. Ignatius London and St. Aloysius in Lancashire. For administrative purposes the Jesuits divided England and Wales into districts that they called Colleges or Missions. The district of St. Francis Xaviour covered South Wales, North Wales, Monmouthshire, Herefordshire, Gloucestershire and Somerset. Later, in 1676 a separate North Wales Mission was formed.

After the Earl of Worcester's death in 1628, his son leased the Cwm to Father William Morton for 99years. Management and profits from both Cwms was entrusted to a local Catholic named Peter Pullen.

In the Monmouthshire and Herefordshire area, Catholics made little attempt to hide their religious practices. Large congregations gathered in Abergavenny to say Mass. Several times a year pilgrimages were taken to the Holy Mountain, the Skirrid Fawr, and Mass was said at the chapel of St. Michael on the summit where a local magistrate claimed to have seen a great crowd with beads in their hands. The presence of a Jesuit College at the Cwm must have been known locally as their cart was sent to Monmouth market regularly for provisions.

This state of affairs lasted for over fifty years. During this time many priests served at the College. The longest serving priest was Father Thomas or John Harris. He became a Missioner at the Cwm in 1639 and was still there thirty-seven years later in 1676, dying just before the raid on the College.

There does not seem to be any record of the Civil Wars (1642-51) affecting the Jesuit College at the Cwm although Pembridge Castle just a mile away was besieged. The Kembles garrisoned the castle for the King. It formed an outpost of the Monmouth defences and suffered considerable damage in 1644, and in 1646, Colonel Birch, the Parliamentarian commander, ordered that it should be slighted.

The Cwm, LLanrothal

The Hereford Times. May 15, 1897.

JESUITICAL BOOKS IN HEREFORD CATHEDRAL LIBRARY.

⁎⁎ FROM AN OCCASIONAL CORRESPONDENT.

⁎⁎ The following appeared in a portion only of our edition last week:—

As I promised in last week's *Hereford Times*, I now send you a copy of a rare and most interesting document which goes to prove that many of the books in the ancient chained library at Hereford Cathedral are from the suppressed College of Jesuits at Combe, Llanrothal, Herefordshire. A very large number of these can easily be identified by the name of Father William Morgan, who wrote his name in German characters. He held the lease of Combe from the Marquis of Worcester. The document in question, which I think clearly locates St. Navarius's College—a matter of some doubt hitherto—is a reminiscence of the days when Herbert Croft, Bishop of Hereford, 1662—1691, was in residence here. The strong effort of the House of Lords to put down Roman Catholicism in England, more particularly the Jesuits, who had one of their houses at Combe, in the parish of Llanrothal, Herefordshire, was occasioned by the report of Mr John Arnold, a Justice of the Peace, co. Monmouth, who lived near to Combe, and Captain John Scudamore, of Kentchurch, who, in their evidence before the House of Lords, 27th March, 1678, gave many particulars to their Lordships.

In the Philips' Library, at St. Michaels' Priory, Hereford, is the original warrant addressed by the House of Lords to Dr Croft, dated

"Die Sabbathi,
"Decembris, 1678.

"Upon information given to this House of a place in Herefordshire called Combe, that the said house and three hundred pounds (per annum) belongeth to the Church of Rome, and that five or six Jesuits commonly reside there, and that in the chapel there mass is said constantly, and that the place is commonly called and known by the name of the Jesuits' College by the Papists. Upon consideration had thereof, it is ordered by the Lords, spiritual and temporal, in Parliament assembled that it be, and is hereby recommended to the Lord Bishop of Hereford, calling to his assistance such Justices of the Peace in the said county as his lordship shall think fit, to inquire into the information aforesaid, and to send for and examine such persons as his lordship or assistants shall think necessary for finding out the truth of the matter concerning the said place called Combe, and give this House a full account thereof as soon as his lordship conveniently can.

"Jo. BROWNE,
"Cleric-Parliamentor."

Bishop Croft appointed Captain J Scudamore to inquire into the affair, and the latter wrote subsequently to Mr J Arnold, Llanvihangel, J.P. The original letter is amongst the Lansdowne MSS. B.M., and is as follows:—

A coppy of Mr Scudamore's letter to Mr Arnold, concerning Combe, in Herefordshire, dated Kentchurch, December 24, 1678.

The Combe, in Herefordshire, hath about £500 per annum belonging to it. All the neighbourhood testify that it is a place to which Popish recusants and priests do often resort, but cannot tell who is proprietor or owner of it. Its situation without, and appartments within, argue it is a place of habitation of such as are fearful of being discovered. It hath fair chambers, to which belongs a study, and in some were found chairs, tables, and standishes, as is usual in colledges. We found a very fair library of books, which may be compared with some of them in the halls and colledges in either of the Universityes. We found about thirty folios, some manuscripts lately written, many English books against Protestant writers, as Laud, Chillingworth, Stillingfleet, &c, &c, not yet bound, and a bundle of Popish Catechisms. The Library was concealed with so much skill, that it was very difficult to discover it; and though they had time enough to remove it, yet we four dDecember 19th when this discovery was made, many papers that mentioned their Society, the Society of Jesus, and the colledge of St Navarius in England. Some instructions for Jesuitical Mission, some memorials left in St Navarius, his colledge in England in the visitation. We found in the frontispiece of ten folios "St Navarius's Colledge." Among other books there was was one very fair folio, printed at St Omer's, 1660, entitled "Historia Anglicanæ Provicinæ Societatis Jesu Collectore Henrico Maco Ejusdem Societatis Sacerdore." The author hath confidence to affirme, p 446. that there are three colledges of the Society of Jesus in England, one of Ignatius in London, Navarius in Wales, and of St Abbysms in Staffordshire or Lancashire, with various houses, and rents belonging to them, which seem to make plain that Combe, in Herefordshire, is St Navarius's Colledge. We found one paper that was a list of the benefactors of the present yeare; also a curious picture of St Navarius, to whose honour this colledge is instituted; many other pictures, also crucifixes, and botles of oyle, reliques, an incense pot, a mass bell, surplices, and other habits; boxes of white wafers, stamps with Jesuitical devices. There is scarce any Jesuitical writers whose works are not here, and scarce an eminent author but Jesuits, as Cardinal Bellarmine, Cardinal Collet, Gregory de Valentia, Gabriel Vasquer, etc, above thirty printed books, containing only orders and decrees, and rules of the Society, whereof fifteen are new, and fairly printed in one volume. We met with the Life of Ignatius Loyola, the founder of their order, not only written with the Lives of Navarius, Quoiles, and the like, famous in the Society, but also the pretended miracles reported by Rebadenira; the like of Ignatius Loyola are set forth in about twenty sheets of curious pictures. Among the papers we found three letters from Rome, from Jo Paulus de Oliva, General of the Jesuit there, upon Jesuitical subjects; and one directed to John Draycott, who is every where in this country reported a Jesuit. Some from Mr Edward Courtnay, that seem to be their provintiale, at London; and one paper writ to him, in obedience to his order, for admittance of some Noviciate into the Society, subscribed by Draycott, Evans, and two other reported Jesuits, whereas, by the rules of their order, all the incomes are administered by the father-rector of the College, we find many papers of account for cloking, travelling, &c. Whereas they are to give annual account to the General at Rome of all they baptize and pervert, we find a paper that is a draught of such an account; thus, 34 baptized, 130 reconciliati: by all of which may easily be judged that St. Navarius Colledge in England is no other than Combe in Herefordshire."

This letter is evidently forwarded to Bishop Croft, who in the beginning of January, 1679, sent a short narrative of the discovery of the College of Jesuits at Combe to the Lords assembled in Parliament. I give extracts from this narrative printed in a scarce pamphlet as follows:—

"A short narrative of the discovery of a College of Jesuits, at a place called Combe, in the County of Hereford, which was sent up unto the Right Honourable the Lords assembled in Parliament, at the end of the last sessions, by the Right Reverend Father in God, Herbert, Lord Bishop of Hereford, according to an order sent unto him by the said lords, to make diligent search, and return an account thereof, &c.

"London: Printed by T. N. for Charles Harper, at the Flower-de-luce, against St. Dunstan's Church, in Fleet-street, 1679."

In the parish of Llanrothall, in the county of Hereford, there are two houses called The Upper and Lower Comes, or Middle and Lower Comes, with a walled court before each of them, having lands belonging to them worth about threescore pounds per annum (they pay taxes at eight and fifty pounds per annum).

One of these houses is a fair gentile house, wherein there are six lodging chambers; each one is a convenient study to it, with a standish left in them, besides several other lodging rooms.

The other house is also a good country house, with several chambers, and studies to some of them, all in very good repair. But the furniture now removed, we cannot find whither.

The remaining dwellers in the houses, who were but under servants, will not confess. They were apparently perjured. For they flatly denied, upon oath, several things, which were made out by others, and then they confessed them.

There are one and twenty chimneys in both houses, and a great many doors to go in and out at; and likewise many private passages from one room to the other.

These houses are seated at the bottom of a thick woody and rocky hill, with several hollow places in the rocks, wherein men may conceal themselves; and there is a very private passage from one of the houses into the wood.

In one of these houses there was a study found, the door thereof very hardly to be discovered, being placed behind a bed, and plaistered over like the wall adjoining, in which was found great store of Divinity books, and others, in folio and quarto, and many other letter-books, several horseloads, many whereof are written by the principal learned Jesuits.

There are several books lately written and printed against the Protestant religion, and many small Popish catechisms printed and tied up in a bundle, and some Welsh Popish books lately printed, and some Popish manuscripts fairly and lately written.

Likewise there is a picture of Ignatius Loiola, the founder of the Society, and the most remarkable actions and pretended miracles of his life, not only written in printed books, but in pictures in several sheets, which pictures refer to Ribadeneira's book of Loiola's life.

One letter seems written by the Provincial to them of this House, wherein complaint is made. "That there was not care enough taken to send young men to Rome to be there bred up in the English College, and for which, he saith, the Pope was much displeased, and threatened to take away their College there, and fill it up with scholars of some other nation and Order."

Two vestments, with some other small matters, were found in two boxes hid in the wood above specified (it seems the other things were but newly removed; and they had begun also to remove the Library, for they carried out and hid in a pigscot adjoining, about two horse loads of books).

Besides those from the College at Combe, the Cathedral Library contains books from the library of St. Guthlac Priory, Hereford, and have no doubt also from the libraries of other local Priories suppressed at the Reformation. It is rare, indeed, to meet with a Library of real monastic books which are here gathered together under most exceptional circumstances, and which might have been destroyed or sent beyond the seas by "whole ships full" or used by "Grocers and soapsellers" of that time and subsequent trials of the Church, during the long period of the civil war. William Blades wrote a very interesting volume in 1881 upon the enemies of books, neglect appearing to be the greatest enemy of all. Happily, now in their new quarter the books will be treasured for ages to come, and the unborn will then feast their eye on those books which are now tenderly cared for.

At the opening of the new Library building by the Archbishop of Canterbury, Dean Leigh said he could find no record since the synod held by Archbishop Theodore, in 673, of any Archbishop performing in public function at Hereford. Neither can our local antiquaries find such a record. I am glad that the Dean has inscribed over the doorway of the new Library a record of Archbishop Temple's official visit in the following terms:—"Hanc Ecclesiæ Cathedralis Bibliothecam Gul. Fred. Powell, A.M., Canon Honor: Gloucstr: et Prebend: Hereford, pietate ac munificentia extructam Dei gloriae dedicavit Fredericus, Archiepisc. Cantuar, Prid; Kal: Mai: A.D MDCCCXCVII.

A Short NARRATIVE
Of the Discovery of a
College of Jesuits,
At a Place called the
COME,
In the County of HEREFORD:

Which was sent up unto the Right Honorable,

The Lords Assembled in PARLIAMENT,

at the End of the last Sessions, by the Right Reverend Father in God *HERBERT*, Lord Bishop of *Hereford*, according to an Order sent unto him by the said Lords, to make diligent Search, and return an Account thereof.

To which is added
A true Relation of the Knavery of

Father LEWIS,

The Pretended Bishop of *Landaffe*; Now a Prisoner in *Monmouth* Gaol.

London, Printed by *T. N.* for *Charles Harper*, at the *Flower-de-luce* against St. *Dunstan's* Church in *Fleetstreet*. 1679.

THE PLOT

Charles I was executed in 1649 and his sons Charles and James were brought up as exiles in France. In 1660, Charles was invited to return to England as King Charles II with the hope that he would help to restore unity and stability to the nation.

The Parliament elected in 1661 was strongly Anglican and Royalist. The Acts of Parliament known as the Clarendon Code that were passed during the next few years were mainly aimed at Puritans, but the terms meant that Catholics also became liable to prosecution. In 1673 Parliament passed the Test Act prohibiting non-Anglicans from holding any civil or military office. Gradually, the tide of anti-catholic feeling began to rise among the general population. The Catholics were falsely accused of starting the fire of London that took place in 1666 and in 1681 an inscription to this effect was engraved on the Monument erected to commemorate this event. The anti-catholic feelings rose to panic in 1678 with the allegations made by Titus Oates, described as the 'greatest liar in history'. Oates was the son of an Anabaptist preacher and was at one time an Anglican clergyman. During his rather colourful and dishonest career, he had been thrown out of the Navy for immorality and had tried to join the Jesuits but had been rejected. In revenge he maliciously revealed an imaginary plot against the King and his subjects. In this alleged plot, the murder of the King was to be followed by a massacre of Protestants and James, Duke of York was to be put on the throne. The panic spread throughout the country and many innocent Catholics were put on trial or died as fugitives. A Jesuit describing the situation, wrote.

Hundreds of innocent people died through the Oates Plot. One Jesuit reckoned that four hundred perished in prison, some of them victims of the plague. King Charles, knowing full well that the plot was a fraud, made no effort stop it. The Jesuits were stunned by this Royal indifference but they never condemned the King. They saw his dilemma, for Charles could have stood for justice only at the risk of a second civil war.

A co-conspirator of Titus Oates was William Bedloe, a Monmouthshire man born in Chepstow in 1650. He had been imprisoned for fraud and theft, and in 1678 had recently been released from Newgate prison. His character was that of a cheat, plotter and informer and according to his own account, one of the 'Principal Discoverers of the Horrid Popish Plot'.

David Lewis, a Jesuit Priest who was eventually executed at Usk; a death that can be directly attributed to the lies told by Bedloe, played an influential part in the life of young William. David Lewis, being impressed by the intelligence of the boy, arranged for him to go to London to be educated by the Jesuits. By the time he was twenty Bedloe was regarded as a convert and he was given the job of travelling to Spain, Rome and Flanders carrying important letters which he opened and forged. He was now known as Captain Bedloe, having managed by fraud to obtain the rank from William of Orange. It was during this time that he met Titus Oates.

During the next five years he lived as an informer and a spy and resorted to blackmail. He was imprisoned several times. Oates and Bedloe gave Parliament detailed accounts of conspiracies that involved leading Monmouthshire and Herefordshire Catholics. According to Bedloe, risings were planned and a great army was to assemble in Radnor and march to Milford Haven where there was to be a Spanish landing. Bedloe became a popular hero and received ten pounds a week from the Royal funds. He was living at the rate of several thousands of pounds a year and entertaining his friends with extravagant hospitality. He added to his income by writing pamphlets in which he attributed far-reaching plots and sensational crimes to the Papists. In 1680 after a short illness lasting four says, William Bedloe died. Titus Oates died in obscurity in 1705.

John Arnold of Langfihangel Court near Abergavenny and John Scudamore of Kentchurch Court near Pontrilas were responsible for collecting evidence against the Roman Catholics in the Monmouth and Hereford areas. John Arnold was the grandson of Sir Nicholas Arnold, who as a reward for supporting Thomas Cromwell at the Reformation, was given Llantony Abbey in the Black Mountains. John, the second son of Sir Nicholas established himself at Llanfihangel in 1626 and his eldest son John who was born in 1634, succeeded him in 1665. John Arnold was a rabid protestant and a Whig politician who had a long- standing feud with the Catholic Earl of Worcester. The Scudamores of Kentchurch Court were the senior branch of the family who had lived in the area since the Norman Conquest. John Scudamore was a lapsed Catholic.

The Magistrates for the counties of Monmouthshire and Herefordshire were split between those who supported the Marquis of Worcester and were Popishly inclined, for example, Henry Milbourne of Llanrothal Court, and those who opposed the Earl such as John Arnold. A Royal Proclamation ordered that the Magistrates were to arrest and bring to trial all priests and Jesuits.

In March 1678 a Commons Committee had considered the danger that the nation was in because of the growth of Popery. Mr Greenhough the Vicar of Abergavenny, John Arnold and John Scudamore all appeared before this committee. Both Arnold and Scudamore told the Committee that the Cwm was a Jesuit residence. The Commons had been informed in 1670 and in 1674 about the existence of the College but the support of the local Justices of the Peace had ensured that nothing was done. However, in the climate of the Titus Oates plot the support of the local gentry gradually faded. The House of Lords took action and a letter was sent to the Bishop of Hereford.

December 1678
Upon information given to this House of a place in Herefordshire called Combe that the said house and three hundred pounds (P.A) belongeth to the Church of Rome and that five or six Jesuits commonly reside there and that in the chapel there Mass is said constantly and that the place is commonly called and known by the name of the Jesuit College by the Papists. Upon consideration that therof it is ordered by the Lords spiritual and Temporal in Parliament assembled that it be, and is hereby recommended to the Lord Bishop of Hereford, calling to his assistance such Justices of the Peace of the said County as His Lordship shall think fit, to enquire into the information aforesaid, and think necessary for finding out the truth of the matter of fact concerning the said place called Combe and to give this House a full account thereof so soon as His Lordship conveniently can.

Jo. Browne, Cleric Parliamentor.

Dr Herbert Croft, Lord Bishop of Hereford was one of the nine children of the Catholic Knight, Sir Herbert Croft of Croft Castle, Herefordshire who sent his third son, Herbert to the Catholic College at St Omers and in 1622, to the English College at Rome. Back in England Herbert Croft was persuaded by the Bishop of Durham to return to the Church of England. Eventually he was made Dean of Hereford and then in 1662, Bishop of Hereford. Despite, or maybe because of his background, he carried out a vigorous campaign against Romanism.

Captain Scudamore of Kentchurch Court was appointed by the Bishop to carry out a raid on the Cwm, which he is said to have done with enthusiasm. He had already accused Henry Milbourne the Justice of the Peace who lived at Llanrothal Court of protecting the College and the Catholic community. Captain Scudamore wrote to the Bishop after the raid as follows.

All the neighbourhood do testify that this is a place to which Popish Priests do oft-times resort. Its situation without, and apartments within do testify that this is a place of habitation of such as are fearful of being discovered. It hath fair chambers to which belong a study and chairs, tables and standishes, as is usual in Colleges, and a fair Library of books which may be compared with them in the Halls and Colleges of the Universities, many of them English books against Protestant writers, as Laud, Chillingworth, Stillingfleet, etc., not yet bound. The Library was concealed with so much skill that it was difficult to discover it, and though they had time to remove it, yet we found many papers that mentioned their Society.

Bishop Croft wrote, *a short narrative of the discovery of a College of Jesuits at a place called the Combe, in the County of Hereford*, which he then sent to the Right Honourable the Lords Assembled in Parliament. This narrative, to which was added, *a true relation of the Knavery of Father Lewis, the Pretended Bishop of Llandaffe, now a prisoner in Monmouth goal*, was printed in Fleet Street, London in 1679.

In the Parish of Llanrothall, in the County of Hereford there are two houses called the Upper and Lower Comes, or Middle and Lower Comes, with a walled court before each of them, having lands belonging to them worth about three score pounds per annum. This Estate did formerly belong to Edward, Lord Marquis of Worcester, who, by lease dated 10th November, in the twelfth Year of King Charles I (1644), did let it for forescore and nineteen years to one William Morton who dying left it to one Robert Hutton, living in St Giles in the Fields, London, styled merchant, which Hutton hath by his lease, dated the second day of February 1677, and sealed and delivered in the presence of William Ireland, John Fenwick, J Groves, let the Lower Comes to one William Williams for one an twenty years at one and forty pounds per annum, and he hath likewise made a letter of Attorney to one Peter Pulton, a servant, intrusting him with the management of the profits of both the Comes, which is dated the 27th day of April 1678, and the Witnesses to it are W. Ireland, John Fenwick and William Cornelius.

One of these, a fair Genteel House, wherein there are six lodging chambers, each one a convenient study to it, with a Standish left in them, besides several other lodging rooms. The other house is also a good Country House, with several chambers and studies to some of them, all in very good repair, but the furniture now removed, we cannot yet find whither.

The remaining dwellers in the house, who were but under servants, will not confess. They are apparently perjured, for they flatly denied upon oath several things which were made out by others, and then they confessed them. There are one and twenty chimnies in both houses, and a great many doors to go in and out at, and likewise many private passages from one room to the other.

These houses are seated at the bottom of a thick woody and rocky hill, with several hollow places in the rocks, wherein men may conceal themselves and there is a very private passage from one of the houses into this wood.

In one of these houses there was a study found, the door thereof very hardly to be discovered, being placed behind a bed, and plastered over like the wall adjoining, in which was found great store of divinity Books, and others in folio and quarto, and many other lesser books, several horse-loads (but they are not yet brought to me, it being Christmas Holy Days, but they remain in a safe hand), many whereof are written by the Principal learned Jesuits. And there were found two paper books in folio, in the form of one written 'Ordinationes Variae Pro Collegio Sancti Xaverii, (Xaverius was the co-founder with Ignatuis of the Jesuits' Order, and his picture was there set up). Ordinations doth not here signify Ordination as we commonly understand it, but orders and rules sent from the Generals of the Jesuits, Caraffa and Paulus Olive, to the Jesuits here inhabiting. As also instructions from the Provincials of the Jesuits living in London unto those here.

The other paper book contains the great benefactors, being Queens, Princes, Nobles, and several others of this and divers other nations, who have contributed towards the foundation of Jesuit Colleges, or the maintenance of them, and likewise the number of Masses appointed to be said for their souls. There was also found a Latin book in folio, declaring, 'That there is in London a College dedicated to St Ignatius, with revenues belonging to it, for the Jesuit Novices in the time of Probation'. One in Wales (which I suppose are these two houses) dedicated to St. Xaverius. A third is (the book saith) 'in Staffordshire or Lancashire, dedicated to St. Aloysius, another prime Jesuit, which Colleges, when shall be reduced to the obedience of the Pope, shall never be altered', as this book directs. This printed book and the other two books in folio I have. There are about fifteen or sixteen several printed books, containing the decrees of the several congregations of that Society at Rome that contain only the rules of the Society of Jesus.

There are several books lately written and printed against the Protestant Religion, and many small Popish Catechisms, printed and tied up in a bundle, and some Welsh Popish books, but in pictures in several sheets, which pictures refer to Ribadeneira's book of Loyola's life.

There is a loose paper dated 1st March, 1652, in which directions were given that an account of the revenue and disbursements should be sent yearly to the College in Rome. It is there also mentioned that the same year there were baptized thirtyfour, reconciled to the Church of Rome, one hundred and fifty five (a great number), of those that were fallen from the church and regained, fifteen, and other matters.

One letter seems written by the Provencial to them of this house, wherein complaint is made 'that there was not care enough taken to send young men to Rome, to be there, bred up in the English College, and for which, he saith ' the Pope was much displeased, and threatened to take away their College there, and fill it up with scholars of some other nation and order'.

In one of these houses lived a mean servant called Peter Pullen, a Papist, yet intrusted with the management of these houses and estates for eight years past, as he confesseth, and was intrusted to receive a rent of £20 per annum from as estate called

Amberley, in the Parish of Monmouth, and another rent of £18 per annum from an estate called Langunville, in the Parish of Dixton, in the County of Monmouth, and to manage them also, part whereof defrayed the expenses of the college, as appears in part by an account book, where there are many leaves cut out (I suppose they had timely notice given them before the order was sent me by the House of Lords, and did therefore do this and remove what they could beforehand), and part paid in money to such Jesuit Priests as were appointed to receive it, but for these eight years that he hath been servant there he never hath made any account unto, nor held any correspondence with the said Hutton, who carrieth the name of this estate.

This Pullen names several Jesuit Priests viz., Prichard, Archer, Harris, Lewis, Price, Humphries and Draicot, who were used to resort thither, and say Mass there, but the Altar, with all the ornaments thereof, was taken down and conveyed away, only the Altar-stone remaining with five crosses cut in it, one at each corner, and one in the middle.

Two vestments, with some other small matters, were found in two boxes hid in the wood above specified. (It seems the other things were but newly removed, and they had begun also to remove the Library, for they had carried out and hid in a pig's cot adjoining about two horse-loads of books).

There were found many bottles of oil, a box of white wafers stamped, several Popish pictures and crucifixes, some relics, a little saint's bell, and an incense pot.

It doth appear by several examinations that on Sundays and Holy Days many Papists did resort to these Comes, and the greater part of Mr Milburn's family near to them, but I do not find that ever he himself frequented it.

The Cwm or Combes was financed at least in part by gifts of land and property given 'for Catholic purposes'. There was a property in Monnow Street granted and conveyed by George Milbourne of Wonastow Court. Another property in Monmouth was granted for the sustaining of certain Jesuits residing at The College of St. Xeveriius at Cwm'. A messuage and 150 acres of land and a wood called Langunville in the Parish of Dixton with an annual value of £28 was for the use of the Jesuits at the Cwm along with three gardens in Monmouth and a meadow at St. Maughans. Four houses and 250 acres of land in the Parish of Llantillio Crossenny in the occupation of Mary Pullan were given by persons unknown for support of the Jesuits at St Xaviers at The Combes, valued at £45.9s.4d, received for ten years by Peter Pullen, 'a known receiver of the Jesuits rents and profits'. Peter Pullen was steward at the Cwm between 1665 and 1681 and appears in the Hearth Tax record of 1671 for the Parish of Llanrothal as being responsible for the rates imposed on twenty chimneys at the Cwm. The Cwm income from all its various sources declined after the raid of 1679.

Although the Bishop's raid on the Cwm was the virtual end of the Jesuit College it survived for another 100 years as a Mission. In 1684 there were four priests at the Cwm, in 1712 seven missioners, in 1750 still seven missioners and in 1771 ten missioners.

Apart from missionary work, the priests were engaged in writing, translating theological and devotional treatise in Latin, Welsh and English. A few works were printed abroad and a small number of Welsh works are still extant.

THE MARTYRS

The madness engendered by the Titus Oates plot resulted in the arrest of over two thousand Roman Catholic priests. Two of these priests were from the Monnow Valley. John Arnold of Llanfihangel Court and John Scudamore of Kentchurch Court, (Plates 5&8) who were instrumental in collecting evidence against the Jesuits at the Cwm, were also busy collecting evidence against all the other Catholics in the district, in particular John Kemble and David Lewis.

John Kemble was born at Rhyd-y-Car Farm, St. Weonards in 1599 the son of George Kemble. His mother was a Morgan of Skenfrith. He was six years old when the Whitsun Riot took place. About 1620 John entered the English College in Duoai and was ordained a priest in 1625. Three months later he returned home and became an itinerant priest tramping about the well-known tracks of the Monnow Valley saying Mass and administering the sacraments in Catholic houses.

Rhyd-y-car Farm, birth place of Blessed John Kemble, 1599.

In June 1630 his brother George took a lease on Pembridge Castle in the Parish of Welsh Newton. After the damage sustained during the Civil War, George Kemble repaired the castle and the family continued to live there. Father Kemble spent much of his time with his brother's family and in his old age probably lived at Pembridge castle permanently. In a corner of the castle there is still a chapel where John Kemble said Mass.

Father Kemble was well known to John Arnold and John Scudamore and believed them to be his friends. At this point it is possible that Father Kemble could have escaped capture as friends warned him that catholic priests were being arrested. But his reply to them was that as he had not many years to live it would be an advantage to him to die for Christ rather than in his bed. So it was, that on a cold January day in 1679, an old man of almost eighty years of age was arrested by John Scudamore and taken the six miles to Kentchurch Court were he was charged and where he spent the night. John Scudamore's wife and children were Catholics and very fond of Father Kemble whom they had known all their lives. The next day he was moved to Hereford Gaol to await trial.

Kentchurch Court

John Kemble was tried at the Spring Assizes on 31st March 1679 and was indicted simply as a seminary priest charged with having offended against Statute 27 Elizabeth I, which equated being a priest ordained overseas with treason. He was found guilty and the verdict was that he should be hanged and drawn.

On 23rd April, the House of Lords ordered that John Kemble, David Lewis and two other priests who had been convicted on similar charges should be brought to London for questioning. Because of his age and infirmity this journey by horseback must have been almost unbearable. It was said that he was strapped like a pack onto his horse. On the return journey from London John Kemble was allowed to walk most of the 135 miles back to Hereford. By early June he was back in Hereford gaol and friends tried to secure a reprieve. While in prison he had many visitors, including John Scudamore's wife and children.

The date for the execution of Father Kemble was the 22nd August 1679. Before leaving prison he was asked if he had any last requests. He wished to be able to finish his prayers and to smoke a pipe for the last time. Mr Digges, the Under Sheriff sat down with him and together they smoked their pipes. Father Kemble was taken to Widemarsh Common, a place of public recreation just outside the City of Hereford bound to a hurdle on which he was dragged, feet first to the place of execution, John Kemble mounted the cart and addressed the large crowd assembled on the Common.

It will be expected I should say something but as I am an old man it cannot be much, not having any concern in the plot, neither indeed believing there is any. Oates and Bedloe not being able to charge me with anything when I was brought up in London, though they were with me makes it evident that I die only for professing the Old Roman Catholic Religion, which was the religion that first made this kingdom Christian.... I beg of all whom I have offended to forgive me for I do heartily forgive all those who have been instrumental or desirous of my death.

After he was hanged his body was cut down and beheaded but not quartered. His nephew Richard Kemble was allowed to have the body. This he placed in a coffin that was taken to Welsh Newton churchyard where it was buried at the foot of the Cross. A flat tombstone marks the grave. Father Kemble's left hand was cut off, possibly as a token of quartering. It is enclosed in a reliquary and venerated at St. Francis Xaviour's Church in Hereford. In the Roman Catholic Church in Monmouth are kept the altar, vestments and missal used by him at Pembridge Castle. Every August, on the Sunday nearest to the anniversary of his death, there is a pilgrimage to his grave. On 25th October 1970 Father Kemble, the Martyr was canonised. (Plate 21)

Jesuit priest, Father David Lewis, was born in 1616 at Aberavenny, one of nine children. His father was Principal of Abergavenny Royal Grammar School which had a reputation for producing men of scholarship. His mother was a strong Catholic.

After his parents died, possibly of the plague, David decided to enter the English College at Rome having been received into the Church of Rome during a visit to Paris. He was then twenty-one and for the next seven years studied philosophy and theology and was finally ordained in 1642.

David Lewis returned to his native Monmouthshire in 1648 and making his headquarters at Llantarnam Abbey near Newport, he visited Catholic houses over a wide area. His generosity to the poor earned him the title Tad-y-Todion, Father of the Poor. A man of learning and considerable eloquence, Father Lewis frequently preached in both English and Welsh.

Twice, during the thirty years that he spent in the area, David Lewis was Superior at the Cwm; first from 1667-1672 and then from 1674-1679 and he was in that position when he was arrested. As soon as Father Lewis realised how serious the danger was and the likelihood of the Cwm being raided, he evacuated all the priests and started hiding the evidence. Four of the six priests living at the Cwm were to die as a result of the Plot. Father Lewis had already been arrested by the time the raid was made on the Cwm by John Scudmore and the Bishop's men.

John Arnold promised an extra reward for the capture of David Lewis, in addition to that offered by the government. This proved too much of a temptation to William James, a servant of David Lewis who led six armed men to arrest him. He took Lewis to the Golden Lion Hotel in Frogmore Street, Abergaveny where William Jones, Recorder of Monmouth, examined him. Father Lewis was charged with having remained in England after taking orders in the Roman Church contrary to the law of Elizabeth's reign. William James swore he had seen the priest at Mass at least 20 times.

Having been committed on a charge of treason, Lewis was given the alternative of spending the night in a guarded room at the Golden Lion or spending the night as Arnold's guest at Llanfihangel Court. As he and Arnold were well known to each other he accepted his invitation. The next morning he was taken to Monmouth Gaol

Llanvihangel Court

where he spent two months. He was given a good lower room for which a friend paid 14/- a week inclusive of fire, candle and linen.

Many highly coloured rumours circulated about Father Lewis and some were published. A pamphlet entitled *A True Relation of the Knavery of Father Lewis* was attached to the account of Bishop Croft's raid on the Cwm. Father Lewis was supposed to have cheated a woman out of her savings by promising to free her father's soul from Purgatory. First of all he said that it would cost £100 but the woman pleaded that she only possessed £30. Lewis agreed he would do it for that, but the woman became suspicious and confided in a friend who alerted the authorities and had the priest arrested.

During May 1679, Lewis was taken to London along with Father Kemble where he was interviewed by Oates and Bedloe and once again denied any knowledge of the Plot. On 23rd May he was returned to Usk prison.

The execution of David Lewis took place on 27th August at Usk. According to tradition the place of execution was on a spot just opposite where the present Catholic Church now stands. His execution was not a popular measure and he was so well known locally that a large crowd gathered to say farewell. For his last speech he took the text from St. Peter's first Epistle. *Let non of you suffer as a murderer or as a thief; but if as a Christian, let him not be ashamed.* He declared he was dying for religion alone and felt no shame.

The gallows were a makeshift affair, so low that a trench had to be dug. In the trench beneath the gallows was placed a stool. After the rope had been put round Father Lewis's neck, the stool was removed. The body was disembowelled but not quartered. Some of those present dipped pieces of cloth into the dead man's blood to be treasured as relics. The body was given a honourable burial in Usk Parish churchyard, the crowd who had attended the execution joining the funeral procession. The grave is very near the Church porch and is covered with a large flat stone, cracked through the middle. No inscription can now be read on this stone but in recent years a replica has been placed alongside this original stone bearing an inscription describing Father Lewis's martyrdom and his canonization. (Plate 22)

Grave of David Lewis, Usk Parish Church

On Sunday 25th October 1970, in the Basilica of Saint Peter in Rome, there was a Solemn Canonization of the Forty Blessed Martyrs of England and Wales by the Holy Father, Paul VI. During the Mass of Canonization, the Westminster Cathedral Choir sang music by William Bird (1543-1623), himself a staunch Catholic and persistent recusant. The Westminster Choir were especially honoured on this occasion, to be permitted to substitute for the Sistine Choir. And so John Kemble and David Lewis, who were executed for their religious beliefs, became numbered among the Saints.

Another priest who had a warrant issued for his arrest by the Justices of the Peace during the Titus Oates panic was Father Andrews. He is described as a Jesuit, although according to Mr Levett he was a secular priest, his name not appearing in any of the Society's lists at that time.

Father Andrews is described as living at Hardwick, which is just south of Abergavenny near the river Usk. He also lived with his brother Thomas at Skenfrith and when threatened with arrest he escaped into the Darren woods where he stayed for about three months. A narrative of the escape and subsequent death of Father Andrews was given in a letter written on 2nd July 1679 to a friend in London and was signed J.D. Skenfrith. Later that year this letter was printed in a pamphlet and no doubt sold to a public eager to read about the evil Jesuits.

A TRUE NARRATIVE

Of that Grand

JESVITE

Father Andrews;

Who Lived at *Hardwick*

IN

MONMOUTHSHIRE

How he Fled into a Large WOOD to Escape

JUSTICE.

How he came to an Untimely END, and the Manner of his

BURIAL.

In a Letter to a Friend in London.

LONDON,

Printed in the Year, 1679.

A True NARRATIVE Of that Grand JESUITE Father Andrews, &c.

SIR,

I Have here given you a Short but Perfect Account of one Father *Andrews* a Jesuit, sometimes Inhabiting at a place called *Hardwick* in *Monmouth-shire*, and sometimes at his Brothers, *Thomas Andrews*'s House in the Parish of *Skenfreth*, about eight Miles distant from *Hardwick* in the same County. Upon the Discovery of the late Plot, Warrants being issued out by several Justices of the Peace, for the Apprehending of the said Father *Andrews*; so that he was forced to abscond from those places above mentioned, and fled into an adjacent Wood, where he lay *Incognito*, for the space of Three Months and upwards; his Food being conveyed to him by a Servant Boy, which his Brother sent daily to him. He finding that place not to agree well with his Constitution, one *Hills* a Priest and a Visiter of his, got him a Private Lodging in a poor Widdows House, whose name was *Jane Harris*. *Hills* came often to Visit him during the space of three or four Days. The poor Woman was imployed by *Hills* to go several times to a Butchers, (who lived in a small Village about half a Mile distant) to buy Meat for Father *Andrews*; she was not to buy much at a time, because he must have it Fresh and Fresh; the sight of a Large Joint was enough to have taken away his Stomack, being a weakly man, and much stricken in Years. This Butcher taking notice of this Poor Womans coming so often to him to buy Meat, which formerly she did not use to do: for she was not in a Condition to buy it for her self; he took an occasion to ask her who it was for; She ingeniously confessed, that it was for an Antient Gentleman who was newly come to lodge at her house; whereupon the Butcher suspecting that he must be either a Priest or a Jesuit, presently went to one Mr. *Arnal* a Justice of the Peace, (and a great Prosecutor of the Papists) and gave him Information what the Woman had said, upon which Mr. *Arnal* went himself with several of his Servants, and some Neighbours to search the House; but old Father *Andrews*, having some private notice of it,

made

(4)

made his Escape before they came. The Widdow Woman was examined what became of the Old Gentleman which Lodged at her House; she said he was newly gone, but whither she did not know, he was a Stranger to her, and had been there but four days. The Justice Committed the Woman to the Common Goal of *Oske*, for the said County, where she now remains. After this Escape Mr. *Arnal* could hear no more of him, till about the 27th of *June* last; and then a Farmer living at *Wengothan* near *Abergaveny*, who having occasion to lay some Hay in a Barn of his, which was formerly a Chappel belonging to some Abby or Priory; and there clearing away some old Stubble-Straw to make room for the Hay, under which he found a place digg'd like a Grave, and newly filled up; whereupon he was at first surprised, and could not tell what to do, at last he thought it his best way to go to a Justice of the Peace, and Inform him of it, supposing somebody might have been Murthered and Buried there. The Justice presently Ordered the place to be searched; and there they found the Corps of a Man who had been newly Buried; he had no Coffin, only a Sheet wrapt about him, with a Cross made of Wax on his Stomach, with several *Beads*, *Crucifixes*, and other *Romish* Fopperies about him. Then presently the *Coroner* was sent for, and called a Jury of *Inquest*, who sate and found the Body had been poysoned, for it was very much swell'd. The Body was exposed to publick view, for two or three days; in which time it was discovered, that it was the Body of the aforesaid Father *Andrews* the Jesuite. Search was presently made, to see if they could find out how he came to be Buried in that place, and how he came to his End; but it could not be done, so that 'tis thought he was privately conveyed thither in the Night, and there Buried, because it was Antiently a Religious Place. This is a Just Account.

I am,

Skenfrith, July the
2d. 1679.

Sir,

Your Humble Servant,

J. D.

MATTHEW PRITCHARD

The appointment of a Roman Catholic Bishop and the formation of some kind of formal structure for the Catholics was one of the lasting achievements of James II during his short reign. The question he faced was should he appoint a Bishop in Ordinary or a Vicar Apostolic?

Initially James was against the appointment of a Vicar Apostolic as it would be 'directly against the King's command; very offensive to the state; provided against by our ancient laws; and extremely dangerous to the Catholics of England'. (*Manusc. of Kirk's Church History in the Westminster Archives*). James asked the Chapter for a clear explanation of the difference between a Vicar Apostolic and a Bishop in Ordinary.

By a Bishop who is an Ordinary is meant one who hath power in Himselfe to govern the flock over which he is sett, according to the common received Rules or Canons of the church and is not revocable at pleasure. On the contrary a Vicar is one who hath no power himselfe, but only the Use or Exercise of the power of the Person whose substitute he is (e.g. an Ambassador or the like); so that what he does, he does not by his own power, but by the Power of the Person he represents, to whom therefore he is at all time accountable as using purely his Power, and both that and himselfe revocable at pleasure. (Westminster Archives).

THE FOUR DISTRICTS

A Bishop took his title from the territory he governed, his See, but a Vicar Apostolic, since they were not 'ordinaries' of their territory were given Sees in other parts of the world, usually Asia Minor and they had neither cathedrals nor chapters. So one of the main reasons against the appointment of a Vicar Apostolic was 'that the King's spiritual and ecclesiastical concerns would lie exposed to the will of a foreign court; his plans might be revealed and his will thwarted; and he would be ill-served as a Vicar Apostolic would be chiefly devoted to the Pope'. (*Westminster Archives*). However, the Holy See considered it would be highly imprudent to appoint a Bishop so long as the Penal Laws were in force in England and Wales.

To begin with, just one Vicar Apostolic was appointed but the overseeing of the whole country proved too much for one man and a request was sent to Rome for more help. The outcome was that in 1688 England and Wales were divided into four districts each of which was given its own Vicar Apostolic.

The London District included all the Home Counties and stretched as far afield as Bedfordshire and Berkshire; the Northern district comprised all England between the Humber and the Tweed; the Midland District filled the area between the London District and the Northern District and the Western District stretched from the west coast of Wales to Wiltshire. Three new Vicars Apostolic were appointed; Bishop James Smith to the Northern District, Bishop Bonadventure Gifford to the Midland District, Dr Leyburn, the original appointee to remain in the London District and Bishop Philip Ellis to the Western District.

This was a sensational event and King James was determined to carry out the consecration of these new Bishops with maximum publicity and splendour. Bishop Gifford was consecrated in the banqueting hall of Whitehall on 22nd April 1688 as Bonadventure, Bishop of Madura, V.A; Bishop Ellis at St James' Palace on 6th May as Philip, Bishop of Aureliople, V.A.; Bishop Smith at Somerset House (then a palace) on 13th May as James, Bishop of Gallipoli, V.A. and Dr Leyburn as John, Bishop of Adramite, V.A.

For just a few short months before the Glorious Revolution of 1688, the future of the Catholic religion looked rosy. The four Vicars Apostolic issued a joint pastoral letter to all the faithful of England. Little did they know that so soon the Church would once again be outlawed and persecution begin

We are concerned, of course, with the Western district. Bishop Ellis was a Benedictine monk, the third son of a Protestant clergyman. He had converted to Catholicism while still a schoolboy at Westminster School and went on to become a monk. He was appointed chaplain to James II when he was Duke of York. It was because of the high esteem in which James held him that he was appointed to the Western district and shortly after his appointment the revolution and the invasion of William of Orange put paid to his plans. Along with Bishop Gifford he was imprisoned in Newgate. On his release he left the country and despite repeated efforts to return to govern his Vicarate he was refused permission to do so by Rome. By 1708 he had been Bishop for 20 years without ever having visited his Vicariate and so he resigned.

The western district was to remain vacant for another ten years. This was mainly because of the controversy between the secular and the regular clergy. Secular clergy are priests who live in the general community as distinct from regular clergy who are members of a religious order and are bound by their rules.

Matthew Prichard was suggested as a possible Bishop for the Western District, an area that was very remote and poverty stricken. The other Bishops were not too keen on this appointment. Matthew Pritchard was a Franciscan monk and they did not approve of a 'regular' becoming a Bishop, feeling that he may have a conflict of loyalty between his duty to his See and his duty to his religious order. The Bishops also considered that the appointment should go to a man of private means as the appointment was not remunerated and the expenses considerable.

In 1713 Rome appointed Father Matthew Pritchard as Bishop of the Western District. He was the first 'regular' to rule in England since the Reformation and the Western District, at last, had a resident Bishop of its own twenty-five years after the setting up of the Vicariate.

Matthew Pritchard was born in 1669 at the Graig in the parish of Cross Ash. This was an ancient house (now mainly rebuilt) on the slopes of the Graig Saerfyrddyn Mountain. He made his noviciate at St Bonadventures, the Franciscan monastery at Douay and returned to his home in the Monnow Valley to become a missioner at Perthir. Although he was appointed as Vicar Apostolic in 1713 it was not until 1715, in a ceremony at Cologne, that he was consecrated Bishop.

Matthew Pritchard worked hard and in great poverty to organise the Western district and remained living at Perthir during his long period in office. After thirty-seven years as Bishop he died at Perthir on 22nd May 1750. He was buried under the communion table of the local parish church of Rockfield. The following letter from Father Abbott was quoted in the Catholic Record Society (ix,165) and tells how a 20th century parish priest of Rockfield almost succeeded in removing all trace of Matthew Pritchard's grave. (Plate 28)

The late incumbent was a bigoted parson. In doing some repairs to the church he had this (tombstone) and two other Catholic tombstones removed, and offered for sale as waste materials! This I heard from some of the Protestant parishioners; so I walked over, and saw the stones reared against the boundary wall. The vicar happened to call upon me, with his wife, a few days after on some business; so I asked him why he had removed the Bishop's tombstone. He said he did not think it right to have a 'Romish' bishop's tombstone there. I said, 'Are you not going to replace it?' He replied, 'no, certainly not.' Then I said, ' I will write to my friend the Rev. Dr. Oliver of Exeter, who has published the history of Bishop Pritchard with a full description of his Lordship's burial there and the inscription on the stone, and I will get him to put a footnote in the next edition to the effect that, through the bigotry of the Rev. – this monument was removed in such a year.' He then said he would have it replaced immediately. I said, 'If you don't I will hand down your name to posterity like Pontius Pilate's in the Creed'. It had been replaced, and his successor, I am told, still repeats the anecdote to visitors.

Bishop Matthew Pritchard's successors were

Lawrence William York	O.S.B	1750
Charles Walmsley	O.S.B.	1763
William Sharrock	O.S.B.	1797
Peter Collingridge	O.F.M.	1809
Peter Baines	O.S.B.	1829
William Ullathorn	O.S.B.	1846
Joseph Hendren	O.S.F.	1848

O.S.B. Order of Saint Benedict
O.F.M. Order of Friars Minor

O.S.F.   Order of Saint Francis.

In 1740 Monmouth and Hereford were taken out of the Western District to form the Welsh District and the first Vicar Apostolic of the Welsh District was Thomas Joseph Brown O.S.B. who lived at Chepstow. Monmouth Catholic Church was opened in 1793 and its first priest was Fr. William Sharrock who became Vicar Apostolic of the Welsh District in 1797.

The Catholic religion survived in the border country. There were still 440 named recusants in the county of Monmouthshire in 1771 compared with 541 in 1676. The area was backward, undeveloped and poor agriculturally with very bad communication. There were no large urban centres with their influences and Welsh was the most common language spoken. Many, if not all of the landed aristocracy were Catholic and their servants and tenants tended to follow their lead. In the first part of the 18th century the two greatest landowners, the Earl of Worcester and Lord Abergavenny were both recusants. Many of the local families like the Vaughans of Courtfield, the Milbournes of Wonastow and Llanrothal and the Jones of Llanarth were resident locally and although not wealthy had enormous influence. It is in the homes of these families that the centres of Catholic worship survived, and in the Monnow Valley the Catholic faith was never really lost. Not being able to erect chapels, worship had to be in private houses, for example in an upstairs room in the Robin Hood Inn in Monnow Street, Monmouth.

The first Catholic Relief Act of 1778 exempted Catholics from most of the penalties to which they were still liable, provided they took the Oath of Allegiance. By 1773 a new chapel had been built in Monmouth. In 1829 the Catholic Emancipation Act was passed giving Catholics the same privileges as those attending Protestant churches.

Within fifteen years of the Act a Catholic church was being built in the Monnow Valley. The remote site chosen was on a steep hill between Skenfrith and Cross Ways.

Not everyone was happy about the Catholic Emancipation Act of 1829 as is shown by this contribution to the Monmouthshire Beacon of 10th February 1838.

' OUR CHURCH' AND 'NO SURRENDER'
Tis now the hour when Popish power
For desperate conflict rallies,
And flings her brand throughout the land
And pours her poisoned chalice.
Now, Britons! now, with dauntless brow,
Back, bold defiance send her;
And swell the cry through earth and sky,
"Our church – and no surrender!"

Remembering all the bloodstained thrall
Of Popish persecution,
O! may ye feel the martyrs zeal
Inspire your resolution!
Yours native land now calls your hand
From slavery to defend her-
Let earth and sky ring back the cry
"Our church – and no surrender"

Shall Priests regain their iron reign,
Our holy churchmen dooming
To rope and rack, to sword and stake,
And molten fires consuming?
To Jesuit knaves shall we be slaves,
Or trust their mercies tender?
No! whilst on high is heard the cry,
"Our church – and no surrender?

Her altars pure shall long endure,
By bigotry unshrouded;
And sacred shine, in light divine,
The shrines of faith unclouded.
As nought on earth can raise her worth
Nor greater glories land her,
So loud be heard our rallying word
"Our church- and no surrender"

Through traitors base her fame disgrace,
O'erawed by mob-debaters,
And dastard flee, or bend the knee
To rebel agitators;
Our maiden Queen enthroned is seen
Our glorious faith's defender,
And raises high the patriot cry
"Our church- and no surrender"

'Perthir'

COED ANGHRED

There were three places in the neighbourhood of Skenfrith where Mass continued to be said during those "horrible days"; the Grove now called New House Farm in Newcastle, Old Hilston and the Graig, Cross Ash. It was to gather up the remnants of these missions that St Mary's Church Coed Anghred was built. It was situated just off a narrow lane that leads uphill from Skenfrith towards Cross Ways known as Lint Lane. The land on which to build a Catholic Church was given by the third Viscount Southwell, (pronounced 'Suthell'). Viscount Southwell was an influential landowner in the area. Through his wife Jane, the daughter of John Berkley of Hinlip, Worcestershire, he had inherited the Manor of Garway.

St. Mary's Church was built with money given by a sole benefactor whose name appears on the inside front cover of the Church Register. This man was Mr William Constable Middleton of Middleton Lodge, Middleton near Ilkley, Yorkshire. The Middleton family had been associated with Ilkley for hundreds of years. William was born about 1763 and died in 1847. In 1825 he built a chapel and established a burial ground at Middleton Lodge that was opened in a ceremony performed by the Rev. Dr Baines of Bath who was soon to become Vicar Apostolic of the Western District.

Although it is difficult to understand why an elderly man from Yorkshire should pay to have a church built in the remote village of Skenfrith, there are certain rather tenuous connections that may be significant.

The most influential Catholics in the Monnow Valley area at that time were, Thomas Wakeman, Viscount Southwell, the Jones family of Llanarth, and the Rev. Thomas Burgess, priest at Monmouth Catholic Church. William Middleton's eldest brother married the daughter of Edward Wakeman of Beckford, Worcestershire. Thomas Wakeman was a solicitor and land surveyor who practised in Gloucester before he came to live in Skenfrith, so it is quite possible that he was of the same family as Edward Wakeman. Thomas was born in 1791, the son of Charles Wakeman who had at one time been steward to the Jones' of Llanarth. Thomas Wakeman bought the Graig in 1839 but he had held land in the Skenfrith area since 1834. He was a keen local historian and intended to publish a history of Momouthshire.

Another member of the Middleton family was connected by marriage to the Jones of Llanarth. William Middleton's son Peter and two of his nephews were vice presidents of the Society of David, a mission dedicated to restoring the blessings of the true religion to Wales. Another of the Vice Presidents was Viscount Southwell.

The Rev Thomas Burgess was appointed as priest at Monmouth Catholic Church in 1836. He was asked by Bishop Baines to set up a school and Herbert and Roger Vaughan of Courtfield became his pupils, one a future Bishop and the other a Cardinal. Thomas Burgess's nephew was Father Abbott who was to become the first priest at Coed Anghred. The Catholic Directory for 1845 reads-

Coedangrol, Skenfrith. A chapel is being built here, and a mission is contemplated for the sake of the remnants of three former congregations in this part of Monmouthshire.

The foundation stone of what turned out to be an example of typical English parish church architecture, was blessed and laid on August 1st 1844 by the Vicar General of the Welsh District, the Very Rev. Dr Thomas F Rooker. The builder was Mr C Lawrence of Monmouth, who was also responsible for building the Infant School in St Mary's Street Monmouth in 1838, the Congregational Church in Glendower Street in 1844 and for restoring the Naval Temple on the Kymin in 1851. The Church was registered with the Quarter Sessions at Usk on March 13th 1846, 'as a place of congregation or assembly for religious worship'. The name of the Church was ' the Church of the Immaculate Conception of the Blessed Virgin Mary'.

After two years the church was finished and on 5th September 1846 there was a notice in the Monmouthshire Merlin advertising the opening of the church.

*The solemn dedication
of the
New Catholic Church at Coed Anghred
Near Skenfrith, Monmouthshire*

Is fixed for the 22nd September. All clergymen attending the procession are requested to bring with them a cassock and surplice.

Morning service. High Mass, Coram Pontifice, will commence at Eleven a.m., Sermon after the Gospel, by the right Rev. Bishop Brown V.A.W

Afternoon service. Vespers and Benediction at Three p.m. Sermon by the Very Rev. Dr Rooker, V.G.

Cards of admission, 5s. 2s.6d. and 2s may be had of Mr T Dubberley, silversmith, Agincourt Square, Monmouth; or at the church on the morning of the dedication.

There are three Inns, Good Stabling, in the village of Skenfrith, near the church.

Refreshments will be provided in the Schoolroom adjoining by Mr Evans, White Swan, Monmouth.

The opening was extensively reported in the Monmouthshire Beacon and the *Catholic Directory* for 1847 described St Mary's as a –'beautiful church, with a good mission house and school house adjoining', but it also added that the means to support the incumbent as yet wanting.

Thomas Wakeman of the Great Graig House sent the following items to the church for the use of the mission, unless he should want them: a silver chalice and paten, one corporal, two mundatories, one alb, amice and girdle, two vestments (one white, one green), two altar stones and one missal.

The following week a full description of the opening ceremony was reported in the Monmouth Beacon.

OPENING OF THE CHURCH OF THE IMMACULATE CONCEPTION OF THE B.V.M.OF COEDANGRA, NEAR SKENFRITH, MONMOUTHSHIRE.

This beautiful church, situated on an eminence above the village of Skenfrith, was solemnly dedicated on Tuesday, the 22nd inst., by the Rt. Rev. Dr. Brown, Bishop of Apolonia V.A. of the Welsh district, assisted by a number of the clergy. Hitherto, the Catholics scattered over this tract of the country, the remnants of congregations, that

The Catholic Church of St Mary's, Coed Anghred, Skenfrith.   W. Price

at no very distant period had their own pastors and chapels, have been deprived, in great measure, of the consolations of religion, by their great distance from any place of worship, and it is lamentable to see how many have in consequence broken away. It may easily be imagined, therefore, with what satisfaction those who still retained feelings of religion, watched the progress of the new building, and with what eagerness they crowded to the ceremony of the dedication. So great was the number that attended from the neighbouring congregations to witness a scene so pleasing in the eyes of faith, that scarcely half of them could gain admittance, though the church was completely crowded. Amongst the company present were Lord Southwell, William Jones Esq, of Clytha, Miss Jones, Messrs Philip, Edward and Wyburn Jones of Lanarth, Mr And Mrs Plowden from Rotherwas, Mr and Mrs Monington from Sarsefield, Mrs Witham, Miss Salvin; the choice of music was most select, and the choir under the skilful management of Mr Henry Field, of Bath was most effective. Miss Whitnall, of Liverpool, whose first ideas on the true character of church music everyone must acknowledge by her powerful tones and pure enunciation of religious feelings, told forcibly upon a people bent down in the solemn act of worship, and the effect was what alone should be aimed at, admiration lost in devotion.

Before eleven o'clock the bell sent forth its tone from the castellated tower, and every place was occupied; the procession advanced from the sacristy, outside the church, to the west entrance chanting the Quam delicia Tabernacula, psalm 83; and passing through the midst of the assembled multitudes, formed around the altar, and the service began. High mass was sung by the Rev. Thomas Shattock, of Prior Park, assisted by the Rev J Dawson of Courtfield, and Rev Wm. Woolett, of Pontypool, as Deacon and Sub-deacon. The Rev J Bonimi acting as master of ceremonies. After the gospel, his lordship, in cope and mitre, advanced to the centre of the altar, and preached a most impressive sermon from 2 Cor.c.6, v.16, "For you are the temple of the living God". After illustrating the zeal of the faithful of all ages in decorating material temples dedicated to divine worship, he took occasion of the spiritual temples of the holy ghost in the souls of men, which it was if infinitely more consequence to decorate by the practice of every Christian virtue, in order to fit them for heaven.

After the high mass there was an elegant cold collation laid out in the new schoolroom by Mr Evans of the White Swan, Monmouth. The poor members of Christ were not forgotten on this occasion, a liberal charity being distributed to about one hundred and twenty of the most needy, "lest they should faint by the way, some having come from afar." The evening service was chanted alternately by the choir and the officiating clergy at the altar with very pleasing effect. The very reverend Dr Rooker, V.G. of Wales, preached an eloquent sermon from Luke 10, v.23, 'Blessed are the eyes that see the things which you see;' showing that the blessing of our Saviour's coming was not confined to those whom he was them addressing, but intended for all future generations to the end of the world; and that his present hearers had great reason to rejoice at the additional opportunity of having the ancient faith of this country, which was the same which Christ and his apostles taught, preached amongst them, and the holy sacraments left by Christ to his church, administered to them. The whole was concluded with the solemn benediction of the Blessed Sacrament; the people separated delighted with what they had seen and heard. The edifice was erected by Mr C Lawrence, builder, of this town, and evinced great taste and ability. It is of the early English order of architecture, and was much admired by the congregation.

Coed Anghred narrowly missed being a place of great importance. In 1852 Joseph Brown the Catholic Bishop of Apollinia and Vicar General of the newly formed Welsh district, was looking for somewhere to build the Cathedral Chapter of Newport. Sites were offered at Chepstow, Usk, Pool Hall and at Courtfield. Among these offers was one to build at Coed Anghred. The final place chosen was at Belmont in Hereford on land given by Mr Wegg-Prosser where Belmont Abbey was built in1859.

When St Mary's Church was built in 1846, provision was made for a resident priest with a house, a school and stables. As a school was built it can be assumed that local catholic children attended to be taught by the priest. The nearest other school in the district was Norton Cross that was originally built as a non-conformist British School. It was not until 1870 that the Elementary Education Act was passed and public education became available to all children at government schools. Fees had to be paid according to age either 3d, 2d or 1d a week. This, combined with the loss of wages from their children, caused great hardship to many parents. It was not until 1891 that contributions towards the cost of elementary education were abolished.

Unlike the children at the elementary school, the children at the catholic school at Coed Anghred received their education free. The Headmaster of Norton Cross school wrote in the school diary on 11th February 1881.

Several children left school since Christmas on account of school fees being raised a penny in the upper standards, they have gone to the Catholic School receiving their education free.
4th March 1881. E Burrows returned on Monday from Catholic School, and on Tuesday he brought his school fees, 2d instead of 3d, so according to the Board's direction, I sent him home for the penny.

In 1881 the Attendance Officer reported that he could not ascertain the number of times the children attended the Roman Catholic School at 'Coed Dangler'. On being asked for the numbers the priest wrote to say that he kept a register that was open to inspection. The Catholic school probably merged with Norton Cross in 1904.

This was not the only school at Coed Anghred. For a short time a much more ambitious project was envisaged. An article marked 'From an unknown newspaper, August 1880.' was sent to Mary Hopson of Tregate Castle from Mill Hill which she kindly passed on to me.

This school was opened at Coed Anghred, near Monmouth, on the Feast of Our Lady's Assumption (August 15th). The object of this school is to prepare for the higher studies at Mill Hill any youth who has a strong desire to study for the foreign missions, in preference to home missions and who is at least sixteen and not more than twenty years of age, has a sound English education and is in good health. The school is placed under the guardianship of Father Marianus, the worthy pastor of Coed Anghred, who laboured for seventeen years in the Foreign Missions. The school commences in the presbytery with four students and a teacher, all of them from Lancashire. To the great delight of the fervent little congregation of Coed Anghred the inauguration of the school was the occasion of a somewhat, to them unusual solemnity. The altar of this beautiful church was decked in its best. F Marianus, attended by the Rector of Mill Hill College and the new students, entered the church by the front door during the singing of the 'Ave Maris Stella'. After the 'Asperges' there was a 'Missa Cantata', as there was sufficient musical talent among the students to sing Webb's Mass in G. The rector of St Joseph's College, Mill Hill, preached, after the Gospel, on the object of the Feast of the Assumption of the Blessed Virgin. He addressed the congregation again in the afternoon after Vespers. He earnestly exhorted them to second by their prayers the important work which was being inaugurated in their midst; and as a mission was about to be given to them by the Capuchin Fathers, he entreated them to act as Apostles by bringing all their friends to come and hear the true word of God. The ceremony terminated with solemn Benediction

There were five students, three entered in August and September and the other two the following May, 1881. There were two teachers. James Hanifan and Richard Joseph O'Halloran who was appointed Master of Discipline in October 1880. Richard Joseph O'Halloran was Irish, born in Cork in 1856. He studied at Dublin and Fermoy and entered Mill Hill in 1875. He was appointed a Deacon in 1880. It would seem that he did not stay long at Coed Anghred. Allegations about his reckless and impulsive behaviour towards some of his students began to reach his superior in London. Despite this, he was ordained priest as a member of the Mill Hill Fathers in December 1880. The logbook of the Society records that O'Halloran left the Society in January 1881. He had been at Coed Anghred for less than three months.

One of the students was a young man from Lancashire called Joseph Cunningham. He was born in 1865, ordained a priest in 1889 and then spent many years in Northeast India as a missionary. Later in his life he wrote his autobiography in which he refers to himself as Austin. He died in 1942 aged seventy-six. This is his description of his arrival at Coed Anghred.

At three o'clock in the afternoon the train drew up at Monmouth station where Austin and his companion alighted. Canon Benoit, who had come from London for the opening of the preparatory college, was on the platform with another priest. This other priest was in charge of the mission where the first apostolic school was to be temporarily opened, the mission of Coed Anghred, some nine miles' walk from Monmouth. There was no railway, so Austin did his first missionary trudge the first day he left home. The party reached Coed Anghred about half past six in the evening. The two youths received a hearty welcome from two other students who were already there, and from a professor who, for the present, was going to inaugurate the course of studies, pending the arrival of another professor or two from Mill Hill. Surely a small community and a humble beginning for a work which has expended so wonderfully!

After a hearty supper and a short but pleasant recreation, the small community assembled in the quaint old church for short night prayers, and by nine o'clock that night, poor Austin, after all his sorrow and fatigue of this eventful day of his life, lay down to rest and slept most peacefully and soundly, until the bell rang next morning for morning prayers. How strange it felt this Sunday morning away from home, and how hard he prayed during the early community mass for his dear father and mother at home! The early part of the morning was occupied in the usual college devotions, breakfast, and recreation. At eleven o'clock there was the parochial sung mass, preceded by procession and prayers, to call down God's blessing on the work of the apostolic school. The priest of the Coed Anghred mission, who was going to act as rector, sang the mass; and Canon Benoit preached a short sermon, explaining to the small congregation of barely twenty souls, the importance of the missionary enterprise which was being inaugurated in their midst, on this beautiful feast of the Assumption of the Blessed Virgin

When the apostolic school had been in existence for about one month a strange event took place. The priest of Coedanghred thought it would be an excellent idea to have a mission preached in the parish. He accordingly brought down from Chester an Irish Capuchin father to conduct the services; and obtained from one of our large Catholic depots some ten or twelve pounds' worth of religious articles to be sold, as usual, at the church door. The mission was to be opened on a Saturday evening. When the Capuchin father emerged from the sacristy to inaugurate the mission, he was startled to notice that the congregation in the body of the church consisted of one old woman and two children. He forthwith announced that he thought a hymn would suffice for that occasion, and that the mission services would begin the next day.

The next day, Sunday, a large number of persons came to the parochial mass, but they were mostly members of the Monmouth congregation, who had driven over to hear the students of the new college sing, and hear the strange new priest preach. Monday, Tuesday, Wednesday and Thursday passed, and scarcely anyone came to the mission. On Friday the good missionary father departed for his home in Chester observing that this mission at Coedanghred was the queerest he had ever been called on the preach.

After this, Austin proceeded without any interruption with his studies, except for a week's retreat in preparation for the feast of St Joseph. The scholastic year came to a close at the end of the following June; and, as it had been decided to discontinue the work of the apostolic school at such an out-of-the-way place as Coedanghred, and to reopen nearer London, Austin was allowed to go home to Manchester for the Midsummer vacation. The school's stay at Coedanghred had been short lived as a document from Mill Hill shows,

The school has been transferred from Coedanghred to Kelvedon in Essex. The little secluded mission of Coedanghred, among the hills of Monmouthshire, was well adapted for an Apostolic School. Moreover His Lordship the Bishop of Newport and Menevia and his Chapter were quite agreeable to let us have the full use of the premises and the land attached to them. But it would have necessitated a considerable outlay of money for the purpose of enlarging the presbytery. This has been providentially avoided by the offer of Kelvedon.

From that time on there was a slow decline in the attendance at St Mary's Church. One of the main problems had always been the 'means adequate to support an incumbent'. There were seven incumbents between 1880 and 1900 and the Catholic population in the district was declining. A statement dated 10th June 1907 was sent from the Diocese of Newport to the Prior of Belmont Abbey.

The Church of St Mary, Coedagnhred, Skenfrith, was opened in the year 1848. It was built, not by the subscriptions of the faithful, or by public collections, but with money given to the Rev Thomas Abbot by a single benefactor. Coedanghred is six miles from Monmouth, and is situated in a scantily populated and inaccessible district, about a mile from the small country village of Skenfrith. There is no railway station nearer than Monmouth. The reason why the church and presbytery were built in this solitary place was that at that time there were, as I am told, some five or six Catholic farmers round about, the neighbourhood being then owned, as it is yet by a Catholic proprietor. The Late Lord Southwell, who then owned the estate, endowed it to the extent of £100. Other small investments by Fr. Abbott and the rent of a few acres of glebe, bring the endowment up to about £90 or £100 a year.

A Catholic cemetery adjoining the Church was established about 1847, and there are a good many interments. It was very soon perceived that there would never be any congregation. The Catholic farmers gradually disappeared. There is now one such family living about two miles away. This is nearly the whole congregation. The average attendance at Mass on Sundays is seven. The loneliness of the presbytery makes it difficult for the priest to keep a housekeeper, or to supply himself with coals etc. The Bishop has been obliged to accept the services of any priest who would consent to live there, with the results too often of the most unsatisfactory nature.

What the Bishop now proposes, is to sell the land and buildings (the latter, including the Church, would probably be pulled down) and apply the proceeds, together with the endowment, to the founding of a new Mission in the neighbourhood. The cemetery, of course, would be reserved, the enclosure wall made secure and the cemetery itself, although closed for interments, reverently looked after.

Finally, in 1910 St Mary's Church Coed Anghred was closed. The last recorded marriage in May 1910 was of, (rather appropriately), Margaret Bennett of the Darren, the place where all those years ago in 1605, the Bishop of Hereford had tried to stop the Catholics gathering for Mass. The last funeral and a baptism were in July 1910.

The Church was not demolished until after the First World War and part of the Presbytery remained standing until the 1950's. The only building now remaining is part of the coach house. Some of the stone taken from the Church was used to secure the churchyard walls and some was taken to the nearby mansion of Hilston. It is understood that stone was taken to Pembridge Castle which had been bought in 1912 by Dr Hedley Bartlett and was being extensively restored.

It was some years before another Roman Catholic Chapel was built in the district. I have been told that for a time Mass was held in a room at the Broad Oak Inn and before that at a bungalow which was built in 1907 by the remaining members of the Catholic church at Lint Hill. This building was converted to licensed premises in 1965 and extended in 1972 and called the Priory Motel. The Motel closed down in 1996 and the building was finally demolished in 1997. By the 1930's the Roman Catholic Chapel, a rather plain wooden building was built at Broad Oak and is still in use today.

It is not easy to find what is now left of St Mary's Church. About half a mile up a steep lane known as Lint Hill that runs from Skenfrith to Crossways, there is a track off to the left. Here is a footpath sign with a chained swan showing that this is part of the Monnow Valley Walk. To the right of this track are some rusted railings and the remains of some broken steps where the entrance drive to the church commenced. When I visited the site a few years ago, the churchyard was completely overgrown and it was impossible to see any sign of the tombstones that had been painstakingly recorded by Mary Hopson in 1984. (Plates 23,24) All evidence of the church had been obliterated. It was therefore a very pleasant surprise to find, on a recent visit, that the owners of the churchyard had erected new fences and cleared away all the brambles and nettles. Most of the tombstones are too weathered to read and many are fallen down or leaning over, but it is possible to see the last remaining evidence of a Catholic edifice in the Monnow Valley.

Coed Anghred Burial Ground

Roman Catholic Church, Broad Oak, Garway

DAN-Y-GRAIG CATHOLIC CHAPEL

On the slopes of the Graig Syfyriddin in the area know as Cwmbaddwr, the valley of the Baddwr, a private Catholic chapel was built around 1870. This was at Dan-y-Graig a house bought by Captain Godfrey Radcliffe, the younger son of Sir Joseph Radcliffe of Rudding Park, Yorkshire. The house had many fine oak carvings and a cabinet alleged to once have been the property of Lady Jane Grey. A report on the opening of this chapel was given in 'The Tablet' on October 16th 1869.

Amidst some of the most beautiful scenery of Monmouthshire, about four miles from the pretty village of Grosmont, there stands a large solitary house, the property and residence of Godfrey Radcliffe, Esq.

Farmhouses and cottages lie grouped at various distances around it; but churches, chapels, and meeting-houses, so thickly scattered in other parts of the country, are not to be seen in this neighbourhood, and the inhabitants seem hitherto to have lived and died without any form of religion whatsoever.

When Mr Radcliffe first brought his family to Dan-y-Graig a few years ago, he was much struck with the spiritual desolation by which he was surrounded. He himself could drive over on Sundays to the nearest Catholic Church, that at Coedanghred, about six miles distant, but his poorer neighbours had no means of satisfying their spiritual needs, and perhaps, from long indifference, scarcely knew they had any. However, some of them told him that if he would build a church they would all come to worship in it.

Such an opportunity of gathering these straying souls into the sheepfold of the church was not to be lost, and Mr Radcliffe determined to do all in his power to satisfy the desires thus awakened, and to find means to "feed these men with bread here in the wilderness".

First of all he fitted up a chapel in his own house, and arranged with the Superior of the Franciscan Monastery at Pontypool, that one of the Fathers from that place should go over to Dan-y-Graig every week to offer the Holy Sacrifice of the Mass on Sundays, and give religious instruction to the people who attended. He then set to work to build a church, in which, after so many years of desolation, men might worship God according to the ancient Faith.

This church, after many sacrifices and much exertion on Mr Radcliffe's part, and with the assistance of several kind friends, was completed a few weeks ago, and was solemnly opened for Divine Worship on the 6th October, within the Octave of St Francis. It is a plain, substantial Gothic building of stone, and consists of a nave and chancel. The high altar, with the tabernacle and throne for the Blessed Sacrament, is of stone, beautifully carved (the work of Mr Radcliffe's own hand), and stands out fair and white, instinctively reminding the worshipers of the first pure altar on which Jesus was adored- the spotless heart of Our Blessed Lady, to whose Immaculate Conception the church is dedicated.

A small altar with a statue of Our Lady, and another with St Joseph, stand on each side of the chancel.

The ceremonies of the day began at eleven o'clock with the blessing, first of the interior of the church, and then of the foundations, by the Rev F Joachim O.S.F., assisted by the Rev Fathers Elzear, Lewis, Fortunatus, and Gerard, and the Brothers Francis and Archangel: After which the doors were thrown open, and the congregation entered the building. High Mass, Benediction of the Blessed Sacrament was given, and the services of the day concluded. Some members of the Principal Catholic families of the county were present on the occasion.

Records of the chapel commence in 1871 and terminate in 1919. The chapel has long been used as a farm building and is now smothered in ivy, particularly on the side nearest the road where it is just possible to see a porch and the remains of a roundheaded door. (Plates 25,26) There was an exterior bell turret on the farmhouse end of the chapel, and another round headed door in the turret wall. Above this door was a niche, flanked by two large windows that could have held a statue of the Virgin Mary. The remains of plaster can be seen on the exterior walls.

Two fields away to the south there is a cemetery that was owned jointly with the family at nearby Glen Trothy where there was also a private Catholic chapel. Ancestors of both these families are buried in the Dan-y-Graig cemetery.

ST JOSEPH'S ROMAN CATHOLIC CHURCH AT GROSMONT

A Catholic church was built in Grosmont in 1910 on the site of what is now the new Rectory. It was a galvanised iron building with a wooden interior. It was only used as a church for eight years, closing in 1918. There is a record of eight baptisms and a wedding in 1914. The first priest to occupy Presbytery was Father Matty followed by Father Rogers who moved from Coedanghred just before the First World War.

Father Rogers moved away from Grosmont to London depositing the keys of the church and the house with the village policeman, P.C. Frampton who was a Catholic. In 1951 the building was dismantled and sent to Llantwit Major.

RETURN TO PEMBRIDGE CASTLE

Thomas Wakeman, who lived at The Graig, Cross Ash and who was a staunch supporter of St Mary's Church, Coedanghred, was also an eminent local historian. He was a member of the Cambrian Archaeological Association whose members met annually at Monmouth for four or five days of visits and lectures. Local members booked tickets for one or more excursions and members from further away took rooms in local hotels such as the Beaufort Arms and the White Swan. Carriages left Agincourt Square at 9 o'clock for tours within a fifteen to twenty mile radius of Monmouth. On Friday, 21st August 1857, Thomas Wakeman was one of the excursionists who travelled up the Buckholt on their way to visit Welsh Newton, Pembridge Castle, Garway, Kentchurch, Grosmont and Skenfrith. The Secretary of the Society wrote a report of the Monmouth Annual Meeting in the following year's Journal of the Association, Archaeologia Cambrensis. For some reason Thomas Wakeman took exception to this article, questioning its accuracy. He therefore wrote his own version of the day's outing and published it privately. A copy can be read in the Wakeman Collection in Newport County Library. Thomas Wakeman gives a very detailed description of the castle as it was in 1857.

Pembridge Castle at the time of Thomas Wakeman's visit   **Newport Library**

On this occasion the excursionists left Monmouth by the old road to Hereford, which ascending a steep hill by the county goal runs along a ridge for about a mile and three quarters, and then enters a narrow ravine through which flows a brook, which is the boundary between the counties of Monmouth and Hereford. The hill on the left is called the Buckholt, on the southern spur of which, overhanging the pass, is a strong British Camp, but so overgrown with wood that to inspect it is impossible, excepting in the years when the coppice is felled.

About three and a quarter miles from the town, having gained the summit of the pass, we crossed the brook and entered Herefordshire. The little church of Welshnewton on the right was not examined. I believe there is nothing very interesting to the antiquarian about it; we here left the road to Hereford, turning off to the left, and in the distance of a mile arrived at Pembridge or more properly perhaps Pembridge's Castle. In the secretary's account he says "the excursionists first halted at Pembridge". This only shows the blunders a person must inevitably fall into who pretends to describe places to which he is an utter stranger, the effect of which is to mislead future excursionists, more especially when such mistakes appear in the journal of a society from where correct information is expected. Pembridge and Pembridge Castle are two very different places. The first is a small town in the northern half of the County of Hereford, at least 25 miles from the latter by the shortest possible route. Every-body at all acquainted with Herefordshire knows that it contains a small borough town called Pembridge, but comparatively few know this little border castle in the parish of Welshnewton, which, however well deserves the attention of the Archaeologist from the extraordinary peculiarities of its construction which are supposed to be unique.

The general idea of the building is a quadrangle, the sides facing the four cardinal points very nearly. In round numbers, it is about forty-five yards from north to south, and thirty-five from east to west. The entrance is on the south side and in its arrangement is very similar to that at Goodrich, only on a smaller scale. Commencing between two towers of unequal size, the smaller one standing on the south-east angle of the enclosure, a dark vaulted passage, thirty-three feet in length, led to the courtyard. In front of this entrance was a drawbridge, which like that at Goodrich, seems to have been contrived so that when drawn up it should exactly fit, and close up the whole front of the gateway between the towers. The bridge no longer exists; and this part of the moat is now filled up to allow of a passage to the interior.

The smaller or right-hand tower is so dilapidated that its exact size cannot be very easily ascertained. It seems to have contained a newel staircase. The passage contained two, if not three gates, with machiolations between them; and two portcullises, the groves for which are so unusually narrow that the frames must have been of iron. On the left, about half way down the passage, a door-way opened into a vaulted room, (twenty-two feet by thirteen) with a narrow lancet window looking out on the moat and bridge, another to the courtyard, and a loophole opened into the passage just within the entrance. There was no fireplace in this room, but one appears in that above it. The vault has fallen in, and also a considerable portion of that of the entrance passage, the right-hand side of which is too ruinous to enable one to state exactly what it originally contained. The most curious thing is a hollow in the wall with a loophole towards the court to which there appears to have been no access but from above. On entering the court a mass of masonry on the right was probably the foundation of a flight of steps giving access to the battlements of the eastern curtain wall. Turning to the left, at the distance of about 30 feet a door between two square-headed windows opens to what, judging from the size of the fireplace, must have been a kitchen, but is now a washhouse. Beyond is another room, now the farmer's dairy. The floors above these rooms are gone, but the beams and joists remain. From the dairy an extremely narrow doorway leads to the court close to the entrance to the principal or keep tower which stands on the south-west angle of the building. The only entrance to this tower at present is by a flight of steps descending from the courtyard into the basement now used as a cellar. There were three floors above the donjon, but they have all disappeared, and the whole is open to the roof. The block of building on the west side of the courtyard and adjoining the keep tower is now the farm house; and has been so altered to adapt it to its present purpose, that the original design of the different parts is not to be easily ascertained. The room immediately adjoining the keep was probably the great hall. It now comprises the farmer's kitchen and a small parlour. The staircase is undoubtedly original. It occupies a square turret projecting into the courtyard. One half the ground floor forms an entrance porch; the steps are solid blocks of oak five feet long. The length of the building, occupied as a farmhouse is sixty feet; but modern windows have been introduced and the front next to the court has been rough-cast; so no idea can be formed of its original appearance. A modern wall from the northeast angle of the house divides the area into two parts or courts. Whatever buildings may have stood in the north court originally, the greater part has disappeared; but what remains is the most curious portion of the whole castle. About 18 feet beyond the north end of the house was a building, the basement of which was an arched vault or crypt to which there is access by a flight of steps outside adjoining the north curtain wall. What superstructure was originally intended for cannot be certainly known; at present the remains of it is used as a receptacle for implements and lumber, which precluded a very minute examination. The northwest angle is supported by a very singular turret-like buttress, about seven feet in diameter of solid masonry. Possibly the adjoining building may have been a chapel, and this extraordinary mass of masonry perhaps terminated in a campanile. The solid turret like buttress we have noticed at the north-west angle of the castle is singular enough, but the termination of the north-east angle is still more extraordinary. It is a solid mass of masonry, the ground plan of which is a quarter of a circle of eleven feet radius, the straight sides projecting form the north and east walls respectively seven feet. This was carried up higher that the ride of the roof of the adjoining building, and so remains. The castle is surrounded by a moat thirty-six feet wide. Outside the ditch on the west side is a terrace 25 feet in width, defended by a banquette of earth. The intention appears to have been to prevent an enemy approaching near enough to discharge missiles into the windows.

For the next fifty years, the Herefordshire Directories show that the Castle continued to be used as a farm. In 1876 Mr William Nelmes was the farmer and "the old castle is now wholly demolished, together with the adjoining chapel, and the park has been ploughed up and cultivated".

Hereford Times August 4th 1906
Lord Glanusk's Herefordshire Estate

Under instructions from Lord Glanusk.
Sale at the King's Head Hotel, Ross. Freehold manorial estate known as

Pembridge Castle Estate. On market to pay death duties and portions to younger sons. 2480 acres producing rent of £1486 p.a.
Offered in 29 lots

Pembridge Castle Farm, 274 acres let at £128.10s was bought by the tenant Mr Thomas Jones at £3000. On this property are the ruins of the historic Pembridge Castle where the famous priest and martyr Father Kemble ministered for over 50 years.

By 1914 the entry reads *Pembridge Castle property of and occupied by Dr Hedley Bartlett. It is being thoroughly repaired and restored to its former condition by the present owner Dr. Hedley Bartlett having been commenced in 1912. Mr Ernest Davies M.S.A. of Hereford is the architect.*

The Roman Catholic connection at Pembridge Castle continued into the twentieth century in a somewhat bizarre way. Dr Hedley Bartlett was a barrister and also a medical doctor. He belonged to an organisation called the Evangelical Catholic Communion whose aims were 'the best and most precious elements of East and West, of Catholic and Protestant should be gathered together in one Evangelical Communion.' These movements were of a 'catholic' type mainly deriving from dissatisfied and unstable elements in Catholicism; they wanted Catholicism without the Pope.

The founders of this group were not satisfied by being simple superintendents of their flocks but gave themselves high-sounding titles and extravagant pretensions. They devised elaborate names for their churches and impressive titles for themselves such as Catholicas, Hierarch, Mar, Metropolitan, Primate, Patriarch. Some of the more ambitious members even bought patents of nobility and university degree from obscure sources In 1919, Mar Jacobs, Bishop of Mercia, raised to the episcopate a Barrister at Law, William Stanley Macbean with the title Mar Paulus, and Bishop of Kent. On the 18th October 1930, Mar Paulus consecrated a fellow barrister who was also a medical practitioner, Hedley Coward Bartlett. He gave him the name and style of 'Mar Hedley, Bishop of Siluria.' He became one of the hierarchies of the Patriarchate of Glastonbury in which the Diocese of Siluria embraced the Principality of Wales and the County of Monmouth.

In May 1945 a very grand ceremony took place in the 12th century chapel in Pembridge Castle. Nine prelates gathered together in full regalia to consecrate a new Episcopal leader, Mar Johannes, Titular Bishop of St Marylebone, an Auxiliary of the Patriarchal Throne of Glastonbury and General Moderator of the Evangelical Communion. Prior to the main ceremony, all the bishops formally merged their respective orders and successions by means of reciprocal consecration 'sub conditione' so as to form one reunited line in the interests of Christian reunion.

In 1972 the Vicar of Welsh Newton wrote to Mr M Watkins who lived on The Doward to ask if he could recollect attending the ceremony at Pembridge Castle in 1945. Mr Watkins replied in a letter to the Rev Windle that he had attended somewhat reluctantly. He was an acquaintance of Dr Bartlett and was asked to attend in his capacity as a Notary Public. He remembers four clergy there one calling himself Archbishop. He was a tall man with an American accent who wore white gloves with rings outside them. Also there was the Prior of Llantony and the Prior or Abbot of Rievaux. The object of this ceremony was for the Bishops to confirm each other in office.

After the ceremony they all moved into the sitting room in the castle where all the celebrants signed the documents. Mr Watkins, as a Notary Public, was asked to certify these documents, but he refused to do anything else but certify that the signatures were of the people who signed them in his presence.

Dr and Mrs Bartlett said goodbye 'to the rest of us' and vanished into the dining room, which used to be the porters lodge, to eat sandwiches. As he was driving back, Mr Watkins passed the rest of the clergy tramping back to Monmouth. He gave them a lift. It was in the days of petrol rationing!

A p.s. to the letter gave the following points.

1. *Dr Bartlett said that he bought Pembridge Castle farm without knowing that there was a castle on it. (Seems extraordinarily hard to believe!)*
2. *He said his sight had gone and that he could not see the Welsh hills from the castle. (confirmed by a neighbour).*
3. *He said that Catherine, widow of Henry V. who married Owen Tudor had lived at the castle for several years towards the end of her life, and he thought he had seen her spirit there. (Could be checked).*
4. *He said he was Bishop of the Lesser Eastern Church which was in communion with the Church of England. (Seems doubtful).*
5. *As to his exercise of his rights as a Bishop I was told that at this period he held a service in the chapel 3 or 4 times a year.*

Dr Hedley (Bartlett), Bishop of Siluria, died in June 1956 aged 93. His cremated remains and those of his wife are buried in the floor of the chapel at Pembridge Castle.

The Chapel, Pembridge Castle

Part Four

River Road and Rail

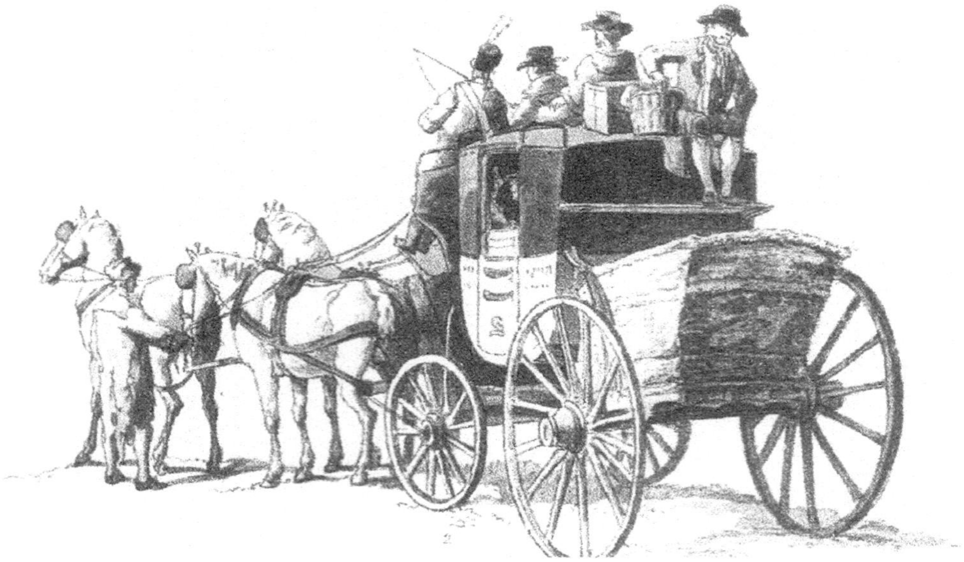

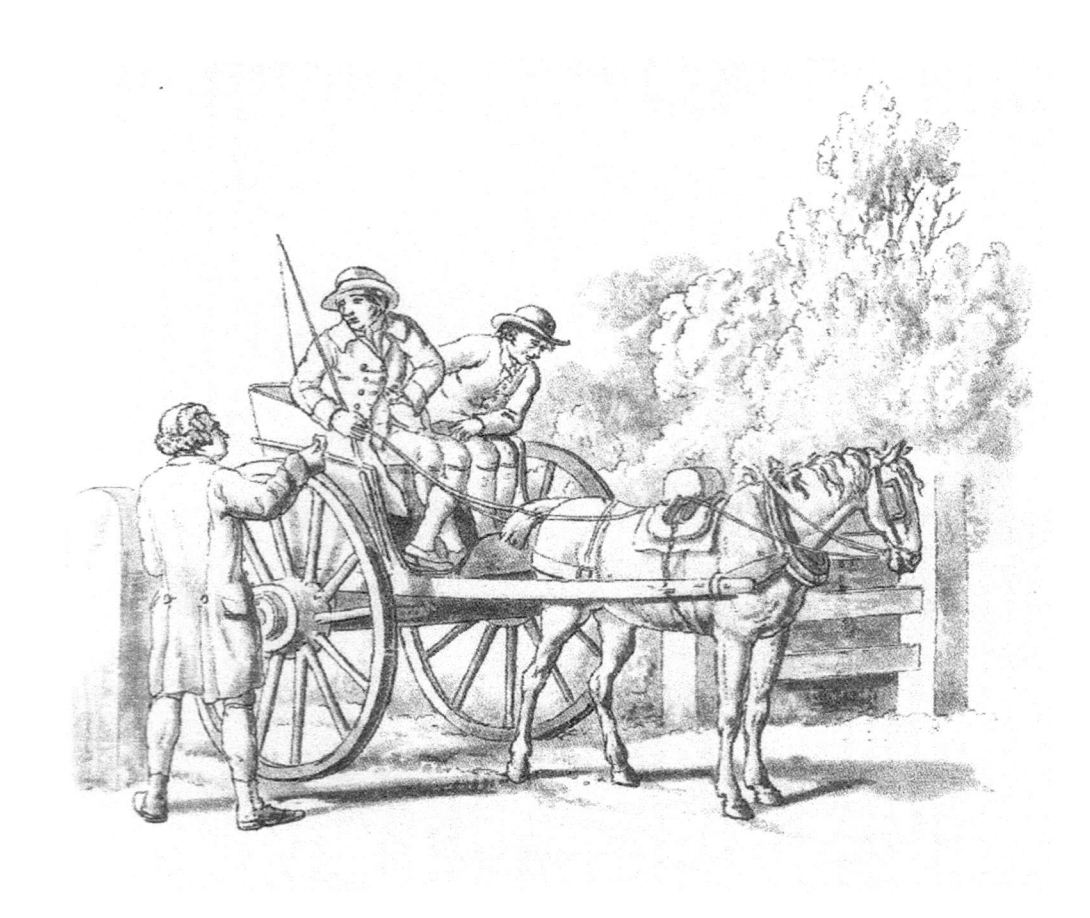

TRAVEL IN THE 18TH AND 19TH CENTURIES

It is quite difficult to imagine as we travel along modern roads, or walk down well surfaced country lanes, just how difficult travelling was until quite recently. Until the 18th century roads were unbelievably bad. There was no national administrative machinery for the construction or repair of public highways. Every parish was responsible for their own roads, and these roads were maintained by the statute labour that each farmer was obliged to provide for six days annually. The work was supervised by the highway surveyor who was selected each Easter at the Vestry Meeting and who had to serve unpaid until the next Easter. The surveyor was responsible for the roads within his parish boundaries and standards varied considerably between parishes. Magistrates could punish surveyors for neglecting their duties and parishes fined for failing to maintain their roads. However, the procedure was cumbersome and rarely effective.

Although the farmers were responsible for providing six days labour annually it would be the poor of the parish who would do the actual backbreaking work of picking the stones off the fields and putting them into the carts provided by the farmers to be hauled to the roads. Here the stones would be broken up and spread over the roads no doubt making a very rocky and uneven surface. Many roads were only broad tracks through open fields and careless drivers, meeting with a large pool of water just diverted onto the cultivated land. The stone collected and intended for road surfacing was often used for the erection of buildings or walls. Dunghills and other rubbish often caused obstructions to the highway.

Most of the roads leading from Monmouth were very narrow and ran between steep banks. The road from Monmouth to Hereford was so narrow that it was necessary to use outriders blowing horns to warn travellers approaching in the opposite direction. When wagons met, the horses were taken out of the wagon going downhill and it was dragged back to a place wide enough to pass. These main roads were described in the Turnpike Act of 1755 as "the great and common highways leading from Monmouth, which were very ruinous and often dangerous to travellers in many parts thereof, and in others so narrow and incommodious that carriages cannot pass each other without great inconvenience and difficulty". In winter and in bad weather wheeled traffic did not attempt to travel and on some roads wheeled traffic was impossible at any time, packhorses being the only method of carrying goods. Along turnpike roads between towns like Monmouth, Ross, Hereford and Abergavenny, passengers were carried by stagecoach. These conveyances were solid and heavily built and could only travel slowly. Goods were carried by stage wagons. These were large, roomy vehicles pulled by several horses and were compelled to have very broad wheels so that they did not make ruts in the roads. Light carriers would transport goods from these stage wagons into the villages. Passengers who could not afford to travel by stagecoach could use one of these stage wagons. Where wheeled traffic was impossible, packhorses would be used.

Because of the dreadful road conditions and the high cost of transporting goods by road, the rivers were used whenever possible. Flat-bottomed barges carried goods along navigable rivers and carried cargoes to and from coastal vessels. It required 240 packhorses to carry the contents of a 30 ton barge. River navigation became increasingly popular and by the beginning of the industrial revolution Britain had over 1500 miles of navigable rivers in use. Improvements took the form of scouring, widening, banking, cutting of lateral canals to by-pass obstructions, the provision of towpaths and the erection of wharves and quayside facilities. This in turn eventually led not only to an extensive canal system but to turnpike roads and to railways as well.

It was during the reign of George II (1727-1760) that the first signs of the coming Industrial Revolution were seen. The new industries were attracting more people to the towns and better medical care meant that the population was increasing rapidly. In 1500 there were less that 3 million people in England and Wales but by 1700 there were 5½ million and by 1750 the population was over 6 million. Because of this rapid growth in population, extra food was needed and therefore better farming methods and the means to transport this increased food production from the countryside into the towns.

Many of the new industrialists were investing their money in land. There was an increasing movement towards accumulating land in large compact estates on which agricultural practises were becoming more efficient. Improved communication was essential if this agricultural revolution was to take place. Although ships could go to America and India with heavy goods, coal and hardware were still being transported strapped to the side of packhorses because wheeled traffic would have stuck in the mud and ruts of English roads. The population in rural communities who lived many miles from a town, and especially those in hilly districts, had serious problems selling their surplus produce and making an income with which to buy the goods they could not produce themselves. Farmers seldom owned the land they cultivated and were often much behind in the rents due to the landlord, sometimes years in arrears. If the landlord insisted on recovering the rent or evicting the tenant then the destitute families would be sent back to the parish where they were born and become a burden on that parish's rates. The landlord would find it almost impossible to find another tenant and so they too were seriously affected.

By the middle of the 18th century the roads in Herefordshire and Monmouthshire were still deplorable and the need to improve communication had become imperative. The river Wye, a tidal river in its lower reaches, had been used for centuries up to Monmouth. From there, sailing barges could take cargoes of up to 40 tons up the river past the rapids to Hereford. The river was almost the only way of conveying goods to Monmouth, Hereford and up the river Lugg to Leominster. The main trade on the river Wye was between Monmouth, Chepstow and Bristol. Barges and trows were the principal boats used, and because of their shallow draft they were able to use the river at most times of the year, sailing regularly every fortnight from Monmouth to Bristol and Gloucester. These flat barges had open holds and had changed little since the 12th century.

THE RIVER MONNOW NAVIGATION

It was about the year 1750, during the reign of George II, that a group of gentlemen who lived in the Monnow Valley met together and decided to do something about the appalling lack of transport and communication in their area. The instigator of this meeting seems to have been William Pitt or Pytt, and the account of the attempt to turn the river Monnow into a navigable river is set out in the back of an account book belonging to him.

William Pytt, who is described as being of Howton, Kenderchurch and Garway, was a prominent man in the area and in about 1716 was appointed by the Receiver General as surveyor and inspector for calculating the rates and duties on houses for the window tax. For this duty he was paid a salary of £60 a year which he received quarterly. It would appear that he had some influential friends because in the year 1722 the following petition was sent to

The most Noble his Grace the Duke of Chandos

Whereas there is a Report that William Pytt surveyor of the Lights for the County of Hereford is in danger of being removed out of the said office – we the persons whose names are here to subscribed being very well Assured that the said William Pytt hath faithfully demeaned himself in the said office for the space of near six years and is very well affected to our sovereign Lord King George and to the Constitution both in Church and State and to your Graces Interests. We therefore make it our humble request to your Grace that you would vouchsafe to him your interest for his Continuance in the same Office.

Sept 12 1722. H Hoskyns   John Williams   John Skipp   Rbt Blodulph
                J Clarke   Thomas Lingen   W Jones   Edw Witherstan
                George Clive Edward Clive   Rbt Mynors   P Hoskyns

William Pytt was married to Elizabeth, the daughter of John and Margaret Noble of Hellens, Much Marcle and they had three children, Noble Walwyn, Elizabeth and Mary. It is unlikely that Mr Pytt was still a collector of taxes when he died in 1752, but he must still have had one of the account books in his possession, for it is in the back of a window account tax book that he copied out the letters he received about making the river Monnow navigable. These letters, which are barely legible, describe in some detail the reasons for undertaking this navigation. The letters describe the state of the countryside in the 1750's and the difficulty of accessing much of the Monnow valley and they support William Pytt in his attempt to make the Monnow navigable.

Sir,

Tis now long since I have heard anything of your very laudable attempt for forming a Navigation by the river Monnow to actively extend Inland Country, that labours under such expensive difficulties in conveying the product of their lands to such different markets having no other way as makes it a wonder how Landlords that have estates there, can possibly get tenants to conduct the husbanding of their several farms.

And yet it is strange, that so many Gentlemen of a knowledge superior to most, and whose positions are very large in that Country, some of whom are by birth in the highest stations, should disregard your endeavours, which are aimed not only at a general Good, but would be in a very particular manner greatly to their own advantage.

But for my part tis to me the greatest wonder of all, that a work so wanting, so feasible and so generally Beneficial has not been done long ago.

Is it not notorious, how great the arrears of the Tenants (some for years) are, which, if not entirely lost, are and can only be recovered by the ruin of families whose fall in time draws on that of the rest by being burdensome to their several parishes.

If no other aid could be obtained by it than helping them to live better and pay better how many would then be rendered happy and by cheerful countenance proclaim about the benevolence of an act so popular and so generally productive of Good.

Such an applause must surely be more satisfactory to a great and generous mind than all the noisy 'adulation' of a mad mob, or the notorious flattery of a venal pen

But it is very well known, that by Navigation this is obtained and more; in course of time as the little Towns upon such a river launch out into some small branch of Trade, or perhaps manufactures; which is not impossible where water, lands, provisions and most materials are so plenty and cheap, and sold to other countries, there will be great consumption by numbers of people, money will circulate and of course everybody will live better, which itself will promote some trade. This though but a small boat traffic, will turn thousands of acres into good tillage, which are now covered with heath and brambles, or where perhaps grows a short grass sufficient only to keep sheep and young or small cattle alive during the summer season. Add to this the Improvements that will consequently be made upon those lands where limestone is so plentiful by conveying coal up the River to make lime or even by bringing lime itself by the same channel for manure.

And what is more, and a greater Improvement to Industry, let us consider that great Mart Bristoll, to which your Navigation will be not only very much shorter than any other River leading to it, but also more constant than that in the Wye by the many locks, which will be as so many Reservoirs to keep water always for a convoy thither and on which may be erected mills for divers uses.

This leads into foreign commerce, whither most of your commodities will go, and surely bring a Return. Thither will go your corn, flour, seeds, grain of every sort, provisions, wrought iron, scrub wood converted into every shape, linen and woollen manufacture, cyder, tyles, stones and paving stone be conveyed.

In return will be brought foreign unwrought iron, coal, lime, all wholesale shop commodities, and salt to supply great part of Wales, and their return though not so large as the export, will more than repay the sum expended on the locks as to render it sufficiently profitable for boats to go up and down.

Will this not give a new face to the Country, will it not convert Barren hills into greater profits and help the fertile valleys that languish for want of near markets. Will not this (I will venture to ask it) double your estates, more maybe, but need not be

said to men of fortune and interest to promote at once their own and a public good; happy circumstances when they are then united; greater hopes there are of its being affectuated. But no doubt if you take a wrong method in your pursuit none will be willing to subscribe any sum (apprehending) when they have so done, they must pay them without profit or to no purpose.

But they should be convinced to the contrary by drawing an Instrument in such a manner as that if it should not take effect, the subscription be voided, only an equal poundage be deducted towards paying the expenses of an attempt to obtain an Act for the purpose, and some responsible merchant in Bristol appointed Treasurer.

I must confess, that formerly in my own mind I treated it as a mere Chimera, so I believe many do now for the same reason (want of thought) or perhaps want of something else, but having considered it more deliberately I am fully convinced, and hope others will be so too.

That it is practicable is without dispute, and in a cheap easy manner, from the cheapness of timber there, stone on the spot the River narrow so as to cause less expenses in wearing.

Rome was not built in a day, but the appearances are so strong in its favour as anything of this land maybe and what interest subscribers will receive cannot be affirmed. Till the locks are finished tis likely there will be none, but I dare venture to say, that when that River begins to bear his burden it will bring forth every year better and better to the satisfaction of every Proprietor, and I made no doubt its paying six per cent if not more.

This letter was copied into the account book giving no clue as to the name and address of the person who had written it, although it is obvious that is was someone who knew the Monnow valley well. There is also a veiled reference to someone who is opposed to the scheme. The next entry copied by William Pytt into his book was the Articles drawn up for the purpose of obtaining an Act of Parliament giving permission to proceed with the navigation on the river Monnow.

Proposal for making the River Monnow Navigable from Monnow Mouth to Grosmont.
  The Subscribers to sign Articles for supporting the expense of Writings etc and procuring an Act of Parliament for that purpose.
Every subscriber to appear at a General Meeting and by a majority of these or their proxies appoint clerks agents and workers with what (money) shall be wanting till the General meeting which shall be held the first Monday in every month and such order made by a majority of them be binding on the whole jointly.
  We, whose hands are hereto subscribed, do severally agree to each of us concerned in an undertaking for making the River Monnow navigable from Monnow Mouth to Grosmont Bridge. For which purpose each of us have deposited in the hands of Mr Pytte of Garway in the County of Hereford gent one pound in order to defray the Indenture and necessary charge of writing and other expenses in forming the said undertaking. And as soon as the Act of Parliament can be obtained for making the said River navigable a proper Draft of Articles of Co-partnership shall be forthwith prepared by the said William Pytte. And the said Wm Pytte shall thereupon summon all the Parties hereto subscribed to meet at Grosmont to consider and settle the same in order to be ? and ?. and the said subscribers shall also deposit and pay into the hands of such person or persons as the majority so meeting shall appoint at that time Ten pounds which said sum of one pound and ten pounds so to be paid shall be deemed and taken as part of the money to be raised in carrying out the said

navigation. And what shall be thereafter further determining about the said proposal by the said majority shall be binding on the whole number of us the said subscribers. And that every and either of us refusing to pay the said Ten pounds shall forfeit the said one pound so deposited and…….also refusing to sign the said Articles when prepared……..shall forfeit and loose the said ten pounds and be utterly discharged from any further concerns therein Witness our hands
Day of   1751
Proposal with Articles for the
River Monnow Navigation Sept 30th 1751
W P: on the Bank of it.

These initials are difficult to read and it is debatable whether they belong to the piece of writing above or the letter that immediately follows. This letter gives a rather optimistic view of the benefits promised by the river navigation. The writer describes how central Wales would be able to use the river Monnow to open up trade with Bristol.

Those two fine valleys of Crickhowell and Combee in Breckonshire raise quantities of grain and would double it had they market within reasonable distance. They now go eighteen or twenty miles in a miserable road to market, by this scheme they will have little more than eight miles and most part by a good road.

Pontrilas, Ewyas Harold and all the Golden Valley in Herefordshire, rich land whose produce cannot always be sent down the river Wye for want of water in summer and sometimes in winter. Again in Herefordshire Kentchurch, Kilpeck, Orcop and Garway and a great part in Irchenfield not to mention the improvement of farms on each side of the river. This is but a short list of places which will be advantaged. For by that river may be conveyed all commodities from Bristol to a great part of Wales by a much shorter land carriage which now are conveyed from Newport, Chepstow and Monmouth and possibly some commodities may return from thence as coarse cloth, stockings, butter and grain so that upon the whole advantages are such as justice ought to put a stop to all opposition

The problems relating to the navigation of the rivers Wye and Lugg are also mentioned in this letter. Both these rivers had severe impediments to navigation as they were usually short of water during the summer and could be flooded in winter. The Lugg navigation is described in the letter as being like a man building a coach in his house and then not being able to get it out without pulling down part of the house. The scheme proposed for the Monnow would have avoided the drawbacks of those encountered on the rivers Wye and Lugg. Because it was proposed to construct several locks, the water would be held back to keep the required depth. The cost would not be great because there was plenty of timber and stone in the locality.

The only letter about the Monnow navigation that has been signed is from John Pritchard who, with his wife Ann, in 1751 was almost certainly living at Campston Hall, Grosmont. He was related to Bishop Matthew Pritchard of Perthir who had died in May 1750 and their family home was The Graig.

September 17th 1751
Sir,
I am very well assured in my own mind that a navigation upon the river Monnow from Monouth to Grosmont is very practicable. What I am not master of but support yet doubt the ability is equal to the undertaking and I think there can be no objection to it, but what might be very rapidly obviated such as are partial or invidious are not worth notice. It must be understandably of great benefit and will have a good effect upon estates at many miles distance. All Crickhowell and a good part of Breckonshire, the Golden Valley and a great part of Herefordshire, that river will undoubtedly find great good attending it by a much nearer market for their timber, grain etc which must of course advance the value of estates by the advantage the County will find from it. For my part I am so much a friend to the affair that I would contribute all my power, but that a little, and have by bearer performed my promise. I wish you all success and assure you the affair has a hearty well wisher to it in J.P

If it is to be I think you are fairly entitled to a Gratuity for the trouble from such as may be.

Yr most humble srvt
J Pritchard
To Wm Pytt Esq at Garway

John Pritchard died in July 1763 and the way John Scudamore of Kentchurch Court acted towards the widow was the subject of a court case White v Scudamore in 1771-1772. At the time of the death of John Pritchard his widow Ann was 70 years of age. She was in poor health and her understanding was impaired. She was induced for the benefit of her health to go and reside at the home of a friend, the Rev. Davies at The Wain for nine months and was attended by a Doctor and was considered incapable of managing her own affairs. John Scudamore was an intimate friend of Ann and John and knew the value of their estate, especially Campstone Hall. He took advantage of Ann Pritchard's state of health and ingratiated himself into her favour, visiting her at the Wain and prevailing upon her to return to Campstone Hall where he persuaded her to sign an agreement drawn up by his attorney to convey her property to him for the sum of £1400. Ann Pritchard was not told the real value of the estate, and had no opportunity to consult with or find anyone who was competent to advise her. After this conveyance all the rents on the estate were increased.

Ann Pritchard died in November 1768 leaving no issue and appointing her great-niece Mary White to manage her estate. The estate solicitors frequently applied to John Scudamore to disclose under what title he had taken possession of the estate and to deliver proof and to account to them for the rents and profits since the death of Ann Pritchard. John Scudamore refused to comply with the request and said Ann Pritchard had not in her lifetime any knowledge or connection with the Whites and so as to secure herself an annuity for life in 1765 conveyed all her interest in the said estate to John Scudamore. Unfortunately, as is so often the case, no papers were found which gave the outcome of the case.

The river Monnow was surveyed in detail by Thomas Bridge on August 27th and 28th 1751. The survey was from Corras Ford above Grosmont to Monmouth giving details of the locks and the fall of the river.

From Grosmont to Duffering fords   5 locks, 8 foot
Garway Weir   2 foot rise
At the Darren Wood   Lock 8 foot
Ruthlin Paper Mill   Weir, 2 foot rise
Fall thence to Tregate ponds   3 foot 7 inches
Thence to Parthir   5 foot 4 inches
Thence below Parthir mill   1 foot 3 inches
Fall of the weir at Monmouth forge   9 foot

MILL ON THE MONNOW, MONMOUTH

There is no indication as to exactly where locks were to be constructed or whether the barges would negotiate a change in river level by being hauled through the sluices of the weirs on the upstream journey, or to shoot the flood of water flowing through them on the downstream journey. These flashlocks, or navigation staunches, as they were called, could only permit small gradients to be ascended and were subject not only to conflicting interest of millers and watermen, but to seasonal variation in the flow of rivers. There were several mills on the stretch of the Monnow that was surveyed for the navigation.

Garway mill dates from at least the 14th century when it was mentioned in the records of the Knights Hospitallers as being a corn mill. Later in 1773 it was recorded as being a snuff mill for grinding tobacco into powder. Whether this was in addition to being a corn mill is not known. The weir is on the river Monnow with a short leat. It is now a private house.

Rather surprisingly, Skenfrith mill is not mentioned in the survey. This is a corn mill built right up against the castle walls. It was still in use as a mill until the 1990's but is now an empty building. There is a short leat to an external undershot water wheel that, until recently, was still in use as a sack hoist. The weir on the river Monnow was badly damaged in the floods of 2002 and has now been removed. The restoration programme to repair the river banks and prevent erosion of the castle walls has now been completed

Ruthlin mill was one of the most industrial mills on the Monnow. From before 1591 to about 1720 it was a corn mill. By 1729 it had been converted into a paper mill. The process for making paper used rags that were pounded with water in a water-powered machine. It was still a paper mill on the tithe map of 1843 when there were about six separate buildings. All that remains is one building converted into a private house. There was a long weir on the river Monnow and a very short leat.

Nothing now remains of the mill at Tregate except the weir although it was still shown as being in use on the 1903 OS map.

There are no remains of Perthir mill which is reported to have been destroyed in 1890. It was a large mill which has been recorded as being a corn mill and a fulling mill and at one time a paper mill. Fulling was part of the process in the manufacture of textiles. The purpose was to felt and thicken cloth to make it more uniform, and this was achieved by soaking the woven cloth and then thumping it heavily with water powered fulling stocks. These mills were also known as tuck-mills, walk-mills or in Welsh, pandy. This mill had a weir on the river Monnow and a very short leat.

Monmouth Forge was an iron forge on the river Monnow at Osbaston. The term forge meant a works were pig-iron was converted by suitable heating in a current of air, and by hammering, using water-powered hammers, into bars of wrought iron. Some of the pig-iron was supplied by the furnace at St Weonards. By 1746 the forge was in the ownership of the Duke of Beaufort. In the mid-nineteenth century the forge was a large complex. There was a smith's shop, a carpenter's shop and a sawpit. There were 21 cottages provided for workers and a 'mansion house' for a manager. Most of the forge buildings were demolished in the 1890's to make way for the hydro-electric generating station and the works sold for scrap. The present weir is of 20th century construction.

The second part of the survey shows the owners on the right and left banks of the river Monnow

The tone of the letters to Mr Pytt seems to confirm support for his proposals against some very strong objection. This objection appears to come from a very influential person whom the writers were at pains not to name. The person most likely to disrupt the plans for the navigation of the river was the Duke of Beaufort. He was one of the largest landowners in the area and owned much of the land on the Welsh bank of the river Monnow.

As one of the letters states "and is it yet strange, that so many Gentlemen of a knowledge superior to most, and whose positions are very large in that county, some of whom are by birth in the highest stations in that county, should disregard your endeavours which are aimed not only at the general good, but would be in a particular manner greatly to their own advantage."

But the most telling clue of all was the following petition which was delivered to the Duke of Beaufort at Stow, Gloucestershire on 23rd September 1751, one week before the inaugural meeting at Grosmont was due to take place.

To the Most Noble his Grace the Duke of Beaufort.
  We whose names are herein subscribed Inhabitants, Tenants and Parishioners of the Town and Parish of Grosmont in the County of Monmouth

Humbly set forth
That the River Monnow has been surveyed from the Lawns to Monnowmouth and found practicable to be made navigable, will be of the utmost service to us and the Country adjacent, humbly beg your Grace will condescend to carry on a work so useful to us and the publik in General and we shall always pray....

Walwyn Cecill	*Thomas Trumper*	*Henry Phillipps*	*William Vaughan*
Thomas Hughes	*Charles Williams*	*James Pytt*	*William Morgan*

Of the men who signed this petition to the Duke of Beaufort four of them had been or would be Mayors of Grosmont. Charles Williams was Mayor in 1749, Henry Phillips in 1754 and 1767, James Pytt in 1757 and 1756 and the Rev Walwyn Cecil in 1759.

The Cecils or Seycylls had a long history in Grosmont. They lived at Lower Duffryn, a large imposing house built in the time of Elizabeth 1. The Cecils were kinsmen of the Marquis of Salisbury and Exeter. Phillip Cecill of Duffryn married Elizabeth Wallwyn of Longworth, Hereford in 1706 (Badminton Papers). His son Walwyn and his grandson Phillip Hastings Cecil were both vicars of Skenfrith.

Thomas Trumper leased the The Lawns, a large farm, which had once been part of the demesne lands of Grosmont Castle, from the Duke of Beaufort. The same family lived in the house for 150 years and were prominent members of the community.

Nothing more was heard of this ambitious plan. Enquiries to the Beaufort estate revealed no further information and they did not seem to have any record of the petition that may or may not have been delivered. There must have been some very disgruntled men in Grosmont during September 1751 but it would seem that without the cooperation of the Duke of Beaufort the whole plan was stymied.

TOLL ROADS

Throughout the middle ages the roads originally laid out by the Romans continued to be the main arteries of trade and the routes between towns and villages. In the Monnow Valley, on a salient position below Garway Hill, a Roman fort was built circa 70 A.D. There would have been a track linking this fort to the nearest Roman Garrison, probably at Blestium (Monmouth). This track would in all probability have followed the river and before passing through Skenfrith made a crossing of the river somewhere near the farm of Lower Duffryn. A letter written in 1828 refers to the foundations of an old bridge across the river Monnow between Lower Duffryn and Demesne farm. This may have been the crossing made by the Romans as it is very near the site of the fort. There is no evidence now remaining of these foundations.

The roads that follow the valley on either side of the river are ancient routes. The river formed part of the border between England and Wales as indeed it still does. This area was part of the ancient kingdom of Archenfield that retained its own laws and customs even after the Norman Conquest.

The roads through the valley must have been in an abysmal condition, for until the late 18th century the only method of travel in these hilly districts would have been on horseback and pack horses. The condition of the heavy local soils also made a difference to the method of travel. As late as 1780 the highways in Herefordshire, after the autumnal rains set in, were impassable to wagons and carts, and for half the year the county families could only visit one another on horseback. Towards the end of April the surface of the roads was in such a dreadful condition that it was levelled by means of 'ploughs', each drawn by eight or ten horses.

As the condition of the road was the responsibility of the parish, very considerable differences prevailed depending on whether the parish officers fulfilled their obligations to keep their stretch of road in good repair. At the Monmouthshire Spring Assizes in 1708 the Parishes of Skenfrith and Grosmont appeared to answer a charge of neglect of the roads, namely failing to maintain their portion of the Abergavenny to Hereford Road. This state of affairs eventually led to the Turnpike Acts which enabled private corporations, by a special Act of Parliament, to put some stretches of main road in good order and to levy tolls on the road users. The money collected would be used for the upkeep of the road and their profit. The name turnpike comes from the description of the type of gate used to regulate the traffic past the toll-house and were usually a long single-armed barrier turning on a pivot. The first gates were probably fitted with spikes (pikes) to prevent drivers from forcing them.

The Toll House Broad Oak Cross Roads — John Blake

HEREFORD TURNPIKE TOLLS

To be taken at the several Turnpike-Gates belonging to this Trust

	From 1st April to October	From 1sr Oct to April
FOR every Horse, Mare, Gelding, Mule, or Ass, not drawing, shall be paid at each Gate	1 ½ d	1 ½ d
BROAD WHEELS		
FOR every Horse, Mare, Etc drawing with broad wheels, at each Gate..................	2 d	2.d
FOR every Horse, Mare, etc drawing with broad wheels, lime for the improvement of land..................	1 d.	1 d.
FOR every Horse, Mare, etc drawing common stage wagons, or carts with broad wheels, at each Gate..................	4 d.	4d.
FOR every Horse, Mare, etc drawing with broad wheels, timber, plank, lime, brick, tile, stone, paving, or any materials for building...	4 d.	8 d.
FOR every Ox, or other Neat Cattle, drawing with broad wheels...	1 d.	1 d.
FOR every Ox, or other Neat Cattle, drawing timber, lime, brick, tile, stone, paving, or any material for building, with broad wheels.	2 d.	4 d.
NARROW WHEELS		
FOR every Horse, Mare, etc drawing with narrow wheels) 1st gate	5 d.	5 d.
(other than common stage wagons) shall be paid 2nd gate	3 d.	3 d.
FOR every Horse, Mare, etc drawing with narrow wheels 1st gate	3 d.	3 d.
loaded with dung, lime or compost for the improvement 2 nd gate of land	2 d.	2 d.
FOR every Horse, Mare, etc drawing common stage wagons with narrow wheels at each Gate	6 d,	6 d.
FOR every Horse, Mare, etc drawing with narrow wheels, lime, 1st brick, tile, stone, paving, or any materials for building 2nd	6 d. 3 d.	1/- 6 d
FOR every Horse, Mare, etc drawing timber carriages with narrow wheels	9 d.	1/6
FOR every Ox or other Neat Cattle, drawing lime, brick stone, tile paving, or any materials for building, with narrow wheels...............	4 d.	8 d.
COACHES, ETC		
For EVERY Horse, &c drawing any coach, chaise, hearse, chair, &c..................	6 d.	6 d.
DROVES		
FOR every Drove of Oxen or Neat Cattle, per Score................	10 d.	10 d.
FOR every Drove of Calves, Hogs, Sheep, or Lambs, per Score....	5 d.	5 d.
ALL TOLLS ON SUNDAY ARE DOUBLE		
Except Carriages going for Lime, Coals, or Charcoal after Sun-set.		

EXEMPTIONS

Tickets being produced from any Two Gates within the Trust, shall be an Exemption for every other Gate for the same day, except Llancloudy and Pontrilas Gates.

Going through the city of Hereford shall be considered as One Gate only, with the same Carriages and Horses.

A Ticket produced from any Stop Gate shall free the adjoining turnpike Gate only to which it is attached, and so alternately for the same day.

Any carriage employed for carrying materials for any public road or highway, or bridge therein, or hauling any earth, soil, or sand, collected or scraped from any part of the Turnpike-roads.

Carriages laden with grain in the straw, hay, materials for fencing, or fuel carried from one farm to another, in the occupation of the same person; implements of husbandry, as fruit carried to the mill to be ground; and cattle, horses, or farming stock, going to or from lands in the occupation of the same person (providing the same be drawn from one parish to the next adjoining parish, or shall not pass upon the Turnpike road more than the space of two miles), shall be exempt from payment.

Horses carrying any clergyman going to, or returning from visiting say sick person, or other his parochial duty; or any horse carrying or conveying any person to or from his usual place of worship on Sundays; or attending the funeral of any person who shall die or be buried in any of the parishes wherein the said roads be; or any horses or carriage employed for carrying the mails of letters and expresses, under the authority of the Post-Master-General – shall be exempt from payment.

Horses belonging to Officers or Soldiers upon their march, or upon duty, or any horses, cattle, or carriages employed in carrying or conveying the same or baggage of any such soldiers, shall be exempt from payment.

And also except for any carriage having taken up building or other materials, which shall be paid for according to the toll paper; any sums previously paid for the same wagon and horses within the same day being deducted.

GATE-KEEPERS –Any Gate-keeper permitting any wagon, wain, cart or other carriage, to be drawn or pass through any Turnpike with any greater number of horses, or beasts or draft, or any carriage constructed or drawn in any manner than directed by the Act; or without such names and descriptions printed thereon as are also directed by such Act, without giving information to the Trustees within one week after, shall forfeit and pay the sum of 40s, for each neglect.

NOTICE IS HEREBY GIVEN, that on the first day of January next, application will be made to her Majesty's Justices of the Peace, assembled at Quarter Sessions in and for the County of Hereford, at the Shire Hall in the City of Hereford, for an order for stopping up as useless and unnecessary, a certain Highway leading from the Village of Kentchurch in the parish of Kentchurch in the said County, towards and unto a certain Wood there called Boulston Court Wood, commencing at or near to a certain Blacksmith's shop in the said Village of Kentchurch, and ending at or near the said Wood called Boulston Court Wood, containing in length *1693* yards or thereabouts, and that the Certificate of two Justices having viewed the said Highway, together with a plan of the same will be lodged with the Clerk of the Peace for the said County, on the first day of December next.

Dated this first day of November, 1838.

JOHN LUCY SCUDAMORE, *Surveyor of the Highways of the said Parish.*

T. N. WEBB, PRINTER, HEREFORD.

In 1772 an Act was passed for widening and altering the roads *'From a place called the Lower Crossways, in the Parish of St Maughans, to the town of Grosmont, in the County of Monmouth'.*

In 1784 The Mayor of Skenfrith owed 13s 4d for the toll and the Mayor Grosmont £4 3s. The Receiver of the tolls reported that since the new Turnpike road had been made about twenty years before, no tolls had been collected, stating, *'for in Grosmont and Skenfrith it is paid out of their own pockets, travellers refusing to pay and demanding to see their authority. I must repeat again what I have said before in the other accounts concerning the inhabitant of Skenfrith about the tolls, for they say that they are in danger of their lives very often by endeavouring to collect them as having no authority.'* They decided to revert to the old way of charging the Mayors with the accustomed rents.

One of the first Turnpike Acts to affect the Monnow Valley was passed in 1771 and was an Act for amending, widening and altering the roads leading from Crickhowell in the County of Brecon to the Cross Hands beyond the New Inn (St Owen's Cross) on the Turnpike Road between Hereford and Ross. (This is where the B 4521 joins the A 49) Also from a place called the Lower Cross Ways in the parish of St Maughans to the Town of Grosmont, and also from the Turnpike Road in the parish of Welsh Newton to Ponttanast (Pontynys, near Longtown) in the parish of Clodock. In 1792 another Act was passed for continuing the terms of the 1771 Act and a third Act was passed in 1813 which allowed for the enlarging of the two previous Acts.

A diversion of new line of Road at or near Broad Oak in the Parish of Garway in the County of Hereford, commencing out of the Road leading there from the Town of Ross to the Town of Abergavenny, and leading through the said Parish of Garway, and through the parishes of Skenfrith and Landilo Cressenny in the county of Monmouth, passing the Southwell Arms Inn, Darren Bridge, Skenfrith Bridge, Norton and Trebella Farms, Kefn-yCraig, Blainlymon Bridge and terminating at or near a place called Cross Ash.

The section of road between Broad Oak and Skenfrith must have been very rough. In 1813, at the Quarter Sessions, James Spencer, Gent was indicted because this road was out of repair. This prosecution was, no doubt, the reason for a totally new line of road being constructed. This work was not done immediately. It was not until 1827 that the following report was made to the Justices at the Easter Quarter Sessions.

29th March 1827…That they had viewed part of a certain common and ancient Kings Highway commencing at the confines of the Parish of Garway where the said parish ajoins Skenfrith and extending to a certain place called Broad Oak in the said parish of Garway in length one thousand seven hundred and sixty yards and in breadth twelve feet. And that they did on the same day visit and inspect certain part of the new highway lately made and substituted in lieu or stead of the indicted Highway which said part of the said new Highway was then in good and substantial repair and condition and likely to continue.

Part of the improvement of this road was the building of a new bridge over the river Monnow near the Bell Inn at Skenfrith. Maps going back to 1577 show an earlier bridge at Skenfrith but there is no description of the earliest bridge or when it was constructed. The following extract from *Bygone Days in the March Wall of Wales* is interesting.

Labouriouse Journey and serche of one John Leylands for England's antiquities geven by hyme as a new yeare's gyfte to King Henri VIII in the XXXXVII yeare of his raygne, begun about 1538.

The River Mone riseth is a place called 'Foresthene' about twenty miles west from Monmouth and the castel of Skenefryth standeth five miles from Monmouth town, on the Mone river, on the very ripe of it. And in times past the river did goe around about the castel dyke. Much of the utterward of the castel yet standeth, the site of it be somewhat lowe; there be a stone bridge over the Mone, a little above the castel yet standeth. Hubert de Burgh, Earl of Kent, was lord of Skenefrythe.

This bridge a little above the castle cannot now be traced but a map, a copy of which is in Skenfrith Church, shows a road along the river and a bridge there which would connect it with the old lane leading up to Garway Church. (There is a local memory of a wire bridge, upstream from the village of Skenfrith, which enabled the local children to cross the river to go to the school in the vestry of Garway church. This consisted to two wires stretched across the river one above the other; one for their feet and one for their hands).

Skenfrith Bridge with the river Monnow in flood

In 1747 a Mr Joseph Austins and a Mr W Seymour attended the Quarter Sessions at Monmouth and asked for the repair of Skenfrith Bridge at the expense of the county of Monmouth. This bridge was described as a gothic bridge with two arches. In 1824 work was begun on the building of a three-arched stone bridge at Skenfrith. Thomas Watkins, the county surveyor, reported to the committee of magistrates on the 9th January 1824.

On attending at Skenfrith I found the masons making their preparations for the erection in the ensuing spring in a regular and workmanlike manner and that a large quantity of stones are dressed. Part of the retaining wall and foundation of one of the piers are laid. The whole preparation I consider to be worth £100.

Samuel Lewis in his topographical dictionary wrote *"in 1825 the village of Skenfrith is intersected by the river Monnow now at last bridged at a cost of £1000 thus shortening the road from London to Milford Haven by seven miles.*

About five years ago I had an interesting conversation with a man who, as a wartime evacuee, had been billeted at Skenfrith. He explained that the stone parapet was lowered on one side of the bridge and wooden railings were erected which could easily be removed. This would have been to enable the 60-foot long RAF transporters known as 'Queen Marys' to negotiate the sharp bend onto the bridge.

The old highway from Ross to Abergavenny went through Skenfrith past the church and over the Norton Brook by bridge and ford. It then went along Brink Lane to Norton Cross where it joined the road from Grosmont. The road continued up the steep hill to Cross Vane, now Crossways. From there the road went past the Boot and Traveller's Seat to Cross Ash. The new road, which was constructed in 1822, went straight from Skenfrith to Norton and then on past Trebella Farm to Cross Ash.

In 1833 during the reign of William IV, the three previous Turnpike Acts were repealed and a new Act passed. The Trustees of the previous Acts had spent a considerable amount of money and there was a deficit on the Credit of Tolls that had been authorised. The money could not be paid off, the interest discharged or the roads kept in repair or improved unless the terms and powers of the previous Acts were enlarged and the Tolls increased and altered. The new Act, applied for by the Grosmont Turnpike Trust, suggested several completely new lines of road that were designed to make the journey from Monmouth to Pontrilas easier and then eventually link up with Hay on Wye.

It was in the 1820's that it became obvious that there were differing opinions about the relative merits of the roads on the opposite sides of the valley. Three Turnpike Trusts were involved; the Herefordshire Turnpike Trust, the Grosmont Turnpike Trust and the Monmouth Turnpike Trust. The Trustees included all the Justices of the Peace for Hereford and Monmouth. At the April quarter Sessions for 1833, the Grosmont Turnpike Trust filed a general statement of the Income and Expenditure of Turnpike roads lately called the Grosmont Turnpike Trust but now called the Ross, Abergavenny and Hay Turnpike Trusts. All these Trusts were involved in the new Act and were concerned with promoting their own schemes for new roads in the valley.

In 1828, Thomas Wakeman of Gloucester (he had not yet moved to The Graig at Cross Ash), was asked by the Trustees of the Grosmont District of Roads to survey the road from Pontrilas to Welsh Newton. This completed survey was sent to Mr John Lucy Scudamore at Kentchurch Court on 25th July 1828 so that he could present it to the Grosmont Trust

Gentlemen.

In obedience to your instructions I have made a survey and plan of the Tunpike Road from Pontrilas to the end of the District in the parish of Llanrothal where it joins the old Hereford and Monmouth Trust.

The line generally is very badly laid out, a worse could scarcely have been found. It abounds in inconveniently short turns and sharp pitches with two long and dangerously steep hills, one at Demesnes in the parish of Garway and the other at

Pembridge castle in the parish of Welsh Newton. The road is so narrow in many parts as not to allow of two teams passing each other. The materials made use of are the common red stones of the county excepting in Kentchurch and the south end of Garway where a sort of limestone is found which makes an excellent road.

From Pontrilas to Kentchurch, a distance of about two miles, the road is in very good repair from thence to the end of the parish it is bad and narrow but Mr Scudamore having kindly undertaken the management of it, for the parish, the repairs have been commenced in a very superior style and under very judicious arrangements made by the gentleman and the scientific mode in which the work is conducted there can be no doubt that in a short time it will be made a very good road throughout.

The road through the parish of Garway is generally very bad. It will require to be lifted and reformed throughout, but it is supposed that there is already nearly sufficient stone upon it when properly broken and spread to do it with a little new stone where wanted and therefore it may be done at comparatively small expense, although from the great length, (nearly five miles) the total amount will be a serious burden to the parish. The hill at the Demesne is at present dangerously steep rising in some places one in 8% and one in nine. This may be materially improved by deviating to the left as shown by the red line in the plan and the acclivity be reduced to one in 16, perhaps less. It will be necessary to throw a bridge over the brook at the bottom of the hill, and two culverts to carry two other small streams. The total expense of this great improvement, I estimate at £320 only, and it having been proposed to do so by subscription I am authorised by Lord Southwell to put down his name for £100. His Lordship will also give the land which I calculate is equal to £100 more. Should the subscription be made up as I confidently expect it will I should propose commencing the work immediately after the harvest.

The Road through the parish of Welsh Newton is extremely bad. The Hill at Pembridge Castle forms the greatest part of it in this parish. The acclivity here is in some places nearly one in seven and it does not appear possible to avoid it by any deviation that can be made without increasing the distance very considerably. The best and cheapest plan therefore will be to lower the crown of the Hill and fill up the bottom, by which manner the acclivity may be reduced to about one in 15, in the best part and I have no doubt the excavation would produce sufficient stone to cover the whole by which a considerable sum would be saved in hauling and quarrying elsewhere. It is hoped a sufficient sum may be raised by subscription to carry this desirable improvement into effect.

In the parish of Llanrothal the road must be lifted and reformed the whole way and a good coat of new stone laid on and a culvert built over the stream at the junction with the Hereford and Monmouth road.

ESTIMATE		£	s	d
Parish of Kentchurch		300	0	0
" Garway	5 miles	737	0	0
Garway,	Demesne Hill	320	0	0
Welsh Newton		100	0	0
Welsh Newton	Extra for lowering the castle hill	310	0	0
Llanrothal		111	15	0
	£	1878	15	0

In this estimate nothing is deducted for the statute duty
Thomas Wakeman   Gloucester 25 July 1828

Work obviously did not start straight after the harvest and Thomas Wakeman wrote again to Mr Scudamore at the end of October.

Dear Sir,

As the season is so far advanced I think it would be perhaps better to defer commencing operations on the Demesne Hill to the spring by which time we may perhaps have obtained a sufficient sum to do the whole. If however the commissioners insist upon its being begun immediately we may commence raising stones for the purpose and mark out the road and if the weather turns out favourable we may form the road which I propose to do 20 feet wide which allowing for sloping of the banks would be about 25 feet between the fences. If no more subscriptions can be obtained we must leave the bridge and alterations at the lower part of the Hill for the present and if the road is stoned 12 feet wide and 9 inches thick in the centre and 6 inches at the sides I should think it might do although I should certainly propose stoning it 15 feet wide if the funds would admit of it being done. Two good culverts will be required to take the water which flows down the dingles were necessary. The fences to consist of a good cop and bank planted with quick and properly fenced with a good substantial dry hedge. As to the time the whole might have been finished during the summer in two months but at this season a great deal will depend on the weather. The sooner it could be formed the better but I should certainly recommend that it should not be opened for travelling before May or June allowing time for the newly made ground to settle and consolidate. As I should consider myself but as an agent in the business I should draw the money as wanted to pay the workmen and as the operations went on.

I am, etc

Gloucester 31st Oct 1828 *Thomas Wakeman*

The closure of the road to Kentchurch and Pontrilas must have made life very difficult for the locals (as it did in 2001 when the Foot and Mouth epidemic closed the road for a couple of months) the alternative route being over Garway Hill and through Orcop.

By 1830 ideas seem to have been forming to improve the line of communication from Monmouth to Hay on Wye. Similar arguments were put forward as had been suggested nearly one hundred years before by the supporters of the river navigation. Letters to the Grosmont Trustees suggested that a good road from Monmouth through Grosmont would help open up the trade coming from Bath and Bristol through to Aberystwyth and North Wales.

The Grosmont Trust made application in 1832 to the Exchequer Loan Commissioners to borrow money on the Tolls collected on their roads. They stated in their application that they were about to have their Act renewed and they would include in the new Act an improved thoroughfare from Bristol and the Passages through Monmouth to Aberystwyth and a proportion of the loan would be expended on this improvement. Mr Fosbrook was engaged to survey the nearest and best line of road from Pontrilas to Skenfrith.

Mr William Fosbrook was tenant of the Tram Inn and was both innkeeper and repair contractor on the Hereford tramway for which he was paid £120 a year and an allowance of £10 4s per mile. He was a man of some substance and a land surveyor by trade. Before being commissioned to survey the roads in the Monnow valley, he had in 1827 been employed by Mr Scudamore to produce a schedule of the land required from Mr Scudamore for the construction of the Hereford railway. Evidently,

Mr Fosbrook found himself too busy with land survey work to continue with the repair contract on the railway as, in 1831 a notice appeared inviting tenders for the repair work, the applications to be sent to Mr Fosbrook himself. At this time no-one was interested but in 1836 there was a further notice which was successful.

MEMORANDUM FOR ROAD FROM PONTRILAS TO SKENFRITH 20TH AUGUST 1832.   PRINTED BY W.FARROR. ROSS

An application was lately made by the Trustees of the Grosmont Road to the Exchequer Loan Commissioners to borrow money on the Tolls collected on their Roads, and it was stated in such application that they were about to have their Act renewed, and that they should include therin an improved thoroughfare from Bristol and the Passages through Monmouth to Aberystwyth, to the Hay and to North Wales, and to pass through the ancient towns of Grosmont and Skenfrith, and to effect which a proportion of the Loan would be expended.

Mr Fosbrook's survey of the nearest and best line of Road from Pontrilas to Skenfrith (although the nearest and best Road for the public accommodation if continued to Monmouth) does not agree with the Trustees application to the Exchequer Loan Commissioners for the following reasons, because unless that Road which Mr Fosbrook suggests from Pontrilas to near Skenfrith is continued down the river Monnow to Monmouth, it is not the nearest Road from Monmouth to Grosmont and Skenfrith.

In case the Road Mr Forbrook had suggested is continued down the Monnow side from near Skenfrith to Monmouth, two horses would draw as much to Skenfrith, Grosmont, Kentchurch and Pontrilas, as four horses can draw on the present roads to either of these places, and in addition there being no hills on the Roads, Mr Fosbrook has suggested that on the Herefordshire side of the river Monnow, the distance would be three miles less from Monmouth to Skenfrith and Grosmont and four miles less distance from Monmouth to Kentchurch and Pontrilas, than the present Roads, or any Roads that can be made by Rockfield, Hilstone and the Boot, to any of these places.

It is submitted to the Commission of the Grosmont Trust, whether the present Road from Pontrilas to Rampant House might not be made use of without any expenditure for the present, and only make a new Road from Rampant House, agreeably to Mr Fosbrook's plan towards Skenfrith, which distance is 2 miles 3 furlongs 10 yards (and the raising of the money being the obstacle with the Grosmont Commissioners) and concluding those Gentlemen whose Estates this Road would pass through, will be so much benefited by the improvement that there can be no doubt of their giving the land required and fencing the Road, and if that be the case, it is suggested that those 4190 yards from the Rampant House to near Skenfrith, be made and stoned only in part so as to make it passable, and stone the other part, and improve the Road on to Pontrilas as the funds increase; by this plan the Road would be soon made passable so as to pay Tolls towards repairs.

In case the Road was made from Pontrilas to near Skenfrith according to Mr Fosbrook's plan and not continued on to Monmouth, it is a question as to whether it would increase the travelling and Tolls, it is presumed it would not be an accommodation to the public or increase the Tolls, unless continued from near Skenfrith to Monmouth, in which case, the Tolls would be increased. If this nearer and leveller communication were opened to Skenfrith, Grosmont, Kentchurch and Pontrilas, who would travel that hilly road from Monmouth by Rockfield, Hilstone to Skenfrith and Grosmont etc., when this nearer and level road is made passable, and also a large and extensive country would be brought three miles nearer, coal and market.

On this line of Road the fine pure lime near and under the Darran Wood, to be used without burning, and lately discovered to have no Magnesia in it, would be taken considerable distance and is of the greatest importance to the landed interests and farmers around Monmouth, Ross and Hereford etc., because the Doward lime is composed of Magnesia which is poisonous to Vegetation, and this country being a silicious sand, requires a calcarious soil to mix with it, to make a good vegetable soil.

To open the Road from near Skenfrith Bridge to Monmouth there would be about 1200 yards of new Road to be made and 988 yards to be widened.

It is submitted to the Trustees of the Grosmont Road, that they should include in their Act of Parliament the road through Skenfrith to Grosmont and under the Castle Hill at Grosmont to the Cap, by which means they will make communication from the neighbourhood of Skenfrith and Grosmont and the extensive estates of the Duke of Beaufort, with the Railroad from Abergavenny to Hereford.

Also a power should be taken in the Act to make the nearest communication to meet the intended new line of road from the Boot, into the Ross and Abergavenny Road, because by the last Act of the Monmouth Commissioners, they have the power to make a new road from the Onion to Newcastle, and whenever that is made and the new Road stated in their last Act, also is made from the Boot to the Ross Abergavenny Road, if continued to Grosmont by the Grosmont Trust, and under the Castle Hill, it will be the nearest Road from Usk, Abergaveny Raglan and that neighbourhood to the Hay etc.

In case the Gentlemen who are interested in the Road from Pontrilas to Hay will subscribe to have that Road surveyed and mapped, it suggested to the Grosmont Trustees whether they had not better have that Road included in the new Act, which will come into the road leading from Hereford to Hay, which is about five miles from the latter place.

If the landed proprietors beyond Pontrilas would give land and fence it, and lend money to improve the present Road from Pontrilas to the Road leading from Hereford to Hay, there can be no objection, if the money be advanced, it would be a most desirable and important thoroughfare opened for the West of England to North Wales etc., and which must pay tolls to meet all expenses and it is submitted that at all events it should be included in the new Act that the Grosmont Trustees intend to apply for the next Session of Parliament

William Fosbrook completed his detailed survey of the roads on both sides of the river Monnow and in several places he proposed completely new lines of road. On the Grosmont side a new line of road was proposed to start at the bottom of the hill into Grosmont going around the castle hill just above the river past the Lawns farm and crossing Cupid's Hill. It continued to Monmouth Cap public house at Llangua and on to Pontrilas; a total of three miles seven furlongs of new road.

On the Herefordshire side of the river the new road was to cross the meadow opposite Skenfrith castle and follow the river closely past Garway Mill, below Cockshot wood and through Demesne farm to join the old road at the Rampart (now Ramping) House, a total length of new road from Skenfrith to Pontrilas being three miles five furlongs.

Although the survey was made from Skenfrith to Hay on behalf of the Grosmont Trust, the line to be taken from Monmouth to Skenfrith was a major consideration

THOMAS TUDOR   1785 – 1855

Monmouth Museum

Any scheme for a road in this area would involve the Monmouth Turnpike Trust. There were two schools of thought about the route this connection should take and lobbying was going on in 1832 to have included in the Act either one of these schemes.

The pamphlet printed in August 1832 by F Farror of Ross, sets out to demonstrate that the route favoured by the Grosmont Commissioners, which was the route through Rockfield and Newcastle does not accord with that proposed by Mr Fosbrooke which followed the river Monnow from Skenfrith, through Llanrothal to Monmouth. Unless the road was continued down the river from Skenfrith to Monmouth it would not shorten the total distance from Monmouth to Pontrilas or avoid the very steep hills. The road through Rockfield and Newcastle to Skenfrith was very hilly and was three miles longer than the proposed road alongside the river. In fact this new road would only require "two horses where four were needed on the present roads".

It was proposed that the new road alongside the river would start near Skenfrith Bridge and 1200 yards of completely new road would have to be made passing under the Darren wood to Llanrothal where it would join the existing road. The road from Llanrothal via Tregate to Monmouth would need widening. The pamphlet continues to point out that if the improvements were made from Pontrilas to Skenfrith and not continued down the river to Monmouth it was doubtful if there would be any advantage to the public as it would not decrease the travelling time and would in fact increase the number of toll gates to be passed through. It was also suggested that the Gentlemen who owned the land over which the road would pass, might be prepared to pay for the section from the Ramping House to Skenfrith. It was thought that these landowners would benefit so much from this shortened route to Monmouth that they would be prepared to give the land and also to stone and fence this new road.

Mr Thomas Tudor, acting on behalf of Mr Lucy Scudamore, attended meetings of the various Trust Commissioners. Thomas Tudor (1785-1855) was born in Monmouth the fourth son of Owen Tudor. He trained as a professional artist at the Royal Academy but he was a man of many talents; he was a land agent, solicitor and agent for insurance, bookseller and surveyor.

In his capacity as a land agent he was responsible for the management of the Kentchurch estate. Between 1822 and 1825 when Mr Lucy Scudamore and his wife were on the continent, Mr Tudor supervised substantial alterations to John Nash's Kentchurch Court, designing a portico in a castellated Gothic style. He had some famous paintings including a Reynolds and a Van Dyke in his house at Wyesham.

Thomas Tudor, acting in his capacity as agent for John Lucy Scudamore, was involved with the decisions as to which line the new roads would take. He wrote to Mr Scudamore on 1st November 1832.

Dear Sir,

As the Commissioners of the Grosmont Turnpike Trust seem really about to do something towards the improvement of their roads, I wish to give you all the information I have obtained on that subject. The Grosmont Trust proposed to the Monmouth Commissioners that the Monmouth Trust should adopt the road from Monmouth to Skenfrith.

I attended a meeting of the Monmouth Commissioners this day when this proposal was taken into consideration and a committee was appointed to enquire into the facts and report on the subject. The road has been surveyed on both sides of the river, but the Surveyor seems rather to recommend the Hilstone side. The best line for the Public will be the best for you to this point (that is from Monmouth to Skenfrith), therefore you need not trouble yourself so far- but the line the Grosmont Commissioners may adopt is very important and therefore should be watched and if possible guided. There is a meeting at Harewood End next Monday when this will be decided on, when I hope you may be present.

I understand it is proposed to improve the present line from Skenfrith to Grosmont and on to Monmouth Cap through part of Mrs James Farm and through part of Llangua Great House Farm. I think it is very important to your interest if a good leading line of road is formed to Grosmont, it should pass on to The Cap for if a road should be opened (as is not improbable) up the Golden Valley The Cap would according to this place be the established Inn upon the road, and on this ground I should think the plan deserves your encouragement. But your communication on the Kentchurch side is of still more importance to you and if the Grosmont Trust will not at present take up the improvement of that line it is very desirable that the <u>power to do so</u> (whenever means can be found for the purpose) <u>should be taken in the new Act</u>.

There seem to me three lines by either of which this improved communication may be effected. The first is under Demains hill to Skenfrith Bridge according to Mr Forsbrook's plan. The second is to cross the Monnow at the foundation of an old bridge near Duffrin (a little above Demains farm) and continue the road by the side of the Monnow to Skenfrith. The third plan is to cross the Monnow at Corras to the Grosmont road at Pontyseal.

Of these plans I think the first is on the whole decidedly the best – each of the others involving the necessity of a new bridge over the Monnow and the last plan through Corras adding to the extent of land in the parish of Kentchurch.

I should have been glad to have talked over these subjects with you but it is impossible for me to come to you before the meeting at Harewood and I have therefore thought it best to write.

In May 1833 the Act of Parliament was passed and included all the recommendations from Skenfrith to Hay but did not mention the road from Skenfrith to Monmouth, and during the next two years estimates were sought for the building of these roads.

The cost of laying a new line of road or for repairing an existing road was considerable as is shown by the work carried out by the Monmouth Turnpike Trust during one year.

Day labour
Cleaning slopes
Scraping the road
Laying stone
Stocking stone
Raising stone in different quarries
Teams for hauling stone
Breaking stone
Repairing turnpike houses
Damage of land
Rent of quarries
Filling and levelling quarries
New tools and repairing old ones
Salaries – Treasurer and surveyor.

The income received by the Trusts was derived from the tolls collected, either by their own appointed toll collectors or by renting out or auctioning the tolls. Parishes would also pay a contribution in lieu of their statute duty

Lord Southwell, a Roman Catholic, was Lord of the Manor of Garway. The Southwell family had a long lineage. John Southwell Esq, of Barham in Essex removed his family to Ireland during the reign of James 1. He had four sons. A descendent was Thomas Anthony, the 3rd Viscount who was born in 1777 and died in 1853. He had a large family, two sons and five daughters. His first son, Thomas Arthur died in 1829 aged 28 and his second son Charles Henry Robert died unmarried. His daughters were Sophia, married in 1830 to Marquis de Choiseul Beaupre; Laura who died unmarried in 1864, Paulina who died young, Matilda-Maria who was married in September 1839 to the Right Hon Richard More O'Ferrall, and the youngest Paulina who was married in 1844 to a Sardinian Count. Matilda-Maria was heir to the Garway estate. The family home was at Hindlip, which is just north-east of Worcester. Early in the 19th century, Thomas Wakeman had been steward to Lord Southwell but by 1835 William Hooper of Ross was the steward of the Manor of Garway. John Lucy Scudamore had written to Lord Southwell on the subject of the new Turnpike roads and Southwell replied on 9th November 1835.

Dear Scudamore,

I have been prevented by absence from home these two or three days past from sooner answering your letter of the 4th. Road making is certainly most conducive to convenience and enjoyment, and frequently also to utility and the improvement of property, and I have little doubt but the opening a communication from Skenfrith to Monmouth on the one hand and the Railroad at Monmouth Cap on the other, would as you observe, benefit our tenants of Garway, but from my ignorance of the locality, I am not aware whether the line stated in the paper you enclosed, and for which a subscription on foot (viz from Tresenny bridge to the Cap by Grosmont) includes the whole of the space to be improved between Skenfrith and the Cap or only a small fraction of it? I have written for some information on the subject and will again have the pleasure of writing to you.

I regret to say that it will again be out of my power to avail myself of your kind invitation to Kentchurch, to join you on an attack on your pheasants. We are unfortunately under the necessity of going to spend the winter on the southern coast, or perhaps even France on account of my youngest daughter's very delicate state of health and we propose leaving home in the course of a few days. My brothers are now in Ireland, but I believe they will both visit this country before the end of the month. I shall not fail to mention your friendly recollection to them when I write. The Bodenhams whom you enquire after, are spending the winter at Rotherwas. I hear that he has been somewhat annoyed by these illiberal attacks, which under the mask of Religion have been levelled against our Whig Politics by itinerant preachers.

Lady Southwell and my daughter write with me for best compliments to Mrs Scudamore and I am dear Scudamore, very sincerely yours. Southwell.

By the following September there had still been no progress towards making a road from Skenfrith to Monmouth alongside the river. Mr William Hooper, Steward to Lord Southwell replied to a letter from Mr Scudamore on 9th September 1836.

Dear Sir,

Since the receipt of your favour of 31st ult I have been in Lancashire, which will account for my silence.

The proposed measure of making a line of road from near Skenfrith Bridge on the left bank of the Monnow River by Llanrothal to Monmouth if you remember, was <u>one of our first great improvements</u> contemplated on the renewal of our late Turnpike Act. – and after battling this point with the Monmouth Gentlemen, we were <u>compelled</u> to abandon it, and <u>to adopt</u> their line from Hilstone to Grosmont and Pontrilas, which Mr Wyatt contended, with others, was the best line from Monmouth to the Golden Valley – instead of following nearly the course of the Monnow from Monmouth and Llanrothal, Skenfrith and Kentchurch to Pontrilas.

I need not touch upon the <u>kindness</u> which allowed the making of a line of road from Rampart House to Skenfrith Bridge – the folly of <u>insisting</u> upon the worst of all bad lines of Road from Monmouth to the Golden Valley.

If a road can now be made from Skenfrith Bridge by Llanrothal and the vale of the Monnow to Monmouth, it shall have my best wishes and support, but I fear its practicality.

I expect Lord Southwell shortly in England and when he arrives, I will lay your letter before him and such other information upon this subject as I an procure.
I remain, dear sir, your obedient servant, Wm Hooper.

To make the road from Monmouth to Pontrilas through Garway and Kentchurch, the shortest and least hilly route, two conditions were necessary. First, an agreement between the Monmouth Turnpike Trust and the Grosmont Commissioners and secondly that the owners of the land and estates through which the road would pass would give their land and help finance the project. Lord Southwell and the farmers in the parish of Garway were in agreement as this route would be of great benefit to them. The land from Skenfrith Bridge to the existing road in Llanrothal on which a completely new road would have to be built belonged to Charles John Kemeys-Tynte.

Charles John Kemeys-Tynte was married to Elizabeth Swinnerton of Wonastow Court. She had inherited considerable property that included land in Llanrothal and Garway. Charles was not a man known for his frugality or philanthropy. He followed his father into Parliament and he lived well in Mayfair, Paris, Hastings and Brighton. Elizabeth died in 1838 and Charles John remarried in 1841 when Cefn Mably was settled on him. He went deeply into debt over the years, mortgaging all his estates, even those in which he only had a future interest, contingent on the deaths of others. Eventually in 1858 this would lead him into the court of Chancery and he had to give up his seat in Parliament and live abroad in Brussels. In his old age Charles retired to Torquay and died with very little personal estate in 1882.

Kemeys-Tynte was approached by John Scudamore asking him to give the land on which to build the new road. He replied from Mount Street, London on 3rd November 1837.

My dear Scudamore,

I have to acknowledge your letter of the 26th respecting the projected new road near Monmouth which will be of great advantage to that part of the country, and in aid of which undertaking I will willingly subscribe £25 but I am informed by my lawyer that my estate at Llanrothal being entailed I am incapable of conveying away any part of it. The Trustees of my Settlement can only do so upon payment of the value of the land.
I am Sir, yours sincerely, C Keneys-Tynte.   Ross, 21st December 1837

Sir,

I beg to inform you that I attended a Meeting of the Gentlemen of Garway respecting your wish of making a road from the Rampart House to Skenfrith, when it was determined that the same, if not continued by the banks of the Monnow to Monmouth, would be of no advantage to the Agriculturists of that district. And I have further to inform you that for these reasons the Rev. Vaughan and Mr Prosser decline either to sell or give their land.

At the same time I was informed that every support would be rendered in making a Road from Rampart House along the Monnow to Monmouth. I have written to Lord Southwell and remain Sir, your obedient servant.   William Hooper.

The failure of Kemeys-Tynte to give his land was very disappointing but the Monmouth Turnpike Trust were equally unhelpful due, most likely to their financial problems. They were seriously in debt. Their expenditure on the repair of roads, the repayment on the Mortgage of Tolls and interest due, exceeded the income they received from the tolls and there was no money to spare for new road building. The amount of income the Trust collected by way of tolls was also falling partly due to cheating and partly by the exemption claimed by post coaches which carried the mail.

The timber wagons passing through Monmouth are an example of one of the ways the turnpike trust was being cheated. Because of the hilly nature of the land around Monmouth it was necessary to use up to six horses to pull these wagons. Tolls were evaded by removing some of the horses before descending the hill into Monmouth and only paying for the horses which pulled the wagon through the toll gate. The other horses would be walked through. This was a serious loss if income. The toll for drawing a timber wagon was 9d for every horse in the summer and 1/6d during the winter. A horse not drawing a wagon but being walked through the toll, summer or winter cost 1 ½ d.

The loss of income from coaches was even more serious. Any horse or carriage employed for the carrying of mails under the authority of the Postmaster General was exempt from the payment of tolls. There were several mail coaches passing through

Monmouth each day. The London to Carmarthan mail arrived in Monmouth at 4 o'clock in the morning, returning a 8 o'clock in the evening of the same day; the North Mail which passed through the town at 8 o'clock in the morning and returned at 2 o'clock in the afternoon and the Gloucester to Abergavenny Mail which arrived in Monmouth at 8.30 a.m. and returned through Monmouth at 7 o'clock in the evening from Abergavenny. The last named coach had been a daily post coach paying annually to the Trust the sum of £124.16s 6d. The commissioners for the Trust suggested in a letter to the Postmaster General that there were quite enough coaches carrying mail and that the Gloucester Abergavenny mail be discontinued, especially as there was no mail carried from Monmouth or Ross to any of the intermediate villages between Gloucester and Abergavenny. The Trustees considered that the mail was not needed, that there was no guard on the coach and that as other mails already travelled the same route they could give all the accommodation required.

A warning to coach drivers!
A Memorial on the roadside between Llandeilo and Llandovery

Nothing was ever done about this road from the Rampart House to Monmouth. The Grosmont Commissioners favoured their own route and the farmers of Garway were not prepared to give their land unless they were able to travel to Monmouth without hills. Perhaps if Mr Kemeys-Tynte's land at Llanrothal Court had not been entailed the road would have been possible, but the resulting impasse brought this rather grandiose plan to a permanent closure.

When the Grosmont Railway (a horse drawn tramway from Llanfiangel to Llangua) was built in 1835 the Railway Company built a toll road from Pandy to Monmouth Cap. At that time there were no roads in this area except for farm tracks. The main road went over the hill past Campston from Monmouth Cap to Llanviangel Crucorney. This new road would have been a great improvement especially for hauliers and coaches.

In 1853 when the Newport-Abergavenny-Hereford Railway was built the old tracks from the tramroad were lifted and sold causing considerable local disruption. The Grosmont Parish Vestry Meeting complained to the Surveyor of Highways claiming compensation for the damage done to the Parish roads by railway contractors or their servants. When the new railway company bought out the tramroad, part of their purchase was the toll road from Penisarplwyf to Llangua. The company sold this road to John Lucy Scudamore of Kentchurch in 1861. It became the subject of much correspondence between the Grosmont Vestry and Kentchurch estate and heated discussion within Parish meetings.

Many years later in July 1897 an article appeared in the local paper, probably the Hereford Times, reporting on a dinner given at the Pandy Inn in honour of Mr John Lewis.

The general public for some years past have been made familiar with the grievance existing by reason of the main road between Hereford and Abergavenny, for the distance of some four miles or so, being intersected by a private thoroughfare known as "The Monmouth Cap" road, which extends between Monmouth Cap and Penisharplwyd Toll Gate. Foremost to do away with this grievance was Mr John Lewis, Great Goytre, who almost single-handed has laboured to do away with the expense and inconvenience incident to a private road and its toll bar; the last toll bar to intersect a main road in the country. The Abergavenny Rural District Council in due course saw its way clear to take over the thoroughfare to be henceforth dedicated as a free highway to the travelling public.

Mr Lewis was presented with a suitable testimonial which took the form of a handsomely illuminated address, enclosed in a massive oak and gilt frame, the work of Messrs Dergeant Bros, Abergavenny, and a purse of gold, containing £19, also a photograph, enclosed in a suitable frame, of the "Old Toll Bar", the work of Mr Houlson, photographer, Abergavenny. The article continued for four columns of newspaper.

Monmouth Troy Station, before and after Beeching! *Monmouth Museum*
The station building has been re-erected at Winchcombe, Gloucestershire

210

RAILWAYS

The plan for a north-south road so long ago amply demonstrates the existence of traffic along routes which border the valley of the river Monnow and although no statistics are available, it is probable that such traffic, whether considerable or not, may have encouraged some of the plans to be put forward in this chapter. All of these plans come into being as a result of the advent of railways in our country from 1825 onwards.

A look at the map shows that the Monnow valley connects the substantial town of Monmouth with Pontrilas, passing through Skenfrith and Grosmont. In railway terms, the two ends of the Monnow valley were connected to the railway network quite some time after the initial development of the steam railway. To the north, on approximately the line of three Tramways – legally Railway Companies, had been built the Newport, Abergavenny and Hereford Railway, opened 2nd January 1854. The three tramways were finally closed in April 1853 and all wagons and other items had to be cleared from the line. All the old 'tram-plates, tie bars and chairs' were put up for sale. The Newport, Abergavenny and Hereford Railway amalgamated with the Oxford, Worcester and Wolverhampton Railway and the Worcester and Hereford Railway to form the West Midlands Railway from 1st July 1860. This company in its turn was absorbed into the Great Western Railway from 1st August 1863 and gave access to South Wales, the Midlands, London and the North and played a significant part in opening the areas it served to improved trade and wider social influences.

To the south, the town of Monmouth had to wait until 12th June 1857 for the arrival of its first trains, via the Coleford, Monmouth, Usk and Pontypool Railway. The Act for constructing this railway was obtained in August 1853 and Crawshay Bailey was the Chairman of the company. The prospectus describes the many advantages of this railway.

The Line is twenty-two miles in length, and commences by a junction with the Newport, Abergavenny and Hereford Railway, near Pontypool; continuing from thence by way of Usk, Raglan, Monmouth and Coleford, to the Iron and Coal Works of the Forest of Dean.

By this means of Railway, two Mineral and Manufacturing districts, containing a population of nearly 500,000 persons, and hitherto practically excluded from mutual intercourse, will be brought into immediate connection, as the transit may be effected in little more than an hour; and the vast iron Works of Monmouthshire and South Wales, consisting of upwards of one hundred blast furnaces, and requiring an intermixture of Forest Ores, will thus obtain the supplies cheaply and expeditiously.

The fine Agricultural district in the centre of Monmouthshire will also be opened to direct and ready markets for its production at both ends of the line; and Timber, Cordwood, Pitwood and Bark (staple articles of produce, both in Monmouthshire and the Forest of Dean), will largely contribute to the traffic.

This railway terminated its journey at Monmouth and another Company built the Monmouth to Coleford section at a much later date.

Victorian travellers wishing to travel to Bristol, London or other destinations by rail had no option but to travel on this railway taking them via Pontypool, Newport and Chepstow, a journey of some 43 miles.

Many previous plans to bring the railway to Monmouth had been thwarted, including a project by Brunel for a line from Ross to Monmouth. The South Wales line was diverted from Chepstow to Newport and the Gloucester line taken from Ross to Hereford, leaving Monmouth isolated. The Monmouthshire Gazette writing in 1851 blamed the Great Western Railway and called it 'a company which has never allowed gross wrong or fraudulent means to prevent the carrying out of their ends'. Strong criticism indeed!

There was real concern in Monmouth that they were missing out on the enormous benefits being brought to towns by the advent of the railway. While most of the towns around had rail connections Monmouth was still isolated. Coaches would take passengers to Gloucester station and meet the trains when they returned. Needless to say, the coach owners had a vested interest in keeping the railways away, but as the arrival of the railway became inevitable, the coach owners concentrated their business in areas where the railways would never reach.

The next approach to Monmouth was quite extraordinary and took the form of an Act for the Worcester, Dean Forest and Monmouth Railway that was passed in 1863. Nothing ever came of the proposals for what would have been a very difficult line.

The next railway to reach the County town was the Ross on Wye and Monmouth Railway that followed what was probably the finest and most picturesque route for any train journey. The route was opened to Monmouth May Hill in August 1873 and extended across the river Wye to Troy station on 1st May 1874.

The third railway into Monmouth was the Wye Valley Railway from Chepstow opened to Troy on 1st November 1876, another picturesque route. This new line from Monmouth to Chepstow shortened the distance from 43 miles via Newport, to only 15 miles making access to Bristol much easier for both commerce and the general public. By 1874 there were plans to build the Severn Tunnel and it was envisaged that the Wye Valley line could play a role in linking Bristol via the tunnel with the North of England.

The fourth and last railway was the Coleford Railway from Monmouth to Coleford which opened 1st September 1883. This was on the line of the Monmouth Railway which had been incorporated in 1810 and was usually referred to as the Monmouth Tramway. It went from Monmouth via Lord's Grove and Newland to Howler Slade, near Coleford in the Forest of Dean with a branch from Lord's Grove to Lower Redbrook. It remained horsedrawn and traffic declined steadily until the 1860's. The line was bought by the Coleford, Monmouth, Usk and Pontypool Railway Company in 1866. In 1876 the Coleford Railway Company bought up all the old 1813 tramway tracks and straightened out many of the sharp curves on the five-mile stretch from Monmouth to Coleford. This railway had an average gradient of 1 in 40 and there were restrictions imposed on the type of rolling stock that could be used. No tender engines were allowed nor carriages over 50 feet long. The Coleford Railway ceased to operate after 31st December 1916 and shortly afterwards the rails were taken up and it is said that they were sent to Flanders to support the war effort.

By the time the last of the railway quartet reached Monmouth they were all being worked by the Great Western Railway that now controlled the lines at both ends of the Monnow valley. The rather sparse population of the valley and the surrounding countryside must have wondered what was to befall them and their remote existence

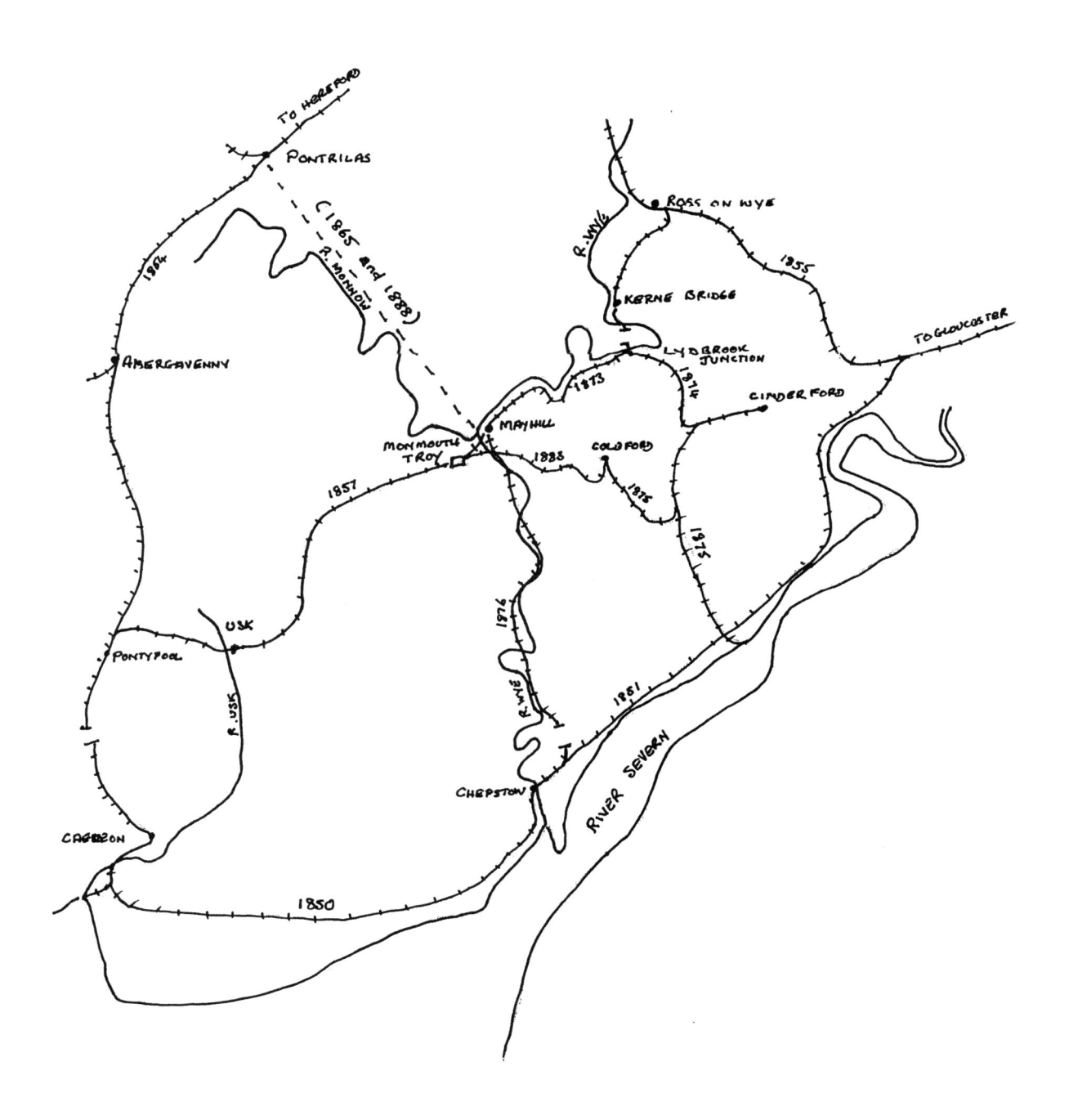

RAILWAYS IN THE MONMOUTH AREA

during the next twenty-five years, while plans were made to join Monmouth and Pontrilas with a railway.

A Public Notice appeared in the Hereford Journal in November 1865 announcing that the Plan and Section of the Monnow Valley Railway was to be laid before Parliament during the Session 1865-6. This Act was to seek powers to make a Railway from Monmouth to Pontrilas – to use portions of the lines of the Coleford, Monmouth Usk and Pontypool and Great Western Companies – to make working and other arrangements with the other provisions affecting those Companies and the London and North Western, Worcester, Dean Forest and Monmouth, Ross and Monmouth and Abergavenny and Monmouth Railways Companies. There would be joint stations at Monmouth and Pontrilas. The Bill would also give the power, by compulsion or otherwise, to purchase lands, houses, and other property, for the purpose of building the railway. The Company could also 'cross, alter, divert and stop all highways, turnpike and other roads, railways, tramways, aquaducts, bridges, canals, streams and rivers with which it may be necessary to interfere for the purpose of the said Act, or any of them'. The engineer for this project would be Mr T Curley FGS and Messrs Apperley were to be the surveyors. One of the sponsors for this undertaking was Crawshay Bailey (1789-1872), the famous ironmaster of Nant-y-Glo. He was Tory Member of Parliament for the United Boroughs of Monmouth, Newport and Usk from 1852 to1868 although it is said that he rarely attended the House and seldom spoke except in Committees. He was very committed to the local railway companies and was Chairman of the Coleford, Monmouth, Usk and Pontypool Railway Company and also the Dean Forest, Monmouth Usk and Pontypool Railway Company.

Until the 1860's, all rails used in the construction of the new railways were made of wrought iron and produced in abundance in the South Wales ironworks. After the introduction of steel manufacture, which was much harder and lasted longer, the demand for iron rails disappeared. By the 1880's iron rails had become obsolete and were replaced by the new superior steel rails. Crawshay Bailey was ageing but would not relinquish control over his Company. His ironworks were in serious commercial and financial difficulties, possibly because of his age and being set in his ways, Bailey would not venture into the new age of steel manufacture and transferred most of his industrial properties to a joint stock company in 1870. Within a month of his death in 1872 the Beaufort ironworks closed down.

Setting up a railway was an expensive business. Before even buying the land or laying any track there was money to be found for the considerable expense of legal fees, procuring an Act of Parliament and the cost of surveying. Money was raised by local subscriptions to shares or by the backing from a contractor who was willing to speculate in the new enterprise, or even hopefully, support from a major existing railway company.

The plans produced in 1865 for the proposed Monnow Valley Railway showed that the railway crossed the river Monnow five times and that at each crossing a bridge with a span of 60 feet and a height of 16-20 feet would be needed. It would be necessary to dig two tunnels at Skenfrith, one 475 yards long and one 275 yards long. Several roads would need to be altered, being either raised to pass over a railway bridge or lowered to go under the railway line.

The main disruption of the intended line of railway would have been to the people living in Overmonnow. After passing through the Castle Field, (now Vauxhall fields), and then over the Scud Brook, the railway passed straight over Drybridge Street and then curved round to the west before passing through a tunnel and emerging near

Monmouth Troy Station. Many houses in and around Drybridge Street would have been demolished including the Britannia Inn and the terrace of houses alongside. On the opposite side of the road the toll house was to remain but all the other houses almost as far as Goldwire Lane would have been affected.

At Monmouth, the Monnow Valley line, after emerging from the tunnel, was to run onto the Monmouth, Usk and Pontypool Railway before entering Troy Station, whereas at Pontrilas, after crossing the Monnow for the final time just a few yards south of Llangua bridge, the Monnow Valley line would join the Great Western (Newport, Abergavenny and Hereford Branch). The total length of the new line was to be 12 miles, 4 furlongs and 6 chains.

Although this line failed to materialise, there appears to have been a serious attempt at construction, because as late as 1959 it was still possible to see the beginnings of the tunnel which was intended to pass through the hill quite near Troy station. Mr Shirehampton in his book entitled, *Monmouth's Railways, a Historical Survey*, writes about the mystery of this tunnel which started to penetrate the hill in a north-westerly direction but was never completed.

Financial problems would seem to be the main reason why this line was never built. The contractor Thomas Savin went bankrupt and the other major sponsor, Crawshay Bailey was in such financial difficulties that he had to sell his Ammanford Works to meet his debts.

An interesting footnote to the story of Troy station is the fact that after many years as a road haulage depot and coal yard, the station building was demolished, stone by stone and rebuilt at Winchcombe on the preserved Gloucestershire Warwick Railway.

The Golden Valley Railway was built between the years 1876 and 1889 running from Pontrilas to Dorstone and then extended to Hay. There are several explanations as to why the Golden Valley is so called although I doubt if any of them are true! Bradley, in his book about the Welsh Borders states that the name comes from the Welsh dwr, meaning water which the Normans interpreted as Dore. The Herefordians concluded that this was Norman/French for Gold, hence the Golden Valley. Yet another explanation for the name Golden is given in the 1876 Directory for Herefordshire which says that in the church at Peterchurch is a rude piece of sculpture representing a trout with a gold chain around its neck which is said to have been taken from the river Dore. From this circumstance the valley is said to have taken the name Golden. In Dorstone the tradition is that a fish was caught in the river Dore with a golden ring it its gills yet again giving the valley the name Golden.

The Golden Valley has a level floor about half a mile wide with pastures and orchards and rising to steeply wooded hills on either side. Travelling northwards from Pontrilas at the southern end of the valley the first parish is Abbeydore with the picturesque Abbeydore church which is the only remaining structure of the grand Cistercian Abbey built here in the 12th century. Half way along the valley is the large village of Peterchurch with its church spire, originally dating from 1320 visible for miles around. Just after the Second World War this spire had become too dangerous to be left untouched and so in 1949 the top two thirds of it was demolished. In 1972 after many years of fundraising and then deciding that to rebuild in stone would be too costly, a new fibreglass replica spire was made in three sections measuring 186 feet in height which was raised into place by the tallest mobile crane then available in Europe. The parish of Peterchurch covers an area of 5000 acres and at the end of the 19th century had a population of about 700. It is still a large village with many new houses built in recent years.

By the mid 1870's the Golden Valley and the Monnow Valley were still rather isolated rural communities with very poor communications with the local towns. Letters were being published in the Hereford Times reminiscent of those of over a hundred years previously about the difficulties the farmers had in getting their produce to market. Timber had to be dragged along very poor roads and cattle and sheep driven by foot to market thus arriving in very poor condition. Fruit took too long to arrive at the local market when sent by wagon. It was suggested that all this could be remedied if a railway was built along the Golden Valley.

Mr C E Lane of Peterchurch is credited with starting the ball rolling which was to end with the building of the Golden Valley Railway. On 21st August 1875 he wrote a letter to the Hereford Times suggesting that a railway taking the direct route from Pontrilas to Eardisley by the most direct route would be easy to build and with the good agricultural resources of the valley would be a good paying line. He urged all the landowners to give their support by selling the land needed for a fair market price.

It is understandable why Charles Edwin Lane was so keen to have a railway through Peterchurch. He had a very thriving business conducted from Albion House being a wholesale and family grocer, provision merchant, linen and woollen draper, tailor and general outfitter; dealer in boots and shoes, china, glass, earthenware, ironmongery, sewing machines, etc., importer of wines and spirits; agent for the Alton Court brewery co. of Ross on Wye, and for Guinness's Dublin stout. A railway would have made the delivery of all these commodities to his emporium very much easier.

The Littlebury's Herefordshire Directory for 1876, published just after the Act of Parliament was obtained for building the railway and before work had begun, was very supportive of the whole idea.

The 'Golden Valley railway' will commence at Dorstone, and run parallel with the river Dore through the valley, joining the Great Western main line at Pontrilas. It is proposed to extend this railway from Pontrilas via the Monnow valley to Monmouth on the one hand, and from Dorstone to Eardisley on the other. The Golden Valley is at the present time a terra incognita *to the vast majority of inhabitants of this country, and yet, perhaps, a more beautiful valley is not to be found in the kingdom. It is environed with hills and mountains, knolls and dells, watered by picturesque streams, and presenting to the traveller some of the most delightful scenery of which England can boast.*

At an inaugural meeting held in the schoolroom at Peterchurch on 30th September 1875 it was proposed 'That the formation of a railway through the Golden Valley is most desirable'. There were however doubters, one of whom prophesied that it was a line starting from nowhere and ending nowhere. This motion was passed and a provisional committee was formed to start fundraising and to negotiate with the landowners. At the next meeting on 26th October, one of the main speakers was Mr Green-Price who prophesied that 'the line was destined before very many years to be made a great line'. It was proposed that the line would continue from Pontrilas southward down the Monnow valley and the Wye valley to Chepstow, through the projected Severn Tunnel and on to Bristol. It would also give access to the Forest of Dean Coalfield. To the north it was proposed to extend the line to Eardisley and have connections to North Wales.

The first Golden Valley Railway Act (39&40 vic cap.cxli), was given royal assent on 13th July 1876 and authorised the construction of a line 10 miles long from

Golden Valley Railway

IN PARLIAMENT—SESSION 1888.

THE GOLDEN VALLEY RAILWAY COMPANY.

Book of Reference.

Book of Reference deposited with the Plans and Sections of the Golden Valley Railway, Ordnance Map and Gazette Notice, in my Office at the Shirehall of the County of Hereford the 30th day of November 1887, at 9-10. a. m.

READ & CRIPPS,
    45, Parliament Street,
        Solicitors.

DYSON & CO.,
    24, Parliament Street,
        Parliamentary Agents.

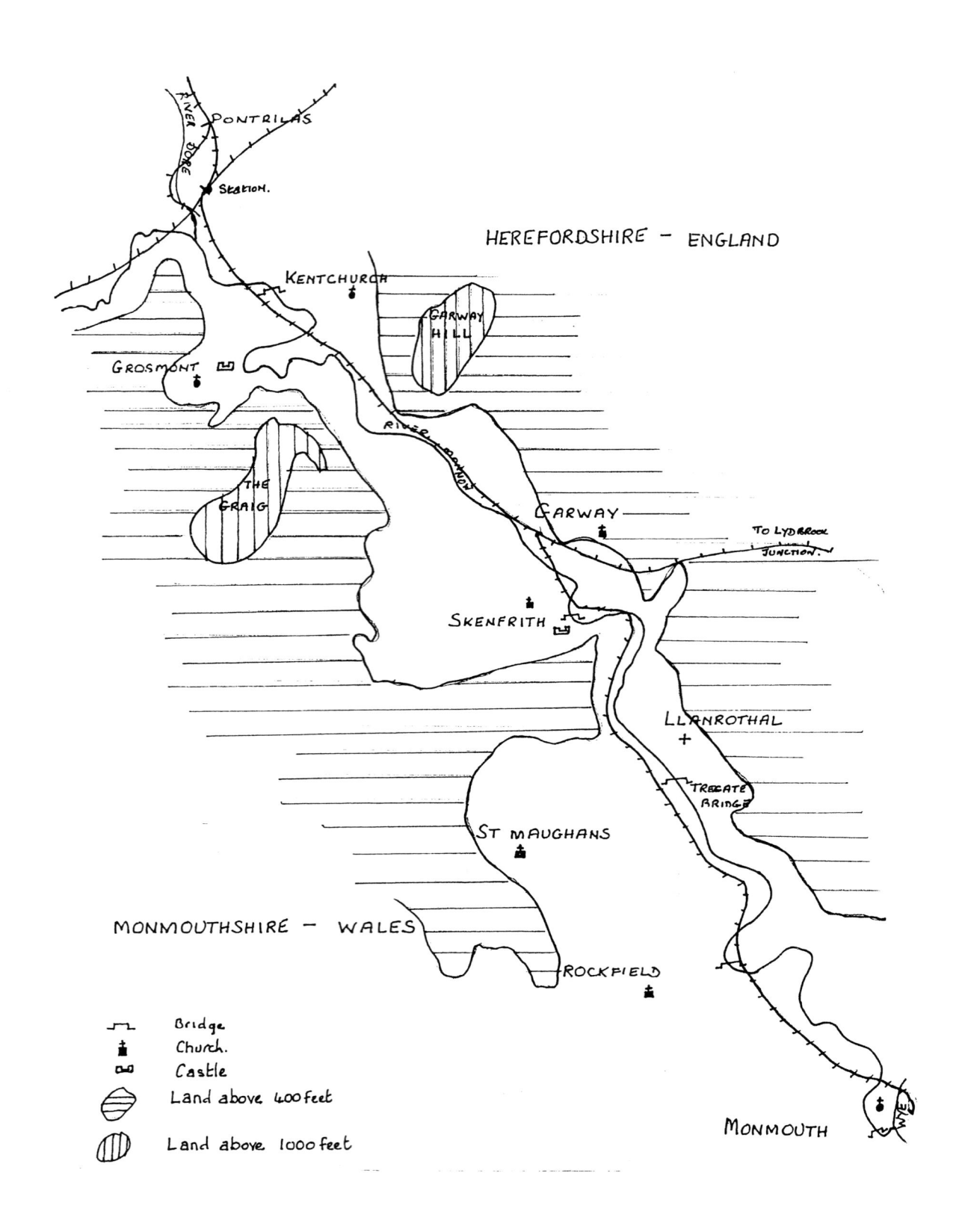

PROPOSED GOLDEN VALLEY RAILWAY EXTENSION TO MONMOUTH

Pontrilas to Dorstone. Lady Cornewall cut the first sod at Peterchurch on 31st August 1876 and work was started at Pontrilas in January 1877.

Seeing this new railway being constructed in the Golden Valley must have excited and aroused great interest in the inhabitants of the Monnow valley for on 21st October 1876 the following report was published in the Monmouthshire Beacon.

There now appears to be every probability that the proposed Monnow Valley Railway from Monmouth to Pontrilas will be carried out. The making of the new line has for some time past been mooted, but it is now taken up in such a spirited and practical manner as to auger well for the carrying out of the scheme. Several meetings on the subject have recently been held in the neighbourhood, the latest was at Grosmont, on Saturday last, when a highly influential number of gentlemen interested in the subject met together to take into consideration the best means of constructing a line to be called the Monnow Valley Railway, and which starting from the junction of the Golden Valley Railway with the Hereford and Newport line at Pontrilas, will run the course of the river Monnow, and form a junction with the Wye Valley line at Monmouth. The course of the proposed line will be as follows;-

Starting from the junction at Pontrilas, the line will infringe upon Cupid's Hill, Great Corras, Castlefields, Lower Duffryn, Trevorney, Garway Mill, the Hill, Skenfrith, Llanrothal, Tregate Bridge, Perthyr Grove, Deepholm, Blackwood, Little Ancre, Ancre Hill (Major), Castlefields, Monmouth Castle, Dialswood and into the Wye Valley Railway on the west bank of the Wye.

The chairman in opening the proceedings, expressed his anxiety to see the line made, and as a first instalment offered to subscribe £2,000 and to take out the value of the land required from him in shares. Mr James Graham followed in a like encouraging manner, and said that while he could not pledge himself in the present incipient state of the undertaking to subscribe largely, he would follow his neighbour's example, and subscribe a couple of thousand and take his land out in shares. Mr Bodenham dwelt upon the encouragement the projected line had generally received from the proprietors of the land through which it would run, and said that he saw no reason why they should not at once proceed with their Bill, and within two-and-a half years the line would be opened. A committee was formed to get the share list filled, and from the hearty manner in which the matter has been taken up there seems no reason why the making of this line should much longer be delayed.

Despite the enthusiasm of these gentlemen it was not until 1883 that the Golden Valley Railway Company deposited the plans for the extension to Monmouth. Securing the necessary private Act of Parliament was very expensive. The cost of presenting the Bill to both houses of Parliament included giving notice of the proposed Bill in the London Gazette and placing notices in the local newspapers. Detailed plans and sections had to be deposited with the clerks of the peace, the town clerks and the parish clerks of any parish through which the railway was to pass. If there was any opposition to the Bill there were hefty legal costs to be paid and the promoters must put their case before the Select Committee of the House of Commons on Railway Bills and then before a Committee of the House of Lords.

On 12th January 1884 it was reported in the Local and district Notes in the Monmouthshire Beacon that -

The promoters of the proposed new line of Railway from Pontrilas to Monmouth are busy in their endeavour to win support for the scheme which next session they intend to lay before Parliament. A meeting a short time ago in Monmouth has been followed by another at Grosmont, the centre of the district which it is believed the line, if constructed, will most benefit. The subscriptions already promised towards the preliminary expenses are very encouraging, and there seems every probability that ere many years have passed the long talked of Monnow Valley Railway may be an accomplished fact. The Great Western Company, we believe, are the only real objectors to the scheme, but any arguments which they can adduce, based as they must be on the desire to prevent competition, will have but little weight with the Imperial Legislature. It may therefore now be taken for granted, in view of the spirited way in which the matter is being pursued that the necessary powers will almost certainly be obtained. It will only then remain for the permission thus conferred to be made use of by the promoters and shareholders.

One of the speakers at the Grosmont meeting expressed the opinion that he did not think the people of Monmouth supported the line as much as they ought. This may be partly accounted for by the fact that a line down the Monnow Valley has been dreamt about for so many years, that it is difficult for people to convince themselves that at length the matter is to be seriously undertaken. If, as the Engineer and Mr Green-Price intimated, the new road might some day become a main line, there would be good reason for Monmouth being expected to render more than ordinary assistance, and taking Mr Jackson's statement that, 'any town that had become a centre of railways generally became a large town itself' as amounting to a truism, it would not be difficult to point out the advantages which would accrue to Monmouth by being made the focus of several systems of communication. The prospect is a bright one and entitles the scheme propounded by the promoters to a proportionate amount of consideration and support.

A combination of these facts may have contributed to the fact that the Bill was promoted in the 1884 session and then inexplicably abandoned.

However, the Directors of the Golden Valley Railway were still determined to promote their plans for the continuation of their line down the Monnow valley to Monmouth. In November 1887 plans were drawn up by Wells, Owen and Elwes, engineers and were deposited with the Parliamentary agents to be considered in the 1888 session of Parliament. In these plans the railway was divided in to six parts. The first two parts were details of how the new line would join the Golden Valley line at Pontrilas station. The third part described the line from Pontrilas to Garway where it would be '*near the western fence of the orchard situated immediately south of the farmhouse known as Great Demesne or Demain, and at a point about 140 yards from the said farmhouse*'. Railway number four was a complete change from anything proposed previously. '*Railway number 4, commencing in the said parish of Garway by a junction with the intended railway number 3, at the termination thereof as above described, and terminating in the parish of English Bicknor, in the county of Gloucester, by a junction with the railway of the Severn and Wye and Severn Bridge company, about 200 yards, measured from the northern end of the platform of the station at Lydbrook Junction.*' This railway was intended to climb by a steep gradient to cross the Garway/Broad Oak road and the Hereford/Monmouth road at Hangar Hill, then proceed by Llangarron and Marstow then across part of Coppet Hill common in the parish of Goodrich to Lydbrook. The line had two tunnels and very sharp curves.

Railway number five was from the junction at Demesne Farm in Garway to Monmouth at '*a point on the bank of the river Monnow 100 yards, measured in a south easterly direction, from the footbridge carrying over the said river the pathway from Vauxhall Farm to the Osbaston Road, near the entrance gates to the cemetery*'.

For Sale and to be Let.

TO be LET, the PONTYPOOL ARMS Beerhouse, Crane-street, Pontypool. Furniture, Fixtures, and Brewing Utensils to be taken to.—Apply to Mrs. Dixon, on the premises.

TO BE LET, with immediate possession, JOAN'S HILL FARM, Fownhope, containing 48 Acres.—Apply to Messrs. Underwood and Knight, Solicitors, Castle-street, Hereford.

CIDER AND PERRY.—Several dozens in bottle of Jones's celebrated Barland and Champagne Perry and Cider; also several Hogsheads for bottling made from the choicest Fruit, and 2,000 gallons of Tankard Cider.—Apply to C. T. Jones, Belle Orchards, Ledbury, Herefordshire.

TO be SOLD or LET, a walled-in GARDEN, (about a third of an acre), excellently stocked with the choicest fruit trees, and situate in the suburbs of Hereford.—Apply to Mr. E. Scooke, 16, Widemarsh-street, Hereford.

TO LET, a COTTAGE, called "Daffy-nant," in the village of Whitchurch, four miles from Monmouth. It is prettily situate on rising ground, with a good kitchen garden behind and a small orchard adjoining. The House consists of two sitting-rooms (communicating with each other), small lobby or entrance, comfortable kitchen, good pantry or larder, underground cellar, good stable for one horse, and a carriage-house with sleeping room over. Within the dwelling-house there are five bedrooms, and the house is now in the occupation of R. Willis, Esq., to whom application may be made for a sight of the premises.

PENNOYRE, NEAR BRECON.
FISHING COTTAGE AND LAKE OF 10 ACRES.

TO be LET on a Yearly Tenancy, or on Lease if required, within 1¼ miles of the Town of Brecon, not far from Pennoyre Mansion, an Ornamental and Picturesque Cottage, standing on the borders of a large Lake known as Lynn Gludy, with Shrubberies, Walks, and Wood adjoining, the whole comprising about 21 Acres. The Cottage will be put in repair; some Pasture Land may be rented in addition, if required.—For further particulars apply to Mr. David Evans, Cradoc, near Brecon, who will shew the Property; or to Messrs. Driver, Surveyors, Land Agents, and Auctioneers, 4, Whitehall, London, S.W.

Public Notices.

SIR JAMES MURRAY'S
CORDIAL FLUID CAMPHOR
Is extensively prescribed as a reviving Tonic, and as the best restorative for weak nerves, Low Fevers, Spasms, Cholera, and Diarrhœa. In this fluid form the dangerous precipitates are avoided which result from the use of Camphor in the solid state, or in tinctures.
Sold by all Chemists, in Bottles at 1s. & 2s. each.

LUCY'S LONDON SAUCE.

Public Notices.

WHEREAS THE GREAT WESTERN RAILWAY COMPANY and JOHN LUCY SCUDAMORE, of Kent Church Court, in the County of Hereford, Esquire, being respectively interested under the provisions of "The Acts for the Inclosure, Exchange, and Improvement of Lands," in the Land and Hereditaments set forth in the Schedule hereunder written, with the Easements and Appurtenances thereunto belonging, and being desirous of effecting an exchange of the same, have made application, in writing, to the Inclosure Commissioners for England and Wales, to direct enquiries whether such proposed Exchange would be beneficial to the Owners of such respective Land and Hereditaments, and to proceed with the same under the provisions of the said Acts.

Now the Inclosure Commissioners for England and Wales, being of opinion that such Exchange would be beneficial, and that the terms thereof are just and reasonable, hereby give notice that they will cause to be framed and confirmed, under their Hands and Seal, an Order of Exchange in the matter of the said application, unless notice in writing, of dissent to such proposed Exchange be given to them by some person entitled to an Estate in, or to a charge upon, the said Land and Hereditaments or any part thereof, on or before the 26th day of July next.

THE SCHEDULE TO WHICH THE FOREGOING NOTICE REFERS.

LAND and Hereditaments in which the above-named GREAT WESTERN RAILWAY COMPANY is interested, situate in the Parish of Groesmont, in the County of Monmouth, and proposed to be exchanged for the Land and Hereditaments hereinafter specified.

No. on Tithe map.	DESCRIPTION.	A.	R.	P.
Part 50	All that piece of Land situate at, or near a place called OldForge together with the cottage (now in ruins), which said piece of land is now in the occupation of the said Company	0	1	21

LAND and Hereditaments in which the above-named John Lucy Scudamore is interested, situate in the Parish of Llangua, in the County of Monmouth, and proposed to be exchanged for the Land and Hereditaments hereinbefore specified.

No. on Tithe map.	DESCRIPTION.	A.	R.	P.
Part 109b	All that piece of Land situate at, or near a place called Monmouth Cap, in the occupation of Joshua Weaver	0	0	16
Part 111b	Ditto, in the same occupation	0	0	35
	Total	0	1	11

WITNESS my hand this 8th day of April in the year of our Lord One Thousand eight hundred and sixty-nine.
Inclosure Commission,
3, St. James's Square,
London, S.W.
H. PYNE,
By Order of the Board.

T. A. DEAN,
COAL, COKE, AND LIME MERCHANT,
BARR'S COURT STATION, HEREFORD, AND MORETON-ON-LUGG.
AGENT FOR IND, COOPE, AND CO.'S BURTON ALES.
T. ALLEN, MANAGER OF THE HEREFORD BRANCH.
OFFICES, 24, CHURCH-STREET,

HUBERT SMITH AND CO.
(LATE FELIX SMITH AND SONS),
ENGINEERS, IRON, BRASS FOUNDERS, AND AGRICULTURAL MACHINISTS,
HEREFORD IRON WORKS—FRIARS-STREET.
REPAIRS AND ALTERATIONS PROMPTLY EXECUTED.

LAWES' MANURES
WERE the first Chemical Manures manufactured and introduced, and have been in use for 28 years with great success.
LAWES' PATENT TURNIP MANURE. DISSOLVED BONES.
LAWES' SUPERPHOSPHATE OF LIME.
LAWES' WHEAT, BARLEY, GRASS, AND MANGEL MANURES.
CONCENTRATED CORN AND GRASS MANURES.

Publications.

SHORTLY WILL BE PUBLISHED, LAND in England, LAND in Ireland, and in other Lands.
A Short Essay addressed to the Men of By CHANDOS WREN HOSKYNS, (M.P. for Hereford).
London: Longman and Co., Paternoster Head and Hull, Hereford, and all Booksellers.

BY ORDER OF THE KING: VICTOR HUGO'S NEW STORY. English Copyright for Gentleman's Magazine. To begin in May. One Shilling.

VICTOR HUGO'S NEW WORK: BY ORDER OF THE KING: A ROMANCE OF HISTORY. See Gentleman's Magazine. On monthly.

Educational Notices.

MALVERN COLL
The SECOND TERM will commence on April 30th.

MALVERN COLL
President and Visitor:
The Lord Bishop of WORCESTER
Head Master:
The Rev. ARTHUR FABER, M.A., late Tutor of New College, Oxford.
Full information on application to ALDRICH, Esq., the Secretary.

ESTABLISHMENT FOR YOUNG L
MISS QUINTIN (near the Lighthouse Leominster (late of Cheltenham cester), PROFESSOR of MUSIC, DEPORTMENT, and EXERCISES, begs her Friends that she has resumed P Avocations at her residence, and that Miss Quintin will be happy to teach under 12 years of age.
Miss Quintin will be glad to receive Young from the country every Friday.
Numerous references can be given, having years' experience in teaching.
Schools attended in Town or Country. of the Organ taught.

USK, THE ROSES.
MRS. WATSON, the Widow of a Clergyman prepared to receive, after Midsummer, or four young LADIES as BOARDERS, with her little nieces who are nine and t age.
An accomplished Governess will reside House.
A Prospectus and Terms with Refer be had on applying to Mrs. Watson, Usk, Mon.

BLENHEIM HOUSE.
THE LEA LINE SCHOOL.
PRINCIPAL: MR. AUGUSTUS IRV

SIGNALS.

NARROW GAUGE.

RED is a Signal of DANGER—STOP.

GREEN—CAUTION—PROCEED SLOWLY.

WHITE—ALL RIGHT—GO ON.

LINE SIGNALS.

1. When the Line is clear and nothing to impede the progress of the Train, the Policeman on duty will stand erect, with his Flags in hand, but showing no signal, thus—

2. If it is necessary to proceed with Caution, the Green Flag will be elevated, thus—

From the Hereford Times 1869

3. If it is necessary to proceed with Caution from any defect in the rails, the Green Flag will be depressed, thus—

4. If required to Stop, the RED Flag will be shown and waved to and fro, the Policeman facing the Engine.

5. Engine Drivers must invariably STOP on seeing the Red Signal.

6. As soon as the Engine passes, the Policeman will bring his Flag to the shoulder.

8. Every Policeman will be responsible for having his HAND LAMP in good order, and properly trimmed.

SEMAPHORE SIGNALS—DAY.

1st. These Signals are constructed with either one or two semaphore arms.

2. The Signal is invariably made on the LEFT HAND side of the post as seen by the approaching Engine Driver.

3. The ALL RIGHT Signal is shown by the LEFT HAND side of the Post being clear, the arm be-

Railway number six would have crossed the Osbaston Road then the Hereford Road near their junction and continued through the area of Monkswell Road, New Dixton Road and Old Dixton Road before crossing the river Wye and running into Monmouth Mayhill station. There were the usual clauses about the company being able to purchase any property they might require. Once again there was a plan to demolish a considerable number of houses in Monmouth to further the cause of railway expansion.

The plans for this railway showed that the line crossed the river Monnow four times and avoided the necessity of having tunnels at Skenfrith by crossing the river twice on the meander. There was to have been a station at Skenfrith that was to be built between the village and the Priory alongside the main road. In 1890, the Skenfrith Church Council, in anticipation of the increased traffic and visitors to the village, asked for additional police supervision in the area if the Monnow Valley Railway was proceeded with and an additional constable was promised.

This Bill was strongly opposed in both Houses of Parliament and thrown out. The following year the Golden Valley Extension Bill was presented to Parliament but this time Railway number 4, the extension from Garway to Lydbrook was omitted. Once again the Great Western Railway strongly opposed the Bill but after a great struggle it was passed.

The Golden Valley Extension Railway Act gave powers to construct a line 12 miles, twenty-two chains long running from a junction with the Great Western Railway at Pontrilas to a junction at Mayhill station, Monmouth. The Company was also given powers to run over the Ross and Monmouth Railway from Mayhill to Lydbrook Junction and then over the Severn and Wye Railway into Lydbrook Junction Station. The Golden Valley Company was to build and work the Monmouth Extension keeping the capital separate. The Golden Valley Company would be financially responsible for the Monmouth extension but the Monmouth line would have no liability for the Golden Valley line.

The need for the line from Pontrilas to Monmouth had always been exaggerated. It is unlikely that the very small population living in the area would want or need to travel out of the area very often especially when most villages were well supplied with their own shops. The other argument was that it would make a direct line from Bristol to Liverpool but this would be over a single-track route using twelve different railway companies. Other routes had proved quicker and more cost effective.

A more serious problem was that the Golden Valley line itself was never financially viable and struggled for many years with heavy debts. The extension from Dorstone to Hay had opened for passengers in May 1889 and had cost far more that the original line from Pontrilas to Dorstone. By 1899 it was decided that the line must close and it was agreed to sell the Golden Valley Railway to the Great Western Railway for £9000. The GWR spent £15000 in relaying and reconditioning the railway and it reopened on 1st May 1901. Passenger services ceased on 15th December 1941 but the goods traffic continued, becoming part of British Rail in 1948. During the war a siding was built between Pontrilas and Abbeydore for the transporting of munitions to and from the Ministry of Supply depot. On 1st January 1950 the line closed to all traffic between Dorstone and Hay followed by the closure of the Abbeydore to Dorstone line on 2nd February 1953. Finally the remaining section between Pontrilas and Abbeydore closed on 3rd June 1957 with all the track, except for the first mile to the Ministry of supply depot, which was in use until 31st March 1969.

The Monnow Valley Extension was never really a viable option and so remained an impossible dream.

EXTRACTS FROM THE MONMOUTHSHIRE BEACON

There now appears to be every probability that the proposed Monnow Valley Railway from Monmouth to Pontrilas will be carried out. The making of the new line has for some time past been mooted, but it is now taken up in such a spirited and practical manner as to augur well for the carrying out of the scheme. Several meetings on the subject have been recently held in the neighbourhood, the latest of which was at Grosmont, on Saturday last, when a highly influential number of gentlemen interested in the subject met together to take into consideration the best means of constructing a line to be called the Monnow Valley Railway, and which, starting from the junction of the Golden Valley Railway, with the Hereford and Newport line at Pontrilas, will run the course of the river Monnow, and form a junction with the Wye Valley line at Monmouth. The course of the proposed line will be as follows:—Starting from the juncton at Pontrilas, the line will infringe upon Cupid's Hill, Great Corras, Castle Fields, Lower Duffryn, Trevorney, Garway Mill, the Hill, Skenfrith, Llanrothal, Tregate Bridge, Perthyr Grove, Deepholm, Blackwood, Little Ancre Hill, Ancre Hill (Major), Castlefields, Monmouth Castle, Dials Wood, and into the Wye Valley Railway on the west bank of the Wye. The Chairman in opening the proceeding, expressed his anxiety to see the line made, and as a first instalment offered to subscribe £2,000, and take out the value of the land required from him in shares; Mr. James Graham followed in a like encouraging manner, and said that while he could not pledge himself in the present incipient state of the undertaking to subscribe largely, he would follow his neighbour's example, and subscribe a couple of thousand, and take his land out in shares. Mr. Bodenham dwelt upon the encouragement the projected line had generally received from the proprietors of the land through which it would run, and said that he saw no reason why they should not at once proceed with their Bill, and within two-and-a-half years the line would be opened. A committee was formed to get the share list filled, and from the hearty manner in which the matter has been taken up their seems no reason why the making of this line should much longer be delayed.

21st October, 1876

Local and District Notes.

The promoters of the proposed new line of Railway from Pontrilas to Monmouth are busy in their endeavour to win support for the scheme which next Session they intend to lay before Parliament. A meeting a short time ago in Monmouth has been followed by another at Grosmont, the centre of the district which it is believed the line, if constructed, will most benefit. The subscriptions already promised towards the preliminary expenses are very encouraging, and there seems every probability that ere many years have passed the long talked of Monnow Valley Railway may be an accomplished fact. The Great Western Company, we believe, are the only real objectors to the scheme, but any arguments which they can adduce, based as they must be on the desire to prevent competition, will have but little weight with the Imperial Legislature. It may therefore now be taken for granted, in view of the spirited way in which the matter is being pursued that the necessary powers will almost certainly be obtained. It will only then remain for the permission thus conferred to be made use of by the promoters and shareholders.

One of the speakers at the Grosmont meeting expressed the opinion that he did not think the people of Monmouth supported the line as much as they ought. This may be partly accounted for by the fact that a line down the Monnow Valley has been dreamt about for so many years, that it is difficult for people to convince themselves that at length the matter is to be seriously undertaken. If, as the Engineer and Mr. Green Price intimated, the new road might some day become a main line, there would be good reason for Monmouth being expected to render more than ordinary assistance, and taking Mr. Jackson's statement that "any town that had become a centre of railways generally became a large town itself" as amounting almost to a truism, it would not be difficult to point out the advantages which would accrue to Monmouth by being made the focus of several systems of communication. The prospect is a bright one, and entitles the scheme propounded by the promoters to a proportionate amount of consideration and support.

12th January, 1884

BIBLIOGRAPHY and REFERENCES

INTRODUCTION
Howell, Raymond, *A History of Gwent, 1988*
Thorn, Frank and Caroline, *Domesday Book Herefordshire, 1983*
Searle, Elsa, *The Rivers of Monmouthshire, 1970*
Sylvester, Dorothy, *The Rural Landscape of the Welsh Borderland, 1969*
Woolhope Transactions 1936, p 147
Monnow Valley River Project.

CRASWALL
Wright, Cecil, *Report of Field Study at Craswall Priory, Herefordshire, 1962*
Woolhope Tranactions 1904
Hereford Times, 1997 and 2001

LLANVEYNOE AND THE OLCHON VALLEY
Baker Gabb, R. *Hills and Vales of the Black Mountain District, 1913*
Howell, John, *History of the Baptist Church at Olchon, 1886*
Llewelyn, Rev F.G. *History of St Clodock, 1919*
Somerville, Chris, *Phillip's Welsh Borders, 1991*
Woolhope Transactions 1897,1916,1932

LONGTOWN
Rowley, Trevor, *The Welsh Border, 1986*
Stanford, S. C. *Archaeology of the Welsh Marches, 1980*
Sylvester, Dorothy, *The Rural Landscape of the Welsh Borderland, 1969*
Woolhope Transaction 1958 p127, 1964 p 67
Hereford Times, 1869
www.longtownmrt.org.uk rescue

CLODOCK
Friar, Stephen, *Companion to the English Parish Church,1996*
Gwilym-John, Rev D. B. *Guide to Clodock Church*
Leonard, John, *The Churches of Herefordshire and their Treasures, 2000*
Llewelyn, Rev F. G. *History of St Clodock, 1919*
Sant, Jonathan, *Healing Wells of Herefordshire, 1994*
Richardson, L, *Wells and Springs of Herefordshire, 1935*

OLDCASTLE AND WALTERSTONE
Baker Gabb, R. *Hills and Vales of the Black Mountain District, 1913*
Bradney, Sir Joseph, *History of Monmouthshire Vol 1 Hundred of Abergavenny, 1907*
Timmins, H. T, *Nooks and Corners of Herefordshire, 1892*
Hereford Times, 2000

LLANCILLO and ROWLESTONE
Bannister, Rev A J. *The Place Names of Herefordshire, 1916*
Coates and Tucker, *Water Mills of the Monnow and Trothy, 1978*
Leonard, John, *Churches of Herefordshire and their Treasures, 2002*
Littlebury's Directory of Herefordshire 1876
Jackeman and Carver's Directory of Herefordshire, 1890, 1914
Woolhope Transactions 1906 p 264

EWYAS HAROLD
Bannister, Rev A J. *History of Ewyas Harold, 1902*
Bradley, A G. *In the March and Borderland of Wales, 1911*
Ewyas Harold WEA Research Group. *Yesterday in Ewyas Harold*
Ewyas Harold Common
Field and Furrow, 1982
Littlebury's Directory of Herefordshire, 1875

PONTRILAS
Mitchell Vic and Smith Keith Western Main Lines, Hereford to Newport 2005
Bannister, Rev A. J. *History of Ewyas Harold, 1902*
Coates and Tucker, *Mills of the Monnow and Trothy, 1978*
Hurley, Heather, *Pubs and Inns and South Herefordshire, 2003*
Mowat, Charles L. *Golden Valley Railway, 1964*
Littlebury's Directory of Herefordshire 1876
Jakeman and Carver's Directory of Herefordshire 1890
Kelly's Directory of Herefordshire 1926

LLANGUA
Cooke, R.A.and Clinker, C.R.
Early Railways between Abergavenny and Hereford. 1984
Friar, Stephen, *The English Parish Church, 1996*
Levett, Fred, *The Story of Skenfrith and Grosmont, Part One, 1984*
Ewyas Harold W E A, *Field and Furrow, 1982*
Woolhope Transactions 1939 p 97

KENTCHURCH
Palmer, Roy, *Folklore of (Old) Monmouthshire, 1998*
Wilson, Roger. *Roman Forts, 1980*
Hereford Times. May 1959
Woolhope Transactions 1989. p 194

GROSMONT
Gibbon, Alex, *The Mystery of Jack of Kent and the Fate of Owain Glyndwr, 2004*
Kissack, Keith, *Monmouth. Lordship Parish and Borough, 1996*
Levett, Fred, *The Story of Skenfrith and Grosmont, 1984*
Rocyn Jones, R. A. *A Guide to St Nicholas Church, Grosmont, 1990*
Kelly's Directory for Monmouthshire 1875, 1884

GARWAY
Hando, Fred, *The Pleasant Land of Gwent, 1944*
Harper, Charles, *The Marches of Wales, 1894*
Coppleston-Crow, Bruce. Personal correspondence
Royal Commission on Ancient Monuments , Volume 1, Hereford South West. 1931
Jakeman and Carvers's Directory for Herefordshire 1914
Monmouthshire Beacon May 1920
Hereford Record Office. Pembridge Castle. Ref C 82

SKENFRITH
Hando, Fred, *The Pleasant Land of Gwent, 1944*
Harper, Charles, *The Marches of Wales, 1894*
Levett, Fred, *The Story of Skenfrith and Grosmont, 1984*
Knight, Jeremy K. *The Three Castles. 1991*
M N J (Late of Blackbrook), *Bygone Days in the March Wall of Wales, 1926*

LLANROTHAL
Clarke, Steve, *Ghosts and Legends of Monmouthshire, 1965*
Hopson, Mary *A Wander Round Llanrothal and Tregate Bridge*
Hancocks, David, *Llangunville (private paper), 1990*
Kissack, Keith, *Monmouth. Lordship Parish and Borough, 1996*

ST MAUGHANS
Coxe, Archdeacon William, *An Historical Tour in Monmouthshire, 1801*
Levett, Fred, *The Story of Skenfrith and Grosmont, 1984*
Phillips, Olive, *Monmouthshire, 1951*

ROCKFIELD
Bradney, Sir Joseph, *History of Monmouthshire Vol.1 Part 1, 1907*
Kelly's Directory of Monmouthshire 1884
Hereford Times, March 2000

MONMOUTH
Kissack, Keith, *Victorian Monmouth*
Kissack, Keith, *The Making of a County Town, 1975*
Kissack, Keith, *Monmouth and its Buildings, 2003*
Stockinger, Victor, *The Rivers Wye and Lugg Navigation, 1996*
Twamley, Louisa Anne, *Twamley's River Wye, 1838*

PART TWO
Addison, C, *The History of the Knights Templar,* 1842
Cooke, A O, *Book of Dovecotes,* 1920
Duncumb, John, *History of the County of Hereford, (Wormelow Hundred),* 1913
Fleming-Yates, J M, *Church of St Michaels, Garway,* 1982
M N T (Late of Blackbrook), *Bygone Days in the March Wall of Wales,* 1926
Moir, Preb. A. L, *Bishops of Hereford,* 1964
Thorn, Frank and Caroline, *Domesday Book Herefordshire,* 1983
Rees, William, *South Wales and the March 1284-1415,* 1924
Rees, William, *Historical Atlas of Wales,* 1972
Rees, William, *The History of the Order of St John of Jerusalem in Wales and on the Welsh Border,* 1947
Seaton, Preb. D A, *A History of Archenfield,* 1903
Webb, Rev J. (Camden Soc.), *Household Roll of Bishop Swinfield,* 1855
Ziegler, P, *The Black Death,* 1969
Rental of the Lands of the Knights Hospitallers in Dinmore and Garway, 1504 (HRO)
St John's Historical Society, Historical Notes on Order Properties, 1985
Poll Tax 51 Edward III (PRO E 179 117/13)
Lay Subsidy 15th 16th Henry VIII (PRO E 179 111/107)
Hereford Assize Roll 1355-6 (PRO JI 1/3312 M6)
Woolhope Transaction 1918-1920, 1927

PART THREE
Bradney, Sir Joseph, *History of Monmouthshire, Hundred of Skenfrith,* 1904
Cape, Rev. Frank, *Two Historic Parishes, Welsh Newton and Llanrothal,* (undated)
Clarke, Arthur, *Story of Monmouthshire, Vol 1,* 1980
Church in History Information Centre, *King James and the Glorious Revolution of 1688, Parts 1 and 2*
Guy, John R, *The Anglican Patronage of Monmouthshire Recusants. Eighteenth Century Gwent Catholics (*Catholic Record Society 1981, 1982)
Hemphill, Dom Basil, *Early Vicars Apostolic of England, 1685-1750,* 1954
Hopson, Mary, *Roman Catholic Burial Ground and Former Church at Coedanghred, Skenfrith,* 1985
    Further to Coedanghred, 1994
    A Wander Round Llanrothal, 1998
Kissack, Keith, *Victorian Monmouth,* (undated)
    Monmouth, The Making of a County Town, 1975
Jenkins, Philip, *Monmouthshire Catholics in the 18th Century,* (Catholic Record Society, 1980)
Levett, Fred, *The Story of Skenfrith and Grosmont, Vol 2,* 1984
Lane, Jane, *Titus Oates,* 1949
Mathias, Roland, *Whitsun Riot,* 1963
Murphy, Paul, *The Jesuit College of the Cwm,* (Severn and Wye Review 1971)
    Catholics in Monmouthshire 1688-1850, (Presenting Monmouthshire No. 29 1970)
O'Keefe, Madge Cusack, *Four Martyrs of South Wales and the Marches,* 1970

Pugh, F H, *Monmouthshire Recusants in the Reigns of Elizabeth and James I* (South Wales and Monmouth Record Society Publication No 4) 1957
Pilley, Walter, *Notes of the Suppressed College of Jesuits at Coombe, Llanrothal,* (Woolhope Transactions 1900)
Smith, T. S, *Herefordshire Catholics and Rites of Passage, 1560-1640,* (Woolhope Transactions 1978)
Thomas, T, *The Welsh Elizabethan Catholic Martyrs,* 1971
Vaughan, Mary, *Courtfield and the Vaughans,* 1989
Whelan, Dom Basil, *History of Belmont Abbey,* 1959
Hereford Record Office, *Narrative of a Discovery of a College of Jesuits,* (Ref X61/1)
Monmouthshire Beacon, 1838,1846 (Monmouth Museum)

PART FOUR

Byles, A. *The History of the Monmouthshire Railway and Canal Company,* 1982
Clarke, A. *The Story of Monmouthshire, Vol. 2* 1979
Cooke, B.A. Clinker C.R, *Early Railways Between Abergavenny and Hereford,* 1984
Croft, J. *Packhorse, Waggon and Post,* 1967
Fox, J. A. *A General View of Agriculture of the County of Monmouth,* 1794
Gray-Jones, W. A. *A History of Ebbw Vale,* 1971
Handley B M, Dingwall, R, *The Wye Valley Railway and the Coleford Branch,* 1998
Hurley, Heather, *The Old Roads of South Herefordshire,* 1992
Jenkins, S C, *The Ross, Monmouth and Pontypool Road Line,* 2002
Kissack, Keith, *Gwent Local Historian,* No 53, 1982
Marshall, Mr, *The Rural Economy of Gloucester and Herefordshire,* Vol 2 1789
M N J (late of Blackbrooke), *Bygone Days in the March of Wales,* 1926
Morgan, P, *The Grosmont Vestry,* 1985
Mowat, C. *The Golden Valley Railway,* 1964
Swallow, M. A. *History of the Development of the Means of Communication in Monmouthshire,* 1932
Trevelyn, G. M. *English Social History,* 1944
Window Tax Authority, HRO
Window Tax Account Book, HRO
Book of Reference and Plans, HRO
Kentchurch Papers, Vol. 3, HRO
Ross Turnpike Trust Minute Book, HRO
Mr. Fosbrook's Plan and Book of Reference, HRO
Monnow Valley Railway, Plans and Sections, HRO
Golden Valley Railway, Plans and Sections, HRO
Memorandum for Road from Pontrilas to Skenfrith, 1832. GCRO
Act for Repairing Road, 1833. GCRO
Monmouth Beacon 1876, 1884, 1889, Monmouth Museum

HRO Hereford Record Office. GCRO Gwent County Record Office.

GLOSSARY

Bordars	One of the lowest ranks in the feudal system performing work for the lord either free or for a fixed sum
Carucates	Alternative name for hide, which was the amount of land which could be ploughed in a year using one plough and supporting one family.
Copyholder	A perpetual tenant under the Lord of the Manor, (copyhold tenure was abolished in 1922).
Corrody	Maintenance for life or fixed allowance in food and lodgings often granted for payment of money.
Cottars	A cottager with small land holding usually 5-8 acres; obliged to provide labour on the lord's farm either free or for a fixed sum.
Demesne	Land retained by the lord for his own use upon which tenants gave free service.
Distrain	Seizure of goods to compel a person to pay money due.
Free Tenant	Tenant who held land from the lord for a fixed rent.
Heriot	Obligation of an heir of a deceased tenant to give the lord the best beast of the dead tenant.
Hundred	Division of a shire. Court meeting held monthly to deal with criminal and minor ecclesiastical matters.
Inquisition	Enquiry into the possessions, services and succession of a deceased person who held land of the crown
Interdict	Ecclesiastical punishment prohibiting participation in the sacrament.
Mark	128 shillings, later 13s. 4d
Medicants	Beggars
Meers	A balk dividing fields or marking boundaries.
Messuage	A house, its outbuildings and yard.
Moeity	One of two parts, often a half.
Murrain	An obsolete word for cattle and sheep disease.
Oblations & Obventions	Donations for pious uses.
Quern	Hand operated corn grinder.
Reeve	A man elected by fellow tenants to organise the daily business of the manor.
Seneschal	A steward with the supervision of several manors.
Sester	A dry or liquid measure.
Suit of Court	The attendance which a tenant was obliged to give at the lord's court.
Villein	An unfree tenant who had a share in the agricultural system of the manor.

INDEX

Abbeydore 30,37,38,120,215
Abergavenny 6
Abergavenny, Lord 159
Aberystwyth 199
Acre 102
Act of Uniformity 123
Act of Union 8
Ainsworth 127
Alderbury, Salop 12
Allensmore 135,136
Allt-yr-ynys 1,30,31
Andrews, Father 152,155
Angel Hotel, Monmouth 95
Apperley, Messrs 214
Archenfield 4,36,60,87,100,190
Arnold, John 29,144,148,150
Arnold, Sir Nicholas 12
Articles of Enquiry 128,129
Austins, Joseph 196

Bailey Crawshay 211,214,215
Baldwyn, Sir Timothy 130
Barry family 77
Bartlett, Dr Hedley 168,175
Baskerville, James 40
Baskerville, Humphrey 40
Baskerville, Thomas 120,136
Baskerville, Walter 40,42
Baskerville, William 132
Beaker people 19
Beaufort John 137
Beaufort, Duke of 51,88,93,94,188
Bedloe, William 143,151
Bell Inn, Skenfrith 70,71,195
Belmont Abbey 39,163,167
Bennett, Bishop Robert 135,151
Bentham, George 43
Berkley, John 161
Bill of Detection 125
Bird, William 152
Bishop in Ordinary 125
Bishop of Hereford 113,135,137
Black Death 116
Black Lion Inn, Longtown 23
Black Mountains 11,12
Blackbrook House 73
Bodenham, Sir Roger 136
Bongam, William 111
Boothby, Martin 77
Bowhaulers 96
Bradney, Sir Joseph 29,44,78
Bridge Inn, Kentchurch 55
Bridge, Thomas 189
Briggs John 73
Bristol 96 184 185
Britannia Inn, Monmouth 215
Broad Oak 59,132,195,220
Broad Oak Inn 168
Brockweir 96

Broom Farm, Llanrothal 76
Broome, William 23
Brown, Thomas 159
Brownrigg, Sir Robert 79
Brute, Walter 18
Brychan 26
Buckholt 76,93
Bull's Head Inn, Craswall 12,14
Burgh, Hubert de 48
Burial Chamber, Bronze Age 19

Campstone Hill 46,185,209
Cap House, Llangua 33
Capel-y-ffin 1,35
Carmarthen 208
Carpenter's Arms, Walterstone 31
Castlefield 55
Cat's Back 17
Catholic Relief Act 126,159
Cave, George 80
Cecil, Walwyn 189
Cecil, William 30
Chambers, G E 58
Charles II 125, 143
Chepstow 96,212,216
Chippenham 87,95,96,97
Chirugion 133
Church Farm, Garway 130
Churchill, Sir Winston 30
Churchwardens 123,127
Cinderhill 88
Civil War 38,60,77,125,132,140,148
Clarenden Code 125,143
Clarke, Steve 87
Clodock 6,11,12,17,21,26-28,195
Clytha Park 84
Coates, Stan 33
Coed Anghred 161-169
Cole, John 42
Compton, Sir William 132
Consistory Court 132
Cornewall, Lady 219
Corras 54,186
Court of Augmentation 120
Coxe Archdeacon Wm 78,81,96
Craswall 6,11-15,21
Crawfurd John 74
Crickhowell 220
Croft, Herbert Bishop 145
Crown Hotel, Hay 21
Crown Inn, Longtown 23
Crusades 101
Cunningham, Joseph 166
Cupid's Hill 48,51,201
Cutta, Isabel 111
Cwm 73,139-142,145,150
Cwmaddoc, Garway 132
Cyprus 104

Dan-y-graig 170
Darren 136,139,152,168,205
De la Billiere 62
De la Hay family 30
De la Hay, John 107
De Lacy, Roger 6,21
De Lacy, Walter 6,7,11
De Molay, Jacques 103,104
De Morgan, Adrian 75
De Payan, Hugh 102
De Pembridge, Gilbert 110
De Swinfield, Richard 113
De Tregat, Robert 77
Declaration Against Popery 126
Declaration of Christian Faith 126
Declaration of Indulgence 125
Demesne Farm 190,210,220
Despencer, Hugh 110
Dinmore Commandery 107,110,111
Dixton, 8,76,87,97
Domesday survey 5,7,8
Dore, river 1
Dorstone 40,215,223
Dovecote 108
Drybridge Street 214
Dyffryn, Lower 189,190
Dyffryn 31,80

Eardisley 216
Edmund of Lancaster 71
Edmund of St Joseph 133
Edward IV 12
Edward the Confessor 4,36
Elizabeth I 123,148
Ellis, Phillip Bishop 157
English Bicknor 220
Englishries 6
Ergyng (Archenfield) 6
Evangelical Catholic Communion 175
Ewias Lacy 4,5,6,11
Ewyas Harold 4,5,36-39
Exchequer Loan Commission 199

Farror, W 200
Festival of Castles 72
Fishponds 109
Fitz Osbern, William 4,44,70,87
Fleming, Sir William 77
Flooding 93
Forest of Dean 33,40,96,212,216
Forge, Llancillo 33
Forge, Pontrilas 40
Fosbrook, William 199,201,205
Fripp, Sir Alfred 74

Gardiner family 65

Gardiner, Bert 65
Gardiner, Fred 63
Garway 7,8,51-62,102,113,130,136
      161,172,181,196
Garway Hill 53,54,63-68,107
Garway mill 109,187,201
Garway, Baptist Chapel 58
Geoffrey of Monmouth 87
Gibraltar Hill 97,199
Gifford, Bonadventure Bishop 156
Glanmonow 62,73,80
Glorious Revolution 157
Gloucester 208 212
Gloucester Abbey 3,7,38
Glyndwr, Owain 49,54,70,78
Godding, Vine 51
Godwin, Earl 4,36
Golden Lion Hotel, Abergavenny 150
Golden Valley 1,215
Goodrich castle 96
Graig 158,185
Graig Methodist Chapel 74
Grandison, John 31
Grandmont, Order of 11,44
Greyhound Inn, Longtown 23
Griffiths, William 139
Grosmont 8, 48-72, 116,172,186,188,195
Grosmont castle 48
Grosmont Railway Co 46,209
Grosmont Tramroad 46
Grosmont Turnpike Trust 197,206,209
Grosmont, St Joseph's R C Church 171
Grosmont, Yorks 11
Gruffydd 4,36
Gunpowder Plot 124,135
Gwent Education Authority 80
Gwent Iscoed 5
Gwent Uwch-Coed 4,5

Haddon G C Architect 34
Hadnock 8
Hardwick 152
Harewood 107,109,110
Harold, Earl 4
Hatterrall Ridge 17
Hatton, Brian 39
Hay 12,40,1997,199,204,215,223
Hearth Tax 132
Hellens, Much Marcle 181
Henry V 18
Henry VIII 123
Henry, Prince 49
Hereford 36,37,40,96
Hereford Abergavenny Tramroad 46
Hereford Cathedral 39
Hereford Museum 19
Hereford Railway 199
Hereford Turnpike Trust 197
Hereford, Bishop of 7
Heyns, Richard 135

Hilston Park 62,78
Holy Land 101
Honddu, river 1
Hooper, William 205
Hopson, Mary 165,168
Horse and Jockey, Rockfield 81
Hospitallers 58,101,113,132,187
Housel bench 27
Hungerstone 135

Ilkley, Yorks 161
Industrial Revolution
Inquisition 104

Jack of Kent 54
Jack, Mr G H 58
Jackson Jeremiah 130
Jackson Mrs of Blackbrook 70
Jackson Peter Rothwell 74
Jackson, Sir Phillip 42
James I 124
James II 125,133,156
Jerusalem 101
Jesuits 123,139,143
John of Gaunt 137
Jones of Llanarth 159
Jones, Father 139

5,44,53-56,113,172,199

Kear, William 40
Keith, Sir Arthur 14
Kember, Father John 60,148
Kemble, Richard 60 140
Kemeys-Tynte, Charles 206,209
Kennedy, Rev James 34
Kentchurch
Kentchurch Court 53,66,144,148
Kilpeck castle 21
Kings Head, Monmouth 95
Kyrle, Thomas 136

Lane, Edwin 216
Laud, Archbishop 26
Lawley, Arthur Ernest 62,80
Lawrence, Mr C 162
Lawrence, Rev W P 39
Le Port, Stephen 110
Le Rous, Thomas 77
Lewis, David 143,148,150
Lewis, John 209
Lewis, Wilfred George 14
Leyburn, Bishop 157
Lillwal, Mr 12,13
Lindsay, Hon John 73
Little Garway Farm 65.117
Liverpool School of Architecture 13
Llancillo 5,7,32-33

Llandaff, Book of 5,7,26,44,52,57,76
  123,136
Llangarron 220
Llangua 8,44-47,201,209
Llangunville 76
Llanrothal 5,76-77,107,114,130,132,139,
  205,209
Llantarnam Abbey 150
Llantillo Crossenny 8
Llantony Priory 29,144
Llanveynoe 6,16-19,21
Llewellin, Rev F G 17
Lollards 17,18
Longtown 6,7,11,12,16,17,21
Longtown Education Centre 24
Loope, George 133
Loyola, Ignatius 139
Lugg river 180,185
Lydbrook Junction 226

Macbean, William Stanley 175
Marcher Lordships 8
Marsh, Leonard 135
Marstow 220
Mary Queen of Scots 124
Mary Tudor 123
Massey, Col. 60
McAdam, Rev Bill 72
Michaelchurch Escley 6
Middleton, William Constable 161
Milbourne family 87,132,144,159
Mill Hill 166
Ministry of Supply Depot 223
Monmouth 1,6,8,86-78,197,199,211
Monmouth Archaeology Society 55,87
Monmouth Bridge 87,97
Monmouth Cap 45,201,209
Monmouth Castle 87
Monmouth County Council 8,88
Monmouth Forge 188
Monmouth Gaol 151
Monmouth May Hill 212,221
Monmouth Priory 76,120
Monmouth Turnpike Trust 197,201,206,207
Monmouth Troy Station 94
Monnow Bridge 87,88
Monnow Cutting 94
Monnow River Navigation 181
Monnow Street 87
More O'Ferrall, Ambrose 62
Morgan, William 135
Mountain Rescue, Longtown 24
Mull, Sir William 77

Nant-y-Glo Ironworks 214
Needham, Sebastian 79
New Inn, Longtown 23
Newbolds, Rockfield 81
Newcastle 78,205
Newcastle Oak 78
Newport County Library 172
Nicholson, Mr T 22
Norton 73,163,197

Oates, Titus 133,143,148,151
Oath of Allegiance 124,125,126,159
Oath of Supremacy 126
Olchon brook 16
Olchon Court 17,18,19
Oldcastle 29-30
Oldcastle Court 29
Oldcastle, Sir John 17
Orcop 68,132,199
Osbaston 188,220
Overmonnow 87,88,93,95

Pandy 209
Pandy Inn 209
Pandy Station 12
Parish Roads 189
Paving Act 88
Paving Commissioners 93,94
Pembridge Castle 59,117,139,140,148,168
Pembridge Castle, Return to 172-176
Pembroke, Earl of 137
Penal Laws 125,127
Penissaplwdd 46 209
Pentecost, Osbern 4,36
Pentwyn mill 84
Perthir 81,132,158,185,188
Perthir mill 84
Peterchurch 12,215
Phillips, Henry 189
Pitt (Pytt), William 181,188
Poll Tax for 1377 116
Pontrilas 197,199,201,214,215
Pontrilas 40-43,51,144
Pontrilas chemical works 42
Pontrilas saw mill 42
Pontrilas Station 12
Pope 123
Popish Plot 134
Population numbers 180
Powell, John 132
Price, Joseph 77
Priory Motel, Skenfrith 168
Pritchard, John 185
Pritchard, Mattew 81,156-160,185
Pritchard, Mr
Privy Council 135,137
Puritans 123
Pytt, James 189

Races 95
RAF transporters 197
Raglan Castle 138
Railways 211-223
  British Rail 223
  Coleford,Usk &Pontypool R'way 211,212,
  Gloucester & Warwick R'way 215
  Golden Valley Extension R'way 221
  Golden Valley R'way 30,40,215,219,220
  GWR 40,47,74, 211,212,214,215,228
  Monnow Valley R'way 97, 214,221
  Newport/Aber/H'ford R'way 40, 209,211
  Oxford/Worc& W'hampton R'way 211
  Ross & M'mouth R'way 212
  Severn,Wye and Severn Bridge R'way 220
  West Midlands R'way 211
  Worc, Dean Forest & M'mouth R'way 212
Ralph, Earl of Hereford 4,36
Recusancy 123,127
Red Lion, Rockfield 81
Rees, Capt. William 42
Riot, The 135-138
Rising Sun, Longtown 23
Rising Sun, Orcop 65
Robin Hood Inn, Monmouth 159
Robinson, Edward 130
Rockfield 8 81-85,158,205
Rockfield Studios 84
Rolls, Mr J E W 79
Roman Catholic School 165
Roman Fort 55,190
Roman Roads 190
Rooker, Rev Dr Thomas 162
Ross on Wye 96.212
Ross, Abergaveny and Hay T'pike Trust 197
Rowlestone 5,7,34-35
Royalists 38
Ruthlin mill 188
Ryd-y-car mill, St Weonards 109,148

Salisbury, Father 139
Sanctuary 102
Sayce family 46
Scudamore Arms Hotel, Pontrilas 43
Scudamore, John 33,43,53,120,133,185,144
Scudamore, Col Edward Lucas 33,44,46
Scudamore, John Lucy 197,205,209
Scudamore, Sir James 136
Seddon, John 52
Severn tunnel 212,216
Sigurdsson, King of Norway 37
Sistine choir 152
Sitsylt, Robert 31
Skenfrith 8,69-75,16,152,160,161,172,201,221
Skenfrith bridge 196
Skenfrith mill 188
Skirrid Fawr 140
Smith, James 18, 156

Society of David 161
Southwell, Vicount 161.205.206
Spencer, James 195
St Beuno 16
St Margaret's 6
St Maughans 8 78-80.139,145,195
St Peters, Rome 152
St Weonards furnace 33,114,188
St Xavier, College of 139
Stanford Bridge 37
Star Brewery, Hereford 42
Statute Labour 179
Swinnerton, Elizabeth 206
Symonds Yat 96

Templars 58,60,101,113
Templars,downfall 102
Tennersfield Farm 118
Test Acts 125,143
Thomas, Father 140
Thomas, George 42
Three Horseshoes, Craswall 14
Tower of London 18
Tower, Garway Hill 65,66
Traveller's Seat 197
Trebella Farm 197
Tregate Castle 76,188
Treville Park 135
Tre-Wyn 29,30
Trothy river 93
Troy House 88
Troy Station 212,214
Troy tunnel 93
Trumper, Thomas
Tudor, Thomas 53,205
Turnpike Act 1755 178
Turnpike Act 1771 195
Turnpike Tolls 192-3

Usk 94,143,151

Vaughans of Courtfield 136,159,161
Vauxhall 87,96,214,220
Vicar Apostolic 125,156,157
Vicar Provincial 133

Wakeman, Thomas 161,172,197,205
Walterstone 5,7,31
Ward, Charles and Kingsley 84
Watkins, Mr Alfred 19
Watley, M 175
Weir Street 97
Wellington Inn, Newcastle 78
Wellington, Alice 135
Welsh Bicknor 8
Welsh Newton 76,107,110,130,150
Welshries 6
Werndee 82
White castle 8,70,116
White Hart, Rockfield 81

White Rocks 63
White Swan, Monmouth 172
Whitfield 136
Widemarsh Comon, Hereford 149
William of Orange 125,143
William the Conqueror 37
Williams, Charles 189
Wilson, G J 42
Winchcombe 215
Window Tax 181
Wonastow 8,145,206
Worcester 133
Worcester, Earl of 137,139,140,144,159
Wright, Cecil 13
Wyatt, Mr 88
Wye Tour 96
Wye, river 87,93,96,180
Wyebridge Street 97

Xavier Francis 139,150

Ynyr, King of Gwent 16